OUTSIDERS IN THE CLUBHOUSE

SUNY Series on Sport, Culture, and Social Relations
Cheryl L. Cole and Michael A. Messner, editors

OUTSIDERS IN THE CLUBHOUSE

THE WORLD OF WOMEN'S PROFESSIONAL GOLF

Todd W. Crosset

STATE UNIVERSITY OF NEW YORK PRESS

Published by
State University of New York Press, Albany

© 1995 State University of New York

For information, address State University of New York Press,
State University Plaza, Albany, N.Y., 12246

Production by Marilyn P. Semerad
Marketing by Dana E. Yanulavich

Library of Congress Cataloging-in-Publication Data

Crosset, Todd W., 1959-
    Outsiders in the clubhouse : the world of women's professional
golf / Todd W. Crosset.
        p.   cm. — (SUNY series on sport, culture, and social
relations)
    Includes bibliographical references (p.   ) and index.
    ISBN 0-7914-2489-8. — ISBN 0-7914-2490-1 (pbk.)
    1. Golf for women—United States. 2. Women golfers—United
States. 3. Sex discrimination in sports—United States. 4. Ladies
Professional Golf Association. I. Series: SUNY series on sport,
culture, and social relations.
GV966.C76 1995
796.352—dc20
                                                                    94-27916
                                                                        CIP

10 9 8 7 6 5 4 3 2

To
Hope Seignious, Betty Hicks
and Ellen Griffen—

Conceivers, creators and defenders
of the Women's Professional Golf Tour

CONTENTS

PART IV
The LPGA as an Agent of Social Change

INTRODUCTION

Cricket had plunged me into politics long before I was aware of it.
When I did turn to politics I did not have too much to learn.

—C. L. R. James, *Beyond a Boundary*

This is a study of a world within our world; an insulated subworld on the fringe of American society. This world revolves around an elite occupation. The shared experience of the work yields a group of people linked not just by a common purpose, but by shared understandings, values, and ideals. Like other subworlds[1] on the fringe of our society, this group's uniqueness strikes some as unusual.

One of the most distinctive aspects of this world is its focus on women within an enterprise historically monopolized by men. This organization, originally created by women, continues to be shaped by its women members. In this organization, women occupy a position of independence. Here women members don't work for anybody, don't punch a time clock, and aren't forced to sign contracts with corporations. They work for themselves. They take vacations when they want. They do the hiring and the firing. There is no network, good old boy or otherwise, which determines their place in the organization or their pay. These women are paid according to how well they perform—strictly merit raises.

Women lucky enough to join this group work in warm, comfortable climes, migrating with the summer sun. Someone else handles domestic chores like cooking and cleaning. Wealthy people give over their most prized leisure facilities and lush parks to this organization

1

every week. Every working day they can take time out to notice the blue sky and the green grass or listen to the birds.

Typically their income is higher than the national average.[2] Exceptional members can become very wealthy through their active participation, making between $200,000 and $400,000 a year. If they fall upon unusually hard times, there always seems to be a benevolent outsider to help defray costs.

In this organization, women are the center of attention. In each town they visit newspaper reporters and television crews report on them and even follow them, seeking interviews. But unlike most admiration for women, these women are not admired for their looks. They are admired by men and women alike for what they do. The admiration is so great that some well-established businessmen envy these women's employees. Although few well-established men actually do "drop out" and hit the road to work for these women, in every city they visit, hundreds of wealthy men pay thousands of dollars for the privilege of sharing a day with one of these women, to watch her do what she does so well, to talk to her, and to be a part of what she does. These women, you see, do what most men can only dream of doing. Nonetheless, because they are women in a male world, they remain outsiders.

The distinctiveness of this world is reflected in the way its members refer to their place in society. They are, they say, "Out Here"—as if it were other-worldly, defying time and space. "Out Here," as if any comparison to the "real world" would be inappropriate. "Out Here," they say, "it is like a fantasy world."

Admirers refer to their organization as "The Ladies Tour." Its formal name is the "Ladies Professional Golf Association," or the LPGA. This is a study of the subworld of professional women's golf. Its primary goal is to capture in words the experience of life on the tour, its tensions and conflicts with the broader culture, and the subsequent resolution of those conflicts through the players' ways of living.

My attention to sport as an area of academic research is motivated by concern—the same sort of concern one might have for a good friend. Supportive, yet critical. I have been involved with sport in some way, either playing it or making a living working in it for as long as I can remember. I am close to sport, but I did not enter this project with either the giddy love for sport that too often reduces serious scholars to romance writers, blind to the injustices and contradictions of sport, or the hostility of the betrayed or failed athlete turned social critic, who sees nothing but exploitation in sport.

My initial interest in sport as a sociological concern arises out of my experience as a collegiate swimmer. I had a successful, albeit undistinguished, career at the University of Texas. Although sport is pretty much the same everywhere in the country, it became clear to me early on that the social meaning of sport varies widely. Nowhere is that lesson more evident than when competing for the University of Texas. Be it high school, college, or professional, Texans take their sports very seriously.

Despite the wide variations in the social significance of sport, the logic of sport is universal. Regardless of race, class, sex, or sexuality, in sport, participants are rewarded according to merit. Theoretically at least, excellence cannot be denied in sport. Indeed, it is this promise of sport which makes it so appealing in a world that promises the same but rarely delivers. It is also this promise that motivates this research.

The meaning assigned to an athletic feat and the significance of the actual achievement as dictated by a sport are often in conflict, particularly when the athletes are women. The contradictions between norms and reality, between expectation and actions with regard to gender in sport were revealed to me decades ago. Swimming is one of the few sports in which men and women train together. Although there are significant differences in performance times, there is little distinction in the training regimes of men and women. As an athlete I became uncomfortable with the notion that women's athletics are something less or different than men's athletics. I am not embarrassed by, actually I point with some pride to, my struggling to stay within a body length of Mary T. Meagher during practice sets of 200 meter butterflies. Keeping up with Mary T. during practice was something of a badge of ability within the swimming world. And Mary T. was only one of many inspiring women athletes with whom I trained. My female training partners have had more of an impact on this study than can be expressed.

I can trace my interest in the LPGA to my career as a swimmer as well. A teammate's younger sister, Kim Shipman, was an exceptional golfer at UT who eventually qualified for the tour. Kim would get me tickets to the LPGA tournament when it came to the Boston area, where I was attending graduate school. It was these excursions to LPGA tournaments and subsequent conversations with Kim that sparked my interest in the life of the tour players.

My desire to do a study of the LPGA can be traced to a specific moment in 1985. I was sitting in the dining room of a country club watching Kim approach the buffet line, feeling somewhat out of place. I probably looked out of place as well. At the time I sported an untrimmed beard and a pasty complexion which comes from spending too many hours in the library. I probably wore a T-shirt and jeans. Kim had spiked hair and wore mid-thigh length shorts. Given other circumstances, neither one of us would have been allowed out of the parking lot of the country club. But this was the week of the LPGA tournament, and all membership and dress code rules were suspended. I watched as Kim moved right to the front of a buffet line. She "butted" in front of country club members who seemed sincerely pleased to allow her in line, almost grateful for the opportunity to be helpful to an LPGA player.

At that time, I was studying gender relations under the direction of Shula Reinharz and Kathy Barry, two eminent sociologists. Through their training I had gained a fairly sharp and critical insight into the workings of the gender order in our society. On the surface the LPGA seemed an anomaly: a place where women hired men to follow them around and perform menial tasks (caddies not only carry a player's clubs but also her name across his back). A place where women moved to the head of the line and wealthy men obliged. Something weird and possibly wonderful was taking place when the LPGA took over a country club and I wanted to understand it. Four years later I started this study.

It is not the sole criterion, but a social researcher's status is often elevated according to the "danger" of their field site. Even the general public seems to perk up and take interest in studies of far-off peoples or the highly secretive criminal world. If danger or difficult access is not inherent to a field site, researchers generally have the good sense to suffer from a lack of funding and painfully make do with limitations which hamper the research. At the very least, it seems obligatory that researchers struggle to track down enough willing and qualified participants to make up a representative sample.

Although I took off after the tour in my pick-up, equipped with all my camping gear, plus a file cabinet and laptop computer, bubbling with the anticipation of roughing it, studying the LPGA proved to be something of a boon to the quality of my life. Far from malaria-ridden jungles or dangerous coal mines, the LPGA floats from one safe, bucolic, manicured country club to the next. At each tournament site, I was awarded a press pass and enjoyed all privileges of the press. I received three free meals a day and an endless supply of coffee. At some tournaments, the meals were prepared and served by the host country club's staff (I was introduced to cold strawberry soup at one tournament). At the very least, I dined on pizza donated by the local pizza parlor. At the end of the day there was usually a free beer or two to be had and cynical but amusing conversations with the local press. The press pass, as it turned out, was better than most academic grants a social scientist could hope to receive.

Folks in and around the tour seemed generally pleased to help me out with my research. All in all, I interviewed sixty people affiliated with the tour in fifty-five interviews. Professional women golfers make up the majority of these interviews. Thirty-four interviews were with active players and three other interviews were with former players. The player's interviews are rounded out by a variety of interviews with caddies, volunteers, staff, and partners. For more details concerning data collection and analysis I invite the reader to look over the methods section in the appendix.

I harbor no special fondness for the sport of golf. I play the game but once a summer, and then rather poorly. Fortunately, this book is not about competitive golf. This book is about life on the LPGA tour. More precisely, it is about the social relations which have developed around the occupation of professional women golfer and the production of elite-level golf.

My ignorance about the sport was more a blessing than a curse. While it clearly caused me to ask some painfully simple questions, which in retrospect are embarrassing, the distance from the sport gave me the perspective of an outsider. Unfettered by the subtleties of the game and thus ignorant of much of the pleasures of watching golf, I was able to observe the world that revolved around the sport without being drawn into it. I do not think I could do the same sort of research on the sport of swimming.

My experience as an athlete, however, was not unlike those of the professionals I studied, and enhanced my understanding of the golfers' lives. There were common understandings about competition, excellence, practice, and travel which made conversation easy. I did not have to discover metaphors in my own life in order to make sense of their experiences. In the voices of the members of the LPGA I heard articulated beliefs I once held. In their words I believe are sentiments shared by all athletes, a sense of justice, and a latent politics: a belief that sport has something to offer far beyond entertainment.

There are probably twenty or thirty books that could be written about life on the LPGA tour. No one book can cover it all. Indeed, one of the difficulties I had in writing this book was deciding what to leave out. Because I chose to focus on the social structures of the tour, the book is somewhat abstract in parts and critical throughout. As such, I think the book misses much of what is fun, colorful, and dramatic about women's professional golf. But I will leave that to the sports writers, the historians, and the biographers. My task as a sociologist is to bring forward the social arrangements which shape the players' lives, to question the logic of these arrangements and suggest what may, or ought to, lie ahead.

This book is divided into four sections. My aim in the first section is to lay out the parameters of the book—historical, analytical, and material. The analysis, as I have indicated, is essentially structural. Chapter 1 defines the levels of the structures and discusses broad themes that run throughout the book. The next two chapters detail the economic and political history of the structures we call the tour. The final chapter in this part details the requirements necessary for entry into and membership in women's professional golf—the material reality of becoming a professional golfer.

The second part details the ideological conflict between being a professional golfer and being a woman athlete in a sexist society. The first chapter of this part introduces the primary social issue for the tour player: the ideology necessary for becoming a female professional athlete is in conflict with what is expected of female public figures. One set of ideological beliefs is a response to the social terrain of professional golf, the other to the mainstream society. The next four chapters examine the "fallout" from the tension between gender and prowess. The primary concern of these chapters is to locate patterns of social behavior which arise out of either the unique qualities of tour life or as a result of conflicts with the broader culture.

The third part focuses on the battle being waged over the symbolic meaning of the tour. In the three chapters which make up this part I discuss the competing ideological explanations of women's athletic prowess. Each chapter details the meaning of women's golf from a particular political/social stance: conventional culture, feminist politics, woman athlete.

In the final part I discuss women's golf in terms of the democratic promise of sport. Beginning with the proposition that all sport holds the promise of equality of opportunity and at certain moments in history has been an institution which spearheads democratic social reforms, I discuss the progress of women's golf. Specifically, I examine the role of women's professional golf in the ongoing struggle against gender, race, and class stratification.

To cite all the people and their contributions to this book would involve writing another volume. I would like to mention my friends and colleagues who put their faith and time into me and this project.

This research began as graduate work at Brandeis University and I am grateful for the advice and encouragement I received from my teachers: Peter Conrad, Kathy Barry, Shula Reinharz, and Egon Bittner. I was lucky to be tutored by one of the finest collections of qualitative researchers under one roof. Alan Klein, although he resides elsewhere, is something of an idol for me, having written two exceptional ethnographies on sport. It is a rare gift to have him as an advisor. I am especially grateful to sport sociologists Mike Messner and Don Sabo, without whose encouragement I would never have begun or finished this project.

I am most grateful to a circle of friends who have heard about the LPGA for five years and listened repeatedly to "sociological insights," all with the endurance that comes only with true friendship. A number of these people have made significant contributions to this project. Jeff Meyerhoff spent a good part of a year transcribing interviews in unusually good humor and turned unmanageable data into sociological riches. For two years Joan Alway met with me monthly to discuss my research. Most of what is theoretically interesting can be attributed to her. Jim Ptacek has served a similar role for the final revision, and his fingerprints will be obvious to all who know him. Ellen Davis served as copy editor, and so much more, for the first draft. Jim Blau helped me clean up the final draft.

Finally, Anne Richmond provided more support than can be imagined. She lived with this project for five years and knows what is on each page of this book without having to read it. In ways that cannot be articulated she has shaped the analysis that follows. I will be forever grateful.

PART I

THE SOCIAL AND HISTORICAL CONTEXT OF THE LPGA

CHAPTER 1

OUT HERE

It is really a fantasy world out here. It is something that you dream about doing. You are your own boss. Especially being a woman, I can't think of any other place where you can do exactly what you want to. I really never felt like I have been harassed by the opposite sex in our world. I have never felt like I was competing with men.

In the corporate world it is a little bit different. There are the men and women competing for the same jobs. We are not. As an organization we are competitive with the men's tour as far as getting sponsors, but as individuals we are competing against other women.

That's why I have stayed out here so long. I don't want to join the real world; it's hard work. This has never been work to me.

—Tara[1]

The expression "out here" is used with such frequency by the players that it hardly causes a ripple in the flow of conversation. In the context of the tour it is a shorthand way to refer to either life on the tour, or the high level of golf played on the tour. "Out here" names a social place or condition and in so doing refers to its uniqueness without drawing undo attention to it. But as is often the case with handy, all-purpose phrases, their power is not what they reveal but what remains hidden. Catch phrases often veil the uncomfortable in the context of polite conversation.

The expression "out here" is a clue toward understanding the women's professional tour. The expression both hides and succinctly captures the social position of the professional woman golfer on a number of levels. Most immediately, it reveals how the players understand themselves as distinct from mainstream society. But within the expression "out here" also resonates the beginnings of a description of the relationship between professional competitive golf and country club golf. Dig deeper and it reveals a legacy of women existing on the fringe of the golfing community. "Out here" speaks to a particular stance of women golfers as being both included and excluded.

RELUCTANT TOLERANCE

From the start of the modern golfing era, women participated. Golf was a European game played by common folks and nobility for centuries before it landed on the shores of the United States. It came ashore in a fashion that would establish it as a popular pastime among both sexes of the upper class. After being introduced to the game while in Europe, William K. Vanderbilt brought the game home. Along with two other investors, Vanderbilt hired Scotsman Willie Dunn to build a golf course on Long Island in the spring of 1891. Dunn built Shinnecock Hills Golf Club. Almost immediately after completion, the seventy original club members of the Shinnecock Hills Golf Club requested Dunn build another nine holes exclusively for the women members.[2]

While some credit can be given to an upper-class flexibility around gender relations, and its European tradition of female participation, the inclusion of women in golf in this country probably has more to do with its institutional base of support, health resorts and country clubs. After Shinnecock, the game quickly spread to the other turn-of-the-century country clubs, spas, and health resorts which catered to wealthy and middle-class heterosexual married men and their families. Both men and women frequented the health spas and country clubs. Other sports whose orgins reside in sex segregated institutions are less open to women's participation. Billiards, for example, has its roots in private coffee houses, pubs, and billiards halls which were the province of heterosexual single men.[3] Baseball, to cite another male sport, has its roots in middle-class, all-male social clubs such as the Knickerbockers, and male-dominated occupations such as shipyard workers and butchers.[4]

Turn-of-the-century resorts developed in conjunction with the health movements of the post-Civil War era. The resorts catered to the rich and urban, supposedly suffering from illness or poor health brought on by urban living. The principle remedy, fresh air, was supplemented by a variety of other methods: rest, rugged hiking and movement, electric shock, baths (hydrotherapy), celibacy, and a myriad of foods. Health advocates like Ralston, Graham, and Kellogg, whose influence on American eating habits is obvious, operated resorts during this period.

The ailing and the infirm were not the only people going to health resorts. Wealthy and middle-class puritan urbanites perceived urban life as energy sapping and ailment producing, which could be combated by an austere and reserved lifestyle. Rural resorts rejuvenated the weary urbanites and freed them from their concern for mental and physical conservation. Immersed in healing waters, healthy foods, and fresh air, urbanites could afford to loosen up and expend moral energy on little vices. By the turn of the century resorts came to represent guilt-free amusement; a decadent atonement for urban life. Saratoga Springs, for example, offered clients healing baths and organized gambling. As historian Harvey Green aptly notes:

> For the purists, the spas were centers of sin and scandal, the antithesis of rational hydropathy and health. But for many middle-class Americans, they were a comfortable compromise, with just enough health-related content to assuage any possible guilt about the costs of rising social status.[5]

Saratoga Springs' oxymoronic mix of puritan cure and speculative amusements is unusual. Most health resorts mixed health treatments with physical amusements. Successful resorts, like Kellogg's in Battle Creek, offered lawn tennis, croquet, bowls, and the like. It was during this period that spas began to build golf courses in an attempt to retain popularity among those leery of the repressive health movement.[6]

The development of Pinehurst Country Club in Pinehurst, North Carolina illustrates the connection between health resorts and recreational golf. In the 1890s James W. Tufts of Boston bought land in Pinehurst with the intention of attracting ailing Northerners to purchase winter homes there. In this regard he retained the services of Dr. George Carver, who argued that the air at Pinehurst had healing powers. Pinehurst did not attract the wealthy Northerners until 1896, after Tufts' son Leonard, along with Dr. George Carver, laid out a nine-hole golf course. The golf course not only encouraged long walks for Carver's patients, but helped attract clients to the Pinehurst resort. In 1900, Tufts and Carver hired a professional who built additional courses. In 1901, Pinehurst hosted an amateur tournament for men, and in 1903, it added a women's tournament. In a relatively short time, Pinehurst gained a reputation as a golf haven, and became a popular stop for wealthy Northerners traveling to and from Florida.[7]

At the time that women were taking up the game of golf at country clubs and health resorts and playing in amateur tournaments, distinctions between the sexes were being emphasized socially. According to popular writings of the time, the country was suffering from a "crisis of masculinity." It was hardly a crisis, so much as solidification of an ideology to restore a patriarchal gender order. The crisis of masculinity played upon the collective fear that the closing of the frontier, urban development, sedentary work, the suffrage movement, and the increase of women in the paid labor force would result in men becoming weak and effeminate.

In the late eighteen hundreds and the early nineteen hundreds, the argument for distinct, separate spheres for men and women was widely advocated as a measure to curb the feminization of men.[8] Country clubs, health resorts, and other mixed-sex settings adopted gender distinctions which, to the contemporary observer, seem quite bizarre. While men and women traveled to health resorts together to find relief from the same urban ailments of tiredness and nervousness, the treatments for men and women were quite different. Men were often advised to endure a rugged lifestyle. Resorts and private country clubs offered male members hunting and fishing lodges to accommodate manly adventures. Meanwhile women suffering from the same ailments were told to take bed rest and put on restrictive diets.[9]

It was during this period that the concept that sport turned boys into men and that athletic prowess is a symbol of manliness crystallized in American culture.[10] For over a century now, sport has been a resource through which men "do masculinity." The structure of recreational golf reflected the sentiment of the day. The masculine image of golf was maintained by keeping women's golf separate from men's golf and thus allowing for distinct social meanings to develop for each sex. Playing time for women was restricted to ensure that no male golfer would cross paths with female golfers. The country club harbored male-only rooms within the clubs, male-only events, and male-only leadership, all of which enhanced the perception that golf was a male domain. Separate tee boxes for women exaggerated and reified the biological distinction of sex. Clubs adopted rules prohibiting women from wearing pants or shorts or manly dress while on the course, highlighting the genderedness of the activity.

Although women have always been participants in American golf and the country club, it has been as outsiders. Nothing illustrates the status of women more clearly for me than the arrangement of the bathrooms in the clubhouse at the LPGA tournament in Rochester. The women's room is inside close to the dining room. The men's room is located down the hall on the outer edge of the building, by a back entry way, with a window overlooking the tenth tee. The architecture reflects the norm: men play golf, and meet their wives in the dining room.

The sex segregation of the country club borders on the absurd. One male amateur and a participant at an LPGA pro-am interviewed related the following when asked about the attitudes of his fellow members toward the women's tour.

> There are alot of guys out there—some of my good friends—that just don't want to golf with women or have women on the golf course. . . . In fact I'll tell you a story. About ten years ago, my daughter was two years old, my good friends belonged to a club. They invited me out one Saturday morning just to socialize. I came out with my daughter, she was young and I was carrying her around. I walked into the grillroom of this very exclusive club with my buddies, and as we approached a group of men playing cards, one of these jerks looked at me and said, "There are no women allowed in the grill room." Now I didn't know how to react. I knew he was referring to my daughter, I was holding her in my arms. Can you believe it, my two-year-old daughter?
>
> I told him if I heard another comment close to that I was going to put his cigar out on his forehead. We got out of there!

Within the golf world women have existed on the periphery. For almost a century they have been limited to weekday playing times, excluded from membership unless married to a man, and barred from holding positions of power. The golfing world reluctantly tolerates the participation of women in golf. Although some of the segregating structures of the country club have been challenged recently, women remain outsiders within the world of golf.

THE SUBWORLD OF PROFESSIONAL WOMEN'S GOLF

On the fringe of the country club as a result of gender, the tour player is further set apart by her relationship toward the game. Although they share the same game, language, and fashions, the world of the professional golfer is qualitatively distinct from the amateur world. Take, for example, the language of the golfing world. Players use phrases like "blasted out of the sand," "drained a ten footer," and "get up and down" to describe what they do. This sort of language is understandable to most within the social world of golf. However, the terms often take on new meaning when they are used on the tour. "Scraping dew," for example, refers to playing golf early in the morning. It alludes to the mark a golfer's swing leaves as the clubhead passes through the dew-laden grass. Within the recreational golfing community it is a romantic image associated with the dedicated amateur. On the tour, it generally has the negative connotation of an early morning tee time. These tee times are filled by weaker players.

The LPGA is really a world within the world of competitive golf. Professional golf is not amateur golf played better. It is qualitatively distinct. Athletes who excel at one level of sport do not move easily to the next level. They do not improve in a linear fashion. Rather, athletes make qualitative leaps from one world to the next.[11] In the case of competitive women's golf, they jump from junior golf, to collegiate golf, to the mini tour, and maybe to the professional tour. Each world has its unique expectations and demands, and distinct structures.

Success at one level does not guarantee success at the next. Nat, for example, did quite well on the mini tour, yet she was struggling with the world of professional golf. Cathy on the other hand, described herself as a "good player in college, but not great or anything." She "wasn't an All-American or anything like that," but after surviving the first year, Cathy bloomed into a consistant top-twenty finisher, leaving collegiate champions in another world.

Professional golfers are not the best collegiate players, but they are the best collegiate players and mini-tour players who were able to make adjustments to the new setting and new expectations. Rookies like Sara seem to understand this process intuitively, giving themselves time to adjust to their new world. In the following quote, she discusses the process of getting adjusted to the tour.

> You are out here for the first year, you do not know what is good for you yet. That is something you learn each time you come to a place. You get to know how much you can play or that you only want to hit the balls for so long. You learn something new at each tournament.
>
> Plus, the veterans know exactly where they are going and how to get around the town they are in. When they go to a new town they know where the post office is and the grocery store. It takes me three times as long to do anything.

Although she was having trouble getting around the cities which hosted tournaments, she was a quick study of what kind of discipline was expected of her on the tour. The qualitative distinction between collegiate golf and the professional tour is clear in Sara's attribution of her rapid improvement to the social expectations.

> When you are out here you don't realize how much practice you are doing. You don't just play eighteen holes. You come out here in the morning and hit balls, then play a round, grab something to eat, and practice for another two hours. It is a routine. At home you just play nine holes or eighteen and when you come in you might put in maybe 30 minutes and then go home. But around here you have got a hundred and forty people who want to do just as well as you or better than you and you see them hitting balls. It is a motivator. You see people (*pointing to the driving range*) out there practicing all the time.

Like most other professional sports, the LPGA is a subworld within a social world. Its members' everyday lives and perspective on the sport only vaguely resemble the majority of those who play golf. Professionals don't just hit it farther, straighter, and with more consistency than mini-tour players or collegiate players, they engage the sport in a qualitatively different fashion. The techniques, attitude, and discipline change with each level of the sport. The very way they think about the game is different. The distinction between the professional and amateur golfers, the staple of LPGA fans, can be extreme.

> Your average golfer wants to improve, but they don't want to change and they don't want to practice. And I don't blame them, practice is boring, *they don't even know how to practice.* They would rather get out on the golf course. (Tara)

It is not that professionals merely do more of it, they do it differently.

Relating across an abyss of incomprehension can become an irritant for some players.

> Fans don't know what it is like to play professional golf because they are only relating to their weekend experiences. They don't know it is a seven-day-a-week job. One guy just asked me what I do with the rest of my week. They just don't know. (Gerta)

The expression "out here" often refers to this distinction between professional golf and other golfing worlds.

STRUCTURAL INSULATION

The professional woman player's isolation within the world of golf and the country club is compounded by her sense of being outside mainstream society. The expression "out here" also captures contemporary players' understanding of their social position.

Being outside the mainstream is the consequence of the tour's structure. The tour is never in one city for more than a week, usually less. Players, caddies, and staff are much more likely to be "on the road" than at home. During the thirty-five weeks that the tour is in season, most players compete in thirty tournaments and stay "out" for four to five weeks at a time. One player described the tour as a "traveling circus," another as a "little bubble that travels from city to city, week after week." The everyday life of the player resembles that of a modern-day nomad.

Like a circus or a production company, the members of the LPGA begin to depend on each other to maintain a sense of continuity. After their golf rounds are completed, players tend to spend time with each other or check in with each other. Val's comparison to other occupations is illustrative of this distinctive aspect of the tour:

> In our environment, we have friends other places only because we go to the tournament sites and we see them once a year. But we are with the players and caddies all the time, all year. So we are going to be going out to dinner and rooming with each other. It is a completely different environment than a business situation. (Val)

In addition to being in constant contact with the people affiliated with the tour, the mobility of the tour inhibits the development and nourishment of intimate relations with people not on the tour. June describes the feelings of isolation as she recounts her transition to tour life:

> I graduate and make the LPGA tour, which was a big, big goal, and then suddenly I was thrown into something I didn't really want. I mean golf is one thing, but what I turned my life into, I didn't know I was qualifying for that. I mean I expected to play a lot of golf but, I also live in a damn van. I live at airports, I am constantly on the phone arranging traveling. I live out of a suitcase and you know I don't have any set routines anymore.
>
> I lost all my friends—well I haven't lost them but it certainly is a different communication with them—some people

call it their support network, but now I see why they say that—I lost my family more or less. I don't have that—It is different. I call them from places I don't even know the area code I'm calling from. (June)

While June may overstate the trauma of turning pro, most players seem to share these general sentiments. The inability to maintain close relations off the tour and the bonding between players isolates and focuses a player's attention on issues of tour life.

The feeling of being away from home as a result of the constant travel is a commonly shared complaint. Again, June dramatically captures the sense of dislocation resulting from the constant travel:

I travel and I travel and I travel. You kind of lose perspective. You're like, where the hell am I, what am I doing? Why am I doing this? Did I ever want to do this? Why do I work so hard to wake up in wherever, to play another round of golf? That is hard, really hard. (June)

The constant travel leads to a sense of groundlessness. Players feel apart from mainstream society, or in their words, cut off from "reality" and relationships.

The worst part of it is not being able to stay in one position for more than two and a half months. Not enough time to build any type of relationship—male or female, sexual or otherwise. Not being able to grow plants, not being able to cook, not being able to ski, not being able to do what normal people do on their days off. (Gerri)

On the professional level, the game is consuming and, as a result, isolating. Players generally spend about six to eight hours a day playing or practicing golf. In some cases, players sustain a routine of eight hours of golf, six or seven days a week, for five to six weeks in a row. The following description of a tournament-day routine by Helen seems fairly typical of an average tour player.

A typical day really depends on what day of the week it is. A tournament day would be: get up three hours before my tee time. If it's late I do try to sleep in because then I don't have all day to get the nerves going, get the adrenaline going. Get up three hours before, get dressed and have breakfast and get out

> to the course about an hour and a half before. Practice: hit balls, chip, putt, putt, chip, hit. And then play.
>
> After I've played the four hours [rounds last about four and half hours] I don't like to stay out there and beat balls for three hours. [An exaggerated reference to some of the other players, most of whom hit for about an hour afterwards.]
>
> Not right away. I do go back and practice, but I like to break it up 'cause I know my concentration. I can't concentrate for an hour before and then four hours on the course, and then go straight back out to the range. Six hours straight, I can't. So I like to break it up. I'll take a break, either I'll go back to my private housing or the hotel or I'll go jogging or go work out or take a nap, do the laundry. I'll do something in between and go back and practice with a fresh mind. (Helen)

In addition to the minimum seven hours at the course playing or practicing, the demands of professional golf shape the way most players arrange their evenings. Many players leave the course with their putters in hand to practice their putting stroke in their hotel room before going to bed. Other players listen to relaxation tapes, to help them "visualize" their game before they retire for the day. Often, before they can even leave the course, they must make an appearance at a tournament-sponsored event.

For many of the better players, there are local publicity and sports news spots to do, and print news interviews to give, in addition to "schmoozing" with sponsors. More experienced and higher-ranked players reiterate Helen's assessment of the time demands but add the entertainment aspect of the sport.

> You figure a round takes five hours to play, four and half, you always practice before and after, that makes seven. It always takes ya an hour or so to get ready, that's eight. And then there are cocktail parties. (Ethel)

The cocktail parties Ethel mentions above, refer to the better players' responsibility to rub elbows with local tournament sponsors.

It is not simply that golf takes so much time, but that the players' sense of time is distinct from broader society. The tempo to life seems unhurried. Their world is task-oriented, not time-driven. Players seem concerned with time only when it stipulates their tee off. Conventional time is the backbone of American society. Industry measures work and profits in units of times. Most people arrange meetings, define the limits of their interactions, eat meals, and arrange golf games according to conventional time. Professional golfers on tour adjust their life according to a round of golf. As Helen points out,

> The tee time determines everything, in terms of what time breakfast is going to be and what time lunch is going to be and what time I'll get up.

As a result, players are more likely to arrange appointments and meet friends according to the completion of a round of golf than a time on the clock.

Most players can keep a fairly good handle on the day of the week because the tour's basic format does not change from week to week. Monday is a travel day. Tuesday is a practice day. Wednesday is a pro-am tournament (a fundraising tournament with local recreational golfers). Thursday and Friday are preliminary rounds of the tournament. Saturday and Sunday are the final rounds. Dates and months are not as clearly defined for the players as days of the week. The LPGA tour lasts for between 35 and 40 weeks each year. It begins in Jamaica in January, and travels to Florida, Hawaii, and Southern California in the winter and early spring. The tour slowly winds its way north and east, hitting New England and Canada in July and August. In September the tour plays the Northwest before heading back into Southern California. By migrating with the sun, players enjoy an abnormally long and pleasant summer but experience a unique sense of dislocation.

Helen, still in her first season, is still grappling with her new-found sense of dislocation.

> For me it's so new, the whole tour. Summer normally for me would consist of being at home and playing and seeing everyone and working on my game. Now it's like almost the fourth of July and I'm—I think I'm going to be in Toledo.
>
> It's different, but I feel it more because I don't have any reference points to say "Oh, fourth of July I will always be in Toledo" or "Memorial Day is in Rochester." It's funny because all my previous reference points are related to being at home or in school or out of school. Everything is sort of changing for me right now. (Helen)

Cathy's caddy and life partner related some instances from his life which nicely illustrate the sense of timelessness one acquires on the tour.

I tell ya, when you get out here for months, there are no holidays. It's not a holiday. It is just one day of a tournament. Like Memorial Day, it was Memorial Day, I didn't even know (*laughs*). I knew it was a holiday, because I wanted to play golf but I couldn't because the course was full. It is funny like that.

I have no idea of the date, I spent time with my family this week. My brother came out and said "Happy June everybody." I had no idea that today was June first.

I called my home once, called my mom from California, to say "How are you doing?" She lives in New York, says "Oh, good, I played golf today." I said, "What do you mean you played golf today?" It was the middle of April and I had no idea. I just assumed that New York was still under snow. You just lose all conception of time, you have no idea. (Cathy's caddie)

The relatively solitary nature of the professional game further contributes to the isolation of the professional golfer. While the practice tee is peppered with conversation between swings, it is generally light banter about golf or tour life. Similarly, conversations with sponsors consist almost exclusively of "small talk" and "shop talk." The golfer is immersed in golf and thus insulated from other social worlds. National and world events often pass by unnoticed.

The most convenient means of gathering information from off the tour are not utilized by some players.

I'm not that much of a TV-watcher type person, sometimes I wouldn't even know what's happening in the outside world unless someone goes "Oh, did you know such and such happened?" And you know, most of the time, I won't even know. (Hattie)

Gerri, a long-time veteran, made this remark about players and current affairs:

I don't know how many of the girls out here read the paper. I read it religiously every day. . . . On a whole, most of the people I associate with read. So we at least have something else to talk about [besides golf].

I would say probably ten [players read]. It's terrible. Cause if they don't read the paper they don't know what's

going on in the world. It's a terrible feeling, but that's the feeling I get out here, is that we don't stay attuned to what's going
on in the rest of the world. (Gerri)

The ability to understand world and national events requires that the
reader or viewer follow the news. Periodic sustained attention is necessary to understanding the larger social worlds outside of professional
golf. It is a luxury most golfers do not have time for. Even off-season
attempts to get caught up can be futile. Denise, in an attempt to broaden
her understanding of the world, attempted to read the *New York Times*
during the winter break. She found, however, that her interest and skill
in comprehending current affairs had atrophied, and she only had the
desire to read the lifestyle section of the newspaper.

The most revealing example of the otherworldliness of the tour
came in a discussion with a golfer's former college roommate. The
roommate, now a medical doctor working in an emergency room, was
in a gallery watching her friend. The evening before, they had spent
some time catching up on each others lives. When the doctor tried to
express the horrors of crack and gang wars, which she dealt with daily,
the golfer's response was, "But isn't Barbara Bush doing a good job
with this?"

In addition to being physically isolated by the relentless travel
and insulated from the everyday reality of mainstream society by the
all-consuming nature of their profession, the players lack control of
and responsibility for themselves. On tour, players don't have to take
responsibility for even their most basic everyday needs. The following
quote from an LPGA staff member speaks to this aspect of tour life.

You know it is funny, it is like a little mini world. You are so
sheltered, you are isolated out here. That is why some people
lose their perspective on everything.

One of my favorite stories is of a player who retired from
the tour, who told me her greatest adjustment to life after leaving the LPGA tour was buying her own hand lotion (*laughs*). I
mean these players are given everything, every locker room is
stocked. All their personal needs are met.

Theoretically, if these girls want to, they could never
spend a nickel. You go into the locker room, there is food for
breakfast, there are hospitality areas, there is lunch. If you want
to eat after golf in the evening, there is usually a function.

This is a tremendously unrealistic world, you are in the
ultimate, the finest country clubs in the country. People are

driving you around. You don't deal with any poverty. We shelter the players from every possible thing. All they've got to do is make their airline reservations and get there.(Staff member)

As a result of this sheltered existence, the players' ability to function outside of their "world" deteriorates. Players suffer from a sort of learned dependence which encourages them to turn to the tour and away from mainstream society for help with the day-to-day issues of getting by. As a result, some players lose their sense of their individual agency. Gerri expressed the tradeoffs of a life with limited responsibilities:

Our world is pretty good. We get catered to every day. Even our shoes get cleaned. The only thing that we have to do is our laundry and make a flight and make a hotel reservation or write a guy [a caddy] a check. There's not a whole helluva lot of responsibility except the responsibility to ourselves.

So I say that it is very selfish, but it is not selfish because it is just what you have to do. If you don't have something to keep your mind [grounded in the world outside of golf] you can get a little lost out here. I don't like to think that I'm spoiled but I know I get spoiled.

I get tired of my dinner being bought every day and I get tired of beer being bought. I get tired of not being able to go in and make my own dinner. I get tired of somebody pampering me all the time.

The players' limited control and understanding of life outside their world is in direct contrast to the responsibilities and pressures they face as athletes. As competition between the LPGA membership improves, players become increasingly focused on golf. The overall level of competition on the tour ten to twenty years ago was qualitatively different.[12] Older professionals frequently noted that the younger professionals are better prepared as golfers, but infuriatingly less adept at life skills. Gerta in her interview suggested the rude awakening many of the players might suffer if and when they leave the tour.

I think most of the players, as a rule, do not appreciate what they have. They don't know what the real world is all about. They haven't had to go out and make a living or had to work and support themselves, as a general rule.

We are treated like royalty everywhere we go. People bend over backwards to make sure your every need is taken care of. Like I said, I don't think they realize that this isn't the way the world really is. People don't kowtow to ya when you [retire]. When you get off the tour and have to go make your own way in the world and you say, I am so-and-so, a golfer, you are going to come across people who don't care, or could care less if they don't know what golf is. It is going to be a real shock if people ever have to do that. So that has been very interesting to observe.

The older players had to "rough it out" through the early years of the tour when players were responsible for more than a good golf game. The players of the fifties and sixties were responsible for event and tour management and thus more connected with the world outside of golf.

Taken in total, today's player experiences tour life as alienating from the rest of the world. But the separateness is not necessarily experienced as something bad. Unlike Gerta and Gerri, most players experience the insulation as a positive aspect of the tour. This freedom from responsibility allows the golfers to focus on golf. Ann's observations epitomized the general feeling of the players on tour. Her comments reflect the awareness of the insulation the players feel, their general acceptance of it, and the comfort that insulation affords the players.

Really the golf tour is out of touch with reality. You are out here and focusing so much of your attention on playing golf, making money out here, surviving out here, that you pretty much lose touch with reality. . . .

People that are close to us, who have an insider's perspective, often take issue with us. They say our life is so easy. They say we don't have to live in the real world. But I wonder what is so bad about that.

OUTSIDERS WITHIN

In her book *Black Feminist Thought*, Patricia Hill Collins describes the position of African American women in our society as "outsiders within." As domestic workers, activists in the civil rights movement, and as intellectuals, African American women have witnessed mainstream culture from the inside without being fully incorporated. For Collins, the "outsider within stance" of African American women in the economic, social, and intellectual spheres serves as the basis of African American women's thought and activism. In many ways the historic position of women golfers resembles that of African American women. Within the various social spheres in which the tour players move—the country club, the golf world, and mainstream society—they remain on the fringe. Although privy to the inside workings of these worlds, and at times even revered, they are not full participants.

The expression "out here" speaks to the players' position in the world as outsiders within. They are outside, yet they are here, on the inside. Their world is arranged so that they are insulated from mainstream society. At the same time, they are part of mass culture. Their approach to the sport is different from the rest of the golf world. At the same time amateurs watch and listen to them when they discuss the fine points of the game. Finally, they are outsiders within the institutional base of their sport, golf, and country clubs on account of their sex. Yet, for a week each summer at many of the finest country clubs and resorts, they are honored guests.

The material reality of being an "outsider within" yields a unique perspective. Being privy to, but not invested in, a social world cultivates a critical eye. Such a stance does not generally inspire devotion. For Collins, this experience of so many black women fosters a shared critical perspective that she labels black feminist thought. While professional women golfers hardly represent a school of thought, they do seem to share a common perspective which can be traced to their position as outsiders within the upper-class, male-focused social world of golf.

Ironically, as sports entertainers, the members of the LPGA must appeal to (or at least not alienate) all the groups from which they seem segregated. Most sport or recreational subworlds and subcultures relish or celebrate their separateness. "Dropping out," the height of commitment in surfing and sail-boarding circles, is not a cherished state on the women's golf tour. Women professional golfers are reluctant outsiders. The tour as public entertainment must develop and maintain mass appeal. At the same time, women golfers are somewhat critical of these social worlds which they are able to observe from within.

Outside yet within the golfing world, the LPGA is never fully separate and alien from the broader culture. For the LPGA necessarily reflects the dominant culture. Indeed, professional golf—with its rigorous work schedule, highly competitive structure, and interaction with the political and financial elite—reflects mainstream and corporate ideals. At the same time, the essence of the tour—women playing sport in a serious fashion—seems culturally distinct from the mainstream. The tour simultaneously reflects social norms and presents an alternative to them. Willis, in a discussion of cultural production, refers to this relationship between mainstream culture and subcultures as the "dialectic of cultural life." When framed in this light, the subworld of the LPGA is not an inconsequential social oddity or an isolated "bubble," but is instead pregnant with social relevance. The LPGA and its members are unwittingly engaged in the transformation of our culture, the injection of political alternatives into the mainstream society, and stretching our notion of what is possible.

CHAPTER 2

OUTSIDERS INSIDE THE TOURNAMENT

At 7:45 in the morning at a tournament site there are few fans. Although the tournament has started, the putting greens are the center of action. Caddies line one side of the practice greens chatting, giving each other a hard time about last night's exploits, or their inability to fully wake up. At this hour there are always a few players on the greens, waiting to begin their round.

Players greet each other with smiles and brief pleasantries as their paths cross. Once they have passed by each other their faces quickly turn serious and focused. Conversations on the putting green are minimal. Their primary focus is on getting ready to play golf.

Flights of players are teeing off into the morning haze ten minutes apart. The caddies and players on the practice green can hear the announcer at the first tee introduce the players.

"Teeing off at 7:50. Originally from Chicago, Illinois. Now residing in San Diego, California. Representing Coral Gables Country Club. A tour professional since 1985. Please welcome . . ."

The introduction is heard by a smattering of spectators. The players take note only of the time. Few wear or carry watches; they count down the minutes prior to their tee time as they practice.

There is a calm to the course early in the morning. It is almost eerie, a calm thick with anticipation. Things are about to happen. Pre-teen boys who will each follow a flight of players carrying a sign announcing their scores, stand huddled in a group near the putting green, conscious of the need for silence. They quietly greet each other in stage whispers, exchanging silent high fives. Rocking back and forth from foot to foot as they wait, they exude energy in their attempt to contain it.

The boys are a sharp contrast to the stance of the players on the putting green nearby, who seem to be able to stand without *any extra movements, wasting no energy. Their movements are calm and deliberate.*

At this hour, the clubhouse belongs to the staff, the waiters, and the bus boys. The lack of formality spills out of the kitchen into the halls and the foyer. No one stops me from roaming, even though I don't have a press pass. A caddy walks confidently into the unwatched press room and steals a long distance call. The rules of hierarchy that are strictly enforced at 11:00 am seem to be suspended at 8:30 am.

With so few spectators around, the underbelly of the tournament is visible. The temporariness of the structures and banners is more obvious. Plastic tables in the sponsors' tent have yet to be dressed. Without the linen, the rather common tables betray the elitism associated with the event.

It begins to drizzle at 8:45. Caddies and players pull out umbrellas. Large colorful umbrellas plastered with logos compete for air rights. From above, it looks like a corporate flower garden. But logos appear everywhere, not just on umbrellas; they are printed on golf bags, stamped on visors, and stitched on sleeves. Around the course, corporations announce themselves on banners, pairing sheets, and on volunteers' clothing. Everywhere there are reminders of cruises, airlines, luxury hotels, and soft drinks. In two hours, against a sea of spectators, the logos will appear to be subtle—gentle reminders of who supports the tournament.

By 9:00, an hour and a half after the first group of players teed off, the course is almost full. For most of the players, the tournament is in full swing. This is of little consequence to the corporate representatives. The corporate tents, lined up like a receiving line around the bend from the main entrance, are just opening. These white carnival tents are plastered with colorful displays, screaming for attention. They are staffed by All-American looking (white and blond) salespeople. In a couple of hours thousands of spectators will walk past them on their way to the course, but at this time only three-quarters of them are open.

At 9:15 I stand in front of one these tents strategically located between the first and eighteenth fairways; two sales representatives are setting up. From here, I watch three golfers hit their approach shots to the eighteenth green. At the same moment, a sales rep informs her co-worker that she had advised their superior, a corporate executive, not to come to the tournament this morning because "nothing would be happening."

—Fieldnotes, July 1993

One of the riddles of women's professional golf is that it exists at all. It seems a minor miracle that women's professional golf could survive for fifty years, let alone thrive in an environment which tolerates but never embraces women playing golf. Why has women's professional golf flourished while professional leagues for women's baseball, softball, and basketball have failed? The answer is the venue of professional golf, the tournament.

The scene above seems to suggest a multitude of competing interests and an indifference to golf on the part of the public and corporate representatives. At first this diversity of aims seems counter to the production of professional golf. But the tournament format encourages this diversity of aims. Ironically, it is the lack of attention to golf which sells the tour.

The tournament is the mainstay of the LPGA. Since 1950, the format of the LPGA tournament has remained essentially unchanged. Central to understanding what distinguishes professional women's golf (and tennis) from the failed attempts to start and maintain other professional sports for women, is the work of two prominent entrepreneurs and promoters of men's and women's golf, George S. May and Fred Corcoran. Their work established two distinct tournament formats which indirectly competed for prominence prior to 1950. Corcoran's tournament organization, with the support of the major golf equipment manufacturers,[1] eventually won out. A comparison of May's tournament format with that of Corcoran's illuminates the logic of the contemporary tournament and why it works for women's professional sports.

PRE-TOURNAMENT PROFESSIONALS

The early golf professionals were mostly European men brought to the United States from Europe by country clubs to help design, build, and care for golf courses and to teach the finer points of the game to the club owners. Some made extra money by giving exhibitions. Golf manufacturers hired the most talented professionals as representatives to help peddle the game and their brand of clubs at exhibitions and clinics. A few women had worked as teaching pros in the early 1900s. In 1934, Wilson Sporting Goods hired the first female representative, Helen Hicks. Hicks did promotional work for Wilson, traveling around the country giving exhibitions and pushing the Wilson clubs designed especially for women. Hicks' work was so successful that Wilson added Opal Hill (1938) and Helen Dettweiler (1939) to their staff. Patty Berg, the 1940 amateur national champion, joined Wilson shortly after she won the amateur title.

The ground work for women's professional tournaments had been laid a generation earlier. The first tournaments played before a paying gallery were held during World War I. The field was comprised of amateurs. The proceeds benefited the Red Cross. Some of these events pitted the top women amateurs against each other and they were warmly received by golf fans.[2]

Although these golfers were technically professionals, they were far from being the tournament professionals of today's LPGA and PGA. There were numerous attempts to create professional golf leagues for men prior to the 1930s. They failed to capture public interest or attract golf professionals, who shunned these risky tournaments for the stability of exhibitions and clinics.[3] For men, the professional tournament circuit began to take shape in the late 1930s and only came into full bloom after World War II. The tournament circuit for women followed the men, hitting full stride in the early fifties.

THE RISE AND FALL OF THE ENTREPRENEURIAL TOURNAMENT

The 1943 All-American Open ("Open" to amateurs and professionals) represents the first professional monied tournament for women. Earlier Open tournaments for women awarded war bonds or merchandise to the winners. George S. May sponsored the tournament at his privately owned Tam o' Shanter club outside of Chicago. May, already a sponsor of a men's tournament, supported a yearly tournament for women for the next decade.

May's events were entrepreneurial affairs designed to generate revenue for the country club. May's vision of professional golf was influenced by the other Chicago-based sport capitalists, Spalding, Comiskey, and Wrigley. The proven approach was to own the sporting facility, produce events, and take the principle profit from the gate and concessions. Owning and operating the facility was the key to success.

May's major contribution to tournament golf was the layout of the All-American Open. He set a standard for the event management of professional tournaments. Prior to May's All-American, management was player focused. May's tournaments catered to the paying spectator. He provided free pairing sheets and numbered jerseys for the caddies so that fans could identify players. He put up concession stands throughout the course and, for a fee, parking adjacent to the course. He also offered preferred seating around the greens at the first, sixteenth, seventeenth, and eighteenth holes (which could be purchased for an additional fee). May's primary concern was the comfort and needs of the spectators willing to pay the price of admission.

The early professionals were both grateful and leery of May. In 1954 professional golfer Betty Hicks wrote:

> Tam o' Shanter's George May is a long-time standing sponsor. Mention of his name brings mixed reactions from the pro's. Famous for his loose purse strings and tight dictatorship, May behaves like a businessman on the brink of bankruptcy when the pay-off for the women comes around.[4]

Because May owned and ran the All-American, his tournaments were never officially sponsored by the professional golf players' organizations. But as long as May put on a tournament the player associations were careful not to schedule conflicting events.

While May's motives may have been self-serving, he deserves credit for seeing the potential entertainment value of women's golf. The failure of the May-style tournaments to catch on undoubtedly had less to do with his energy and creativity than it did with the nature of the sport. May took his lead from the promoters of football and baseball. Yet the differences between golf and these sports made it difficult for his model to work. Individually owned golf courses were rare. Even if there were a consortium of course owners, players operated independently (without the need for teams, managers, or promoters) and therefore were difficult to control. Corcoran once wrote that golf "operates upside down" in comparison to other sports. "The players have to pay to tee off, and they use facilities constructed for the use of the amateur owners who, occasionally, agree to open the gates."[5]

In contrast to May, Corcoran took his lead from Hollywood and advertising executives. Unlike May, whose approach to the sports business was like a stadium owner selling tickets for seats, Corcoran used athletes and golf tournaments much the way newspapers use news—to sell space in the public eye. Corcoran never promoted golf strictly as entertainment. The golf tournament, for Corcoran, was the medium through which a celebrity, local Pol, manufacturer, charity, town, or product gained exposure. He sold the event.

CORCORAN'S TOURNAMENT

For many decades the golf manufacturers had understood the value of retaining professional golfers to enhance exposure of their golf prod-

ucts. Wilson, Spalding, and other manufacturers hired golf professionals to travel across the country to offer clinics and demonstrations under
the pretense of promoting the game.[6] As with other sports, sporting
goods manufacturers also promoted their products by sponsoring
leagues and contests and sought endorsements from leagues and organizing bodies.[7] Wilson Sporting Goods and the other manufacturers
were carrying on this tradition by pouring money and assistance into
the competitive tours.

For manufacturers of golfing equipment, a tournament circuit was
ultimately a better value than retaining players as manufacturer representatives. The cost was minimal because many tournaments were
sponsored by local chambers of commerce or benevolent organizations.
With a solid tournament circuit in place, the cost of retaining a player
representative was reduced, because the salaries of better players would
be paid for through prize monies. Tournament players began to see
themselves as independent operators, so manufacturers were relieved of
representative travel costs and per diems. The only potential problem
manufacturers faced was loss of control over the players. They solved
this problem by funding the salary of the tournament director and
retaining a core group of influential players. In 1937, they hired Fred
Corcoran as tournament director for the men's circuit. He served in
that capacity for over a decade.[8] Then, in 1949, the manufacturers
rehired him to organize the women's tour.[9]

One of Corcoran's prewar contributions to the professional golf
tour was the first financially self-sufficient tournament. Prior to 1937, the
PGA guaranteed the players' purse to entice communities to sponsor
tournaments. Corcoran, who had spent a decade organizing amateur
tournaments in Massachusetts, understood the potential revenue a tournament produced for a community. Corcoran was able to switch the
responsibility onto the community to come up with the purse under
the pretense that the revenue generated by seventy professional golfers
eating in restaurants and sleeping in hotels would generate three times
the minimum $3,000 purse.[10]

Corcoran witnessed the tremendous boost competitive golf got
in the mid-1930s from Bing Crosby. In addition to being a famous movie
comic and song-and-dance man, Crosby was a sports entrepreneur
associated mostly with horse racing and golf. To raise money for charity, Crosby orchestrated the first celebrity pro-am tournament, a pre-
cursor of the modern golf tournament. The teaming up of celebrities
and professional golfers in a mock tournament was extremely successful. Amateur golfers, celebrities, and community leaders paid exorbitant
fees to participate in the tournament. Although these funds were

directed toward charity, there were spin-off benefits for professional golf. The celebrities not only enhanced the athletes' status by appearing with them, they increased attendance, which increased the proceeds for charity and the exposure for professional golf.

The potential power of this type of charity event became clear during World War II, when golf was again used to raise money for the Red Cross. Using a celebrity pro-am format, Bing Crosby teamed up with movie co-star Bob Hope, professional golfers, and various others, including Fred Corcoran, to raise millions of dollars for the war effort and the Red Cross.[11] At the end of the war, Corcoran replaced the war effort and war bonds with civic pride and charities such as hospitals or youth programs.

Turning professional golf into a charity represented more than community altruism, it was smart business. At that time donations to charitable organizations were fully tax deductible. Local businesspeople not likely to benefit directly from a golf tournament were more easily persuaded to contribute to the tournaments with these tax deductions as an incentive. In addition, a good charity attracted the hundreds of volunteers and essential in-kind donations needed to run a tournament. Further, a charity with broad reach and many volunteers acted as a promotional vehicle for the tournament. As such, Corcoran transformed a potentially labor-intensive event into a no-cost operation. By appealing to the altruism of a community to put on a tournament, Corcoran obtained all the advantages of May's approach: a tournament site, capital, and event management.[12]

CELEBRITY PRO-AMS AND THE ADVENT OF CELEBRITY STATUS

Possibly even more significant than the charity component of contemporary professional tournaments is the celebrity aspect of pre-tournament pro-ams. Amateurs and celebrities pay large entry fees to mix with professionals in a mock tournament. Since the success of the Crosby "clam bakes," the celebrity pro-am has been the financial core around which most professional golf tournaments are built.

Celebrity status was a fairly new phenomenon in the 1930s, a direct consequence of the burgeoning communications industry. Celebrity status differs from other forms of status in that it is not tied to position or achievement. A celebrity acquires status by virtue of being known. Celebrities enjoy a particular type of charismatic power. They give status to others simply by appearing with them. When the political and the economic elite mingle with celebrities from the entertainment industry, they are cashing in on each other's claims for prestige and credibility.[13]

The Crosby pro-ams, or "clam bakes" as they were affectionately called, also provided Hollywood celebrities the opportunity to boost each other's status. To be seen in public or on film rubbing elbows with professional athletes, community leaders, and most importantly, other movie stars and celebrities, they enhanced their standing in the celebrity system.

By becoming a vehicle for media exposure, golf benefited as well. Celebrity admiration of the professionals' skill enhanced their standing in the public eye. Golfing celebrities like Crosby, Bob Hope, and President Eisenhower did as much or more for professional golf's popularity as did the superior play of Walter Hagen, Bobby Jones, Gene Sarazen, or Patty Berg.

Celebrities did more than help publicize the game. They shaped the manner in which professionals viewed themselves. Early on in the development of the game, professional golfers understood that their celebrity status could be exchanged for financial gain. They realized that people came not just to see good golf, but to see them because they were celebrities. Their status grew more by standing in the reflective glow of Hollywood stars and by engaging in other acts and antics to capture the attention of the media apart from playing a good golf game. It wasn't long before golfers learned the tricks to getting into the limelight. Golf "personalities" like Didrikson or Hagen became celebrities in their own right.

Like all forms of power, celebrity status can be traded or transformed into economic and political power.[14] This credibility can be sold, used to influence, or employed to increase their own fame. In this regard, the renowned sociologist C. Wright Mill noted that the star "system is carried to the point where a man who can knock a small white ball into a series of holes in the ground with more efficiency and skill than anyone else thereby gains social access to the President of the United States."[15] It was clear to Corcoran that if manufacturers could use tournaments to sell golf products, gain political influence, and boost status, tournaments could also be sold as an advertising medium for non-golf-related merchandise.

In the postwar economy of the 1940s and 1950s, American manufacturers could not rely on war-torn Europe or Asia to buy American goods. The American manufacturing community turned to advertising to convince the usually stingy American consumer to buy material goods. As tournament director of the PGA and the LPGA, Corcoran orchestrated the first non-golf-related corporate sponsorship of professional golf tournaments. For the men's tournament, Corcoran arranged for Palm Beach Clothing to sponsor tournaments. A few years later he orchestrated a transcontinental series of women's tournaments sponsored by Weathervane Ladies Sports Apparel.[16]

Corcoran's extrapolation of Crosby's celebrity tournaments to tournaments funded by the advertising of clothing foreshadowed the immense corporate involvement in contemporary professional tournaments. However, professional golf was not able to take full advantage of corporate interest in athletes until the late 1950s. Up until that time, the major media wire services, AP and UPI, followed a policy of using the name of the city or town to distinguish a tournament. They argued that using the name of the corporate sponsor was a cheap way to avoid paying for newspaper advertising. In the late 1950s, the newspaper industry reversed its policy and agreed to call tournaments by the name of their corporate sponsors. This change meant that by sponsoring a national sporting event, a corporation gained tax-free exposure to a target market in the name of charity.[17] In the end, professional golf, the charities, and the corporations benefited from this arrangement.

GENDER AND THE TOURNAMENT

It is not a mere coincidence that the two major professional women's sports, golf and tennis, have tournament formats. They share a common history of women's participation among the upper classes. But the transition from upper-class amusement to a form of mass entertainment came by way of the tournament.

What separates women's golf from women's softball and, for that matter, Corcoran's tournaments from May's, is that Corcoran did not rely solely on the entertainment value of the sport. At a women's baseball or basketball game, the athletes are necessarily the central focus. They play in a confined space for a limited period of time. The conflict between gender expectations and women competing in athletic endeavors is on the surface at these events. Despite feminine outfits, feminine team names, and other overt attempts to feminize women's sports, the conflict between social norms and the actions of women athletes are too great.[18] Historically, women's sports have difficulty drawing spectators. Leagues or events dependent on the revenue generated from the gate are financially suspect.

Corcoran did not sell golf solely as entertainment. Instead, he sold the golf tournament as a medium through which a person, community, or corporation could buy exposure. Gallery seats, Pro-am tournaments, and the pre- and post-tournament festivities were the focuses of interaction, access to which could be sold. Corporations, politicians, and radio and movie "personalities" found tournaments a worthwhile investment. As such, the success of a golf tournament was not dependent on revenue from the gate.

The golf tournament, as an event, quickly evolved into a celebration of corporate capitalism and consumer culture. The tournament has become the county fair of the corporate world—a kind of corporate celebration of itself and its products. The golfing competition at a golf tournament is like the cotton candy and carnival rides at a county fair. It is something nearly everyone takes in, but it is inconsequential to the primary theme of the event—celebration of community. For some, the golf tournament is merely an excuse around which the social world of the country club amuses and celebrates itself. From this perspective, the players seem to be outsiders at their own tournament.

This position is vividly illustrated in the field notes which begin this chapter. The sales representative's comment that "nothing was happening" stands in stark contrast to how much was happening for the players. The difference is perspective. The sales rep meant that no other executives or major clients would be at the tournament site. Business, on the executive level, was not going to take place that morning.

Not being the constant center of attention has its benefits. Less attention is paid to athletic prowess. The gender conflicts, inherent in women's baseball and basketball, dissipate. Furthermore, because a tournament stretches over a number of days, there are plenty of opportunities for the athletes to engage in compensatory acts to assure fans of their femininity and to affirm the sponsoring community. Players spend time with sponsors, participate in the festivities, and make an effort to draw attention to the communities' benevolence by associating with the tournament charity. The subversive qualities of professional women golfers within the country club setting are muted by the corporate-sponsored tournament format.

But the transformation of the tournament into a corporate celebration is not simply a benign reflection of market forces, as this chapter might seem to suggest. Such an explanation is devoid of human intentionality. Ongoing within and around the business of golf is a political struggle. Corcoran's successful effort to win the women's professional golf tour away from the players for the benefit of the golf manufacturers and how that shaped the tour is the subject of the next chapter.

CHAPTER 3

RADICALS AMONG
THE POWER ELITE

*If I am ever tempted to complain about the strain of tournaments
and the woes of traveling, I remember the poor girls back home
slaving over hot stoves and cold typewriters.*

*Men pros on the tournament trail haul their wives along to
tend to washing and ironing, packing and unpacking, shoe shining,
sock darning and map reading. We members of the Ladies P.G.A.
are our own slaves.*

—Betty Hicks, "Saturday Evening Post" Jan 23, 1954

For twenty years, the official version
of LPGA history has marked its beginnings in 1950 with eleven charter
members, including Patty Berg and Babe Didrikson Zaharias. While
this is technically correct, the LPGA, in fact, was preceded by the
Women's Professional Golf Association (WPGA), which was chartered
in 1944. Today the WPGA is rarely mentioned in LPGA literature, and
when it is, it is benignly described as a false start. At risk of being lost in
this muddle of revisionist history is the political battle for control of
women's golf.

The name change from the Women's PGA to the Ladies PGA was
not, as some claim, simply aesthetic, and the transition from the WPGA
to the LPGA was anything but smooth. In fact, the name change is a
lasting remnant of a battle for control of the women's tour and marks a
shift in power from the players to the golf manufacturers. This rocky

transition in the infancy of the tour illuminates the primary political interests of professional women's golf, which can be found throughout its fifty-year history.[1]

THE WOMEN'S PROFESSIONAL GOLF ASSOCIATION

The 1940 Western Open marks the birth of professional competitive women's golf, when Patty Berg won the tournament and received a war bond worth $100. There were other professional women golfers prior to 1940. They were professional in the sense that they were excluded from amateur tournaments, but these teaching pros and reps of golf equipment manufacturers did not have the opportunity to compete for prize money. Berg first attracted media attention when she won the 1940 National Amateur Championship. Her declaration of professional status was national news, and may have been the catalyst for the creation of the early professional tour.[2]

Organized professional competitive golf got off the ground in 1943. Following on the heels of George May's 1943 All-American Open for women, the first monied tournament for women, three professional women golfers formed the WPGA. In 1944, the organization was incorporated. Hope Seignious was the energy and the brains behind the organization. She teamed up with Betty Hicks, the 1941 amateur champion, and Ellen Griffen, a physical education professor at the Women's College of the University of North Carolina. Hicks, the only recognizable name among the three, was named president. Seignious was secretary-treasurer and acted as tournament director. Griffen was vice president. The primary goal of the organization was to organize and promote professional tournaments for women. The WPGA also arranged promotional tours for Hicks in 1946 and 1947. She promoted the sport, giving clinics to physical education professors, high school teachers, students, and amateurs.[3]

The early years of the WPGA were difficult. Amateur women's golf associations hindered the development of the WPGA.[4] Although the amateur bodies had come to accept or at least tolerate the men's professional tour by 1945, they had difficulty accepting the women as professionals. Amateur bodies pressured country clubs not to host WPGA tournaments. Early tournament sites for women were most often public courses. This schism between amateur organizations and professionals continued well into the sixties. In addition to a lack of support from the women's amateur organizations, the men's professional organization was unwilling to help the women get off the ground. A 1945 Seignious proposal for the WPGA to become a branch of the PGA was rejected. Then the powerful Golf Manufacturers Association, a group made up of the major sport and recreation equipment makers and crucial to the development of the PGA, turned down Seignious' 1946 request for aid.[5]

The response of the PGA and the golf manufacturers reflected the prevailing social winds. Seignious' vision of professional golf was conceived in the war era, when women replaced men in the factories and on the ball fields. But the postwar era was not conducive to maintaining this change. Postwar government and industry dedicated themselves to creating jobs for men and restoring a gender order. The late forties were notable for an inordinate number of marriages and births, suburban sprawl, and a temporary decrease of women in the paid labor force. The time was not ripe to begin a professional women's golf tour.

Despite the lack of support from within the golf community, Seignious managed to put together the first three United States Opens. In 1946, with the aid of the Spokane Washington Athletic Round Table (a civic group), the WPGA co-hosted a U.S. Open in Spokane. The 1946 U.S. Open was played for $19,700 in war bonds. In 1947, with much of her own money, Seignious sponsored the U.S. Open in her hometown of Greensboro, North Carolina. Seignious added the first winter professional money tournament in Tampa that same year. The Tampa contest was the WPGA's first money event, with a purse of $3,000. The final WPGA-sponsored U.S. Open took place in Atlantic City in 1948.

Hicks recalls that those early tournaments "were not exactly overrun with pros." She names only seven women as players in the 1947/48 tournaments other than herself and Seignious: Patty Berg, Helen Dettweiler, Mary Mozel Wagner, Kathryn Hemphill, Betty Jameson, Helen Hicks, and Babe Didrikson Zaharias. The rest of the tournament fields were filled with local amateurs.[6]

In those early years, players not only played golf but took an active role in the management of the tournaments. Every member was part of a committee responsible for some aspect of the tour. Players coordinated travel, made rulings, determined pin placement, and orchestrated the press coverage. Player management and operation of the tour was extensive up until the late sixties.

In March of 1947 a meeting of the membership was held to map out the future of the WPGA. Hicks called it disastrous and the undoing of the organization. Tension arose over who should be the tournament director and the responsibilities of that position. The membership, Hicks writes, "refused to let anyone in their own organization have any permanent role in tournament management."[7] Hicks' analysis is probably a bit simplistic, but points to a larger issue—tension over the control and general direction of women's professional golf.

Although there are no records of the WPGA meetings,[8] it is reasonable to suspect that tensions arose between the players representing manufacturers and the less well-established tournament players; between those who wanted payment for performance and those who wanted payment for appearance and peddling equipment. As was the case with men's golf, early women professionals made the bulk of their income from representing golf manufacturers. Even as late as the early fifties, it was not clear to women professionals that competitive tournament play would ever be as lucrative as exhibitions and club pro work.

But the WPGA was founded with the objective of promoting the sport and not golf products. The differences in vision can be illustrated by the type of promotional tour the WPGA sponsored as compared to the tours of manufacturers' representatives. The WPGA funded a golf promotional tour for Betty Hicks in 1946. Hicks traveled to colleges and high schools and put on clinics for teachers and students for the sole purpose of promoting the game of golf. In contrast, Wilson and the other golf manufacturers financed exhibition tours to promote their products.[9]

After the tumultuous meeting of 1947, the WPGA drifted into the 1948 season with little or no growth. Nonetheless, the foundation of professional women's golf had been laid. The tour consisted of seven tournaments which included the May's All-American Open, the Western Open, the Texas Open, the WPGA U.S. Women's Open, the Titleholders, the Tampa Open, and the Hardscrabble Open. Seignious, who had acted as tournament manager prior to 1947, continued to manage and organize the WPGA U.S. Open in 1948 held in Atlantic City. There continued to be some sort of formal organization, as records indicate Helen Dettweiler replaced Betty Hicks as president.[10]

THE BABE

If professional women's golf was adrift in 1947, it was kept afloat by the media's coverage of Babe Didrikson Zaharias. Didrikson Zaharias was the star of women's golf in the forties. She played as an amateur in 1946 and 1947, winning at least fourteen tournaments in a row.[11] In 1947, she turned pro. Her Olympic fame and crass, but charismatic, personality carried over into golf. She promptly became the leading money winner on the tour and its main attraction.[12]

Fred Corcoran, the former tournament director for the PGA and business manager for Ted Williams, Sam Snead, and other spots figures, was Didrikson Zaharias' manager. She hired Corcoran immediately after she won the 1947 British Women's Amateur title. In addition to Babe's dominating the professional circuit, winning the 1947 and 1948 WPGA U.S. Opens, Corcoran arranged for Babe to tour the country giving exhibitions. She played before large galleries and attracted considerable attention. Her combination of talent and wit was irresistible.

Although there are numerous accounts of Didrikson Zaharias' antics, one shall suffice here to illustrate her talents. In 1948, at the WPGA U.S. Open in Atlantic City, she threatened to spend the weekend in New York City if the pot was not sweetened. Local businessmen quickly offered another thousand dollars to any player to break a score of 300 for the tournament. Didrikson Zaharias won the National Open and $1,200 in prize money. But her score of 300 was one shy of the bonus prize. Despite having complained so loudly earlier in the week, she brushed aside falling short of the bonus prize by saying, "Oh well, it would have put me in another income-tax bracket."[13]

THE COUP

External pressures on the WPGA began shortly after Didrikson Zaharias joined the tour and the disastrous meeting in March of 1947. In the winter of 1947, Wilson representative Patty Berg approached the PGA for aid in organizing tournaments for the women. Although a member of the WPGA, Berg was not an officer and it is not clear if she made her request in the name of the WPGA. Berg's request was tabled.

Within a year Berg's employer, L.B. Icely, president of Wilson Sporting Goods, began to back the ladies tour. According to Fred Corcoran, Icely approached him in Chicago in the winter of 1948 to ask if he might be interested in organizing a professional tour for women. Corcoran, who had been an effective PGA tournament manager for many years, agreed to take on the task. By employing Corcoran, Icely accomplished an organizational coup. Because he was Babe Didrikson Zaharias' manager, Corcoran could assure the manufacturers of the presence of "the Babe" at official events. Didrikson guaranteed media attention, which helped to loosen the purse strings of potential sponsors. The rest of the field would follow the money. By controlling the biggest name in women's golf, the manufacturers and Corcoran effectively gained control of professional women's golf.

Corcoran was a logical choice for another reason: he had experience. A decade earlier, he transformed the men's tour for the benefit of the manufacturers. In 1937, Corcoran was asked to replace Bob Harlow as tournament director of the PGA. Although he officially was employed by the PGA tournament bureau, Corcoran was informed in no uncertain terms that his salary was fronted by the golf equipment manufacturers. The PGA players revolted against the replacement of Bob Harlow, the popular, long-time tournament director. The player revolt ended when the manufacturers' player representatives were told to pull their support for Harlow or risk losing valuable manufacturer sponsorship.[14]

In contrast to his tenure as PGA director, Corcoran never pretended to be an employee of the WPGA or the LPGA. He was hired by Wilson and later was paid by a consortium of golf equipment manufacturers to help run the women's professional golf tour.[15] The players met with Corcoran at the Tampa tournament in February of 1949. The professionals present, the majority of whom were manufacturers' representatives, agreed to appoint Corcoran as tournament manager. Berg was elected president.

Betty Hicks refers to this transition of power from Seignious to Corcoran as a "kind of coup."[16] In Corcoran's account, it is clear that Seignious was overpowered by the manufacturers.[17] The new leadership called Seignious, who was not present at the Tampa tournament, to ask if she would pass along the organization's charter to the newly elected officials. Not surprisingly, Seignious, who had invested her energy and money with little or no return and had asked for help from the manufacturers a few years earlier, felt little compulsion to remove herself from the organization and turn it over to the manufacturers. She declined to relinquish the charter. Corcoran called his attorney, Lee Eastman, to ask for advice on how to operate without the charter. Eastman suggested Corcoran sidestep Seignious by merely changing the name of the organization and applying for a new charter.[18]

In May of 1949, at the Eastern Open, the organization was formalized under the name Ladies Professional Golf Players Association (LPGPA). Six players signed this agreement. Louise Suggs, who was unable to attend the Eastern Open, was invited to join the organization. The seven charter members of the LPGPA were Patty Berg, Betty Jameson, Babe Didrikson Zaharias, Helen Dettweiler, Bettye Mims Danoff, Helen Hicks, and Suggs. At least four of the seven were either under agreement with a manufacturer and/or represented by Corcoran.

By 1950, it was clear that the WPGA was no longer functioning and that Corcoran and the manufacturers were running the women's tour. In 1950 the organization was renamed the LPGA and new papers were drawn up. The revised organization was broader in membership than the LPGPA. Eleven players were charter members, including the founding WPGA president, Betty Hicks. Berg retained her position as president, Dettweiler was named vice president, Betty Jameson was elected secretary-treasurer.

BATTLE LINES

Although the LPGA represented a coming together of the WPGA members and the LPGPA, there was one noticeable difference between the WPGA and the LPGA. The LPGA relied heavily on outside, non-golfer, male management professionals, while the WPGA was player managed.

Hicks was reluctant to forget the past and the hard work done by Seignious, Dettweiler, and herself. In an article written for *Sport Magazine* in 1950, she continued to call the organization the WPGA or "WPGA the second." She gave vice president Dettweiler, a former WPGA president, primary credit for forming the new constitution and relegated Wilson representative Berg to a figurehead position. Hicks' article points to the continued tension between the independent, self-sufficient old guard of the WPGA and the manufacturers and their player representatives in the LPGA. Here is a sample of the article:

> That is why, as this is written, WPGA-the-second is in the process of actually being organized. The ringleader is Helen Dettweiler, whose faith in women's ability to implement the democratic process is unshakable.
>
> At a Chicago meeting in August, the pros formed a straight-thinking committee to draw up a constitution and by-laws for the new association. Incorporation is expected by the year's end. Patty Berg is president. Helen Dettweiler is executive vice president, or whatever title one prefers to give the officer who handles the broom and dustpan.[19]

Also illustrative of continuing tension over who controls the tour are her comments about the role of Corcoran after the transition from the LPGPA to the LPGA.

> Next year should be the biggest in the history of women's golf. Though Corcoran was trumpeted in as tournament manager

with the news he would line up 20 tournaments in 1950, he actually produced six which had not been in the schedules previously. The speculation that there will be 20 to 30 events in '51 is therefore not based on what Corcoran already has signed for the girls, but [what the WPGA officers tell Corcoran to do].[20]

The powers that be, however, were working hard to forget the past and shape the future. The editors of *Golf World* made it a point to correct Hicks shortly after the 1950 article appeared and reaffirmed that Corcoran was indeed in charge and directing a new organization called the LPGA.[21]

Unbeknownst to Hicks and the other players, the manufacturers had limited the number of tour events. Regardless of the players' wishes, there would not be thirty tournaments. Wilson's management instructed Corcoran to limit the annual contests to twenty to ensure that their player representatives had time to travel to various golf clubs across the country to promote their golf products.[22] The new LPGA actually lost the opportunity to play a tournament in Sarasota, which had raised $4,000 to host an LPGA event, because Corcoran could not guarantee that players under contract to the manufacturers would be able to show up.[23] Also illustrative of the players' lack of control is the LPGA's failure to incorporate. Although this seemed to be the players' desire, the golf manufacturers' legal advisors recommended forming an association.

The struggle over control was not completely lost by the WPGA faction. Remnants of the WPGA and the vision of Hicks and Dettweiler can be found today in the strictly enforced rules which prohibit players from receiving appearance fees. Unlike professional tennis, where appearance fees are not-so-subtly paid under the table, and professional road racing, where appearance fees are openly demanded by top runners, the LPGA requires their membership to play solely for prize money. LPGA members can only receive appearance fees for non-LPGA related events.

As time passed, the WPGA, Seignious, Dettweiler, and Betty Hicks received less credit for their work in the cultivation of professional golf and the conflicts were all but glossed over. A 1958 account of the history of women's golf, written by former pro and Wilson employee Lois Hayhurst, claims Seignious "decided to withdraw from her position."[24] The literature produced by the LPGA for the fortieth anniversary of the LPGA makes scant reference to the independent work done by the WPGA. Even Patty Berg, as late as 1989, continued to hold fast to the standard answer to questions regarding the name change—"Fred thought it sounded better."[25]

Berg's and Hayhurst's accounts gloss over a tension which consistently crops up throughout the history of the tour. This conflict can be loosely described as the tension between those who see professional golf's primary attraction as pure competition and those who envisioned its power as an entertainment business and an advertising tool.[26] In all spectator sports there exists a tension between sport and showmanship, between play and display.[27] The conflict is not an "either-or" debate. The debate is over the emphasis and amount of control the players, as athletes beholden to the principles of fair play, should exert over the spectacle of competition. In what form should professional sport be presented to ensure honest effort, yet create enough drama or interest to attract public attention? The conflict often pits players against each other and players against sponsors and management, as they wrestle with how much control to give up in exchange for financial gain and institutional stability. This tension can be found throughout the history of the LPGA.

THE MANUFACTURERS' TOUR

Under Corcoran's direction, the number of events tripled from seven in 1948 to 21 in 1951. The most impressive were the Weathervane Tournaments, sponsored by Alvin Handmacher, a maker of women's sportswear. The contest was played at four sites over the country. The players competed in individual tournaments and for an overall prize for the best play over the four tournaments. Handmacher, in exchange for sponsorship, used the events to sell his sportswear. In addition to putting up the money for the four tournaments, Handmacher also signed Didrikson and other professional golfers as manufacturer representatives to promote his goods.

While Weathervane symbolized the type of sponsorship Corcoran brought in, the Bauer sisters represented the type of players Corcoran brought to the tour. The two sisters, although good players, were not as talented as Suggs, Berg, or Didrikson. Their primary asset was their beauty. The Bauer sisters added sex appeal to the tour, a portrayal Corcoran never failed to discourage.

Corcoran and the manufacturers were clearly in control of the tour by 1950. Corcoran represented the three major draws, Didrikson and the Bauer sisters. Three other stars, Berg, Louise Suggs, and Marilynn Smith, were tied to the manufacturers. Through this core group of players, Corcoran and the manufacturers could dictate the terms of any agreement. But the players found ways of resisting. In

1953, they actually orchestrated a sit-down strike at a Handmacher-sponsored event. Although their demands only concerned playing conditions and did not represent a threat to the power structure, the fact that they resorted to a locker room sit-down strike is illustrative of the players' independence and, simultaneously, their lack of input.

The growth of the tour, orchestrated by Corcoran and the golf manufacturers, hinged on Didrikson. Didrikson dominated the tour in the early fifties. She continued to perform exhibitions before large crowds and became synonymous with women's golf. The crowning accomplishment of the Corcoran/Didrickson era came in 1953, when the USGA agreed to sponsor a Women's U.S. Open. Women's professional golf had officially arrived.

The increasing stability of the women's tour reflected a broader theme within American culture—namely, that the postwar pressures for women to return to the domestic sphere were unrealistic. Despite the postwar propaganda, working women did not want to leave the work force. In fact, by 1952, two million more women were at work than in the peak years of the war effort.[28] Women's professional golf represented a symbolic alternative to the dominant images found in popular culture and may have more acurately reflected women's reality.

But the tour was overly dependent on Didrikson's status. In the midst of unprecedented growth and acceptance, the young tour remained extremely vulnerable. In 1953, tragedy struck. Didrikson was diagnosed with cancer. Handmacher and the golf manufacturers pulled their support for the tour shortly thereafter.[29] Without funding for Corcoran's position and a major sponsor, control of the tour fell back into the hands of the players.

THE PLAYER'S TOUR

Old tension between the players and outside control again became apparent in this transition. In 1954, Hicks took a jab at Corcoran and the previous management of the tour when the players discovered that their organization was not incorporated.

> There has been other evidence that the association was in want of an efficiency expert. We had long been told we were incorporated in New York; investigation revealed that the secretary of that state had never heard of us. . . . Last July, Betty Jameson matter-of-factly advised us that the bylaws which had presumably been in effect had never been approved.[30]

Similarly, the manufacturers were leery of player management. A cover letter, dated February 1954, accompanying a copy of the organization's by-laws from Henry P. Cowen, president of the MacGregor Company, to Louise Suggs, urged her to convince the players not to tamper with the by-laws. The attitude of the manufacturers toward the players is captured in the following piece of advice concerning the transition of power:

> Just be careful about making a lot of changes. A lot of thought and attention, as well as legal advice, went into this original draft so don't let the "radicals" upset things.[31]

Despite the mutual suspicion, player management proved effective throughout the 1950s. Clearly the work of Corcoran and the manufacturers did not go to waste. Although the number of tournaments increased only moderately over the next decade, from 21 to 26 in 1959, the prize money increased significantly. Annual prize money increased from $50,000 in 1952 to $200,000 by 1959.[32] Players cultivated local contacts originally established by Corcoran and the golf manufacturers. Although it was a decade before another major sponsor supported the LPGA, the grassroots commitment to the tour was strong and lasting. The players' personal touch with local golf enthusiasts and civic leaders paid off. For some civic groups and communities, sponsoring an LPGA tournament event became a central annual event.

Just as Babe Didrikson symbolized the LPGA in the early fifties, Mickey Wright epitomized the tour for the next decade. Wright was far and away the best golfer of the time and is considered by some the best woman golfer of all time. She was quiet and smart. Unlike Didrikson, whose golfing prowess was somewhat ancillary to her showmanship, Wright's skill was the show.

It was during Wright's tenure that the LPGA was first televised. Wright's ability induced Sears and Roebuck, a major seller of sporting goods, to sign on as the television sponsor of the 1963 Women's U.S. Open. That same year, Wright won a record thirteen tournaments. The tour expanded with Wright's supurb play and television exposure. Annual competition prize monies grew from $200,000 in the late fifties to $500,000 in 1966. The number of events climbed as high as thirty-seven. Trouble lay ahead, however.

In 1965, without notice or explanation, Wright went into semi-retirement, and just as suddenly the growth of the LPGA slowed.[33] This slowdown can no doubt be partially attributed to the social turmoil of the late sixties and the lack of household names on the tour, but the main problem was the management style of the players. The players were still reluctant to centralize management and control and relied on local civic groups and golf enthusiasts to produce events. The decentralized power which characterized player management did not adapt well to the television era. Sears and Roebuck pulled their television sponsorship after three years and the tour was unable to land a stable television sponsor to replace them. The annual purse failed to grow over the next five years, and even more dramatic, the number of tournaments fell to 21 in 1970 and 1971, the same number that Corcoran had arranged in 1951.[34]

THE CORPORATE TOUR

The LPGA was rescued by Colgate Palmolive in 1972. Colgate became the anchor sponsor of the tour and directed the LPGA's entrance into the television era. Colgate's motives for supporting the LPGA were not totally charitable. Colgate anticipated the women's recreation and sporting boom of the 1980s and was attempting to get a headstart on the competition, particularly Procter and Gamble, which monopolized daytime television advertising.

In addition to their advertising plan, Colgate purchased numerous midsized sporting goods manufacturing companies in the early seventies. During 1973, Colgate Palmolive of Great Britain acquired Craighton Golf Club Company, Penfold Company (golf balls), E. J. Price (golf bags), and Pickards (golf gloves). In 1974, they purchased Ram Golf Corporation, makers of clubs, balls, and bags.

Their plan was essentially threefold. First, promote women's sports to increase women's participation and interest. Second, use this increase in participation to increase the sales in the company's recreation and leisure divisions. Third, use female sports stars created by their sports promotion, with whom the growing active female population will identify, to sell Colgate's line of household products.[35] This strategy proved to be mutually beneficial to Colgate and the LPGA. However, even with the new growth this relationship brought, all was not well at the LPGA.

While Colgate gave the tour an image boost and strong corporate sponsorship, internally the player management of the tour was proving inadequate. The tensions between sport and business which had festered under the surface of the tour since 1954, came to light in an internal conflict. Indeed, had it not been for Colgate's sponsorship, the tour might have dissolved in the early 1970s.

In 1972, the young star and budding media favorite Jane Blalock was accused of cheating (improving her line on the greens when replacing her ball) in three successive tournaments by fellow players. The LPGA leadership assigned four neutral observers to watch Blalock during a tournament. Based on the testimony of the four observers, the LPGA leadership voted to expel her from the LPGA for one year. Blalock sued the LPGA.

The basis of Blalock's suit was not her innocence, but rather the legitimacy of the punishment—competitors denying her access to making a living. She appealed to the court to protect her rights as a participant in the free market system. In its defense the LPGA argued that its action was motivated by its members' desire to protect the sanctity of the sport. Their action reflected an assumption of obligations that went with the position of athlete; obligations so basic to sport they were never explicitly stated in the by-laws of the organization. The case highlights the divergent interests of sport and business which again threatened the LPGA.

Player management proved to be woefully inept at handling this crisis. Players chose sides in the controversy and accused each other of perjury, slander, and ethics violations. The press painted the LPGA leadership as harsh and unfair and Blalock as a helpless victim. In 1973, the court ruled in favor of Blalock; the suspension was in fact an antitrust violation. The LPGA unsuccessfully appealed the decision. By the end of 1974, the leadership of the LPGA was divided and weak. The court cases had drained the treasury and the organization teetered on the edge of bankruptcy.

In the summer of 1975, the president of the LPGA, Carol Mann, pleaded with Ray Volpe, a vice president of marketing for the National Hockey League, to take over as commissioner of the LPGA. So broken and tired was the player leadership that Volpe was given carte blanche to reshape the organization. Volpe dismantled the player-controlled executive board that managed the tour and developed a player council whose power was strictly advisory. The player council was composed of a president, vice president and five player representatives. These players represented groups of players divided into cohorts determined by the years a player had been on tour (0-2, 3-5, 6-8, 8-10, and 10 or more). In place of the executive board, he established a board of directors composed of four players, the commissioner, and five volunteers from the corporate world or the golf establishment. Structurally, Volpe ensured that he and corporate representatives were firmly in control of the management of the tour.

In addition to reshaping the core of the LPGA's structure, Volpe assembled a management staff. Prior to Volpe's direction, the tour was managed by the players, an executive director, and an administrative assistant. Volpe added a full-time media staff, a public relations director, a publicity coordinator, and he assembled a marketing group (People and Properties).

The hiring of Volpe represented not only a relinquishing of tour control by the players, but a reemphasis (à la Corcoran) on golf as spectacle rather than competition. Under the direction of Volpe, the tour was transformed from the centerpiece of small-town civic events to a national media phenomena and an advertising medium. Volpe relocated LPGA headquarters from the country club setting of Atlanta to the media capital of New York. Like Corcoran, Volpe emphasized the "sex appeal" of the players. Jan Stephenson, Laura Baugh, Cathy Reynolds, Judy Rankin, and other attractive golfers were highlighted by the Volpe marketing team.

It did not matter that Baugh never won a tournament and never finished higher than fifteenth in the annual rankings during Volpe's tenure. Although clearly a good golfer deserving of professional status, she was never a great golfer. Nonetheless, like the Bauer sisters a generation earlier, Baugh became a well-known golfer. Her stunning good looks, a pin-up poster, and Volpe's marketing of the tour through her accounted for her status.

Likewise, Volpe used Stephenson's beauty to promote the tour. Stephenson, like Baugh, employed her good looks to turn a profit. Unlike Baugh, Stephenson became one of the finest golfers in the 1980s. Between 1981 and 1987, she finished in the top ten five times and won sixteen tournaments. Sadly, as a result of Volpe's marketing, she will be best remembered by many for her non-golfing attributes.

Similar to the previous periods of growth, the Volpe era was associated with one exceptionally talented player—namely Nancy Lopez, from whom the tour received a huge boost in the late seventies. In 1978, her first full season, Lopez won eight tournaments, including a record string of five in a row. Her accomplishments were expertly promoted by Volpe. Lopez quickly became a national hero as her rags-to-riches story reverberated through the popular media. But like Stephenson, Lopez' best golfing performances came later. In 1985, Lopez' per-round average (70.73, an LPGA record) was a full stroke better than her play in 1978. But as a result of Volpe's expert handling of the media, she will remembered most for her rookie season.[36]

By skillfully using the media, Volpe was able to cultivate corporate sponsors. Volpe aggressively courted sponsors by offering more services and involvement. Special sponsor packages enabled corporations to simultaneously advertise to a target market, entertain buyers, put on employee functions, and demonstrate social responsibility. Corporate sponsorship, which accounted for only 10% of the LPGA's backing in 1975, jumped to 40% in 1978.[37]

The centralized control of the organization allowed Volpe to make other sweeping changes. He instituted a pension plan for players who remain on the tour for ten or more years. This retirement plan was the first of its kind for an individual sport. He established licensing of the LPGA logo and products. These structures and programs instituted by Volpe continue to serve as the bases of the LPGA today.

Most players who lived through the Volpe era admit that he pulled the organization from the brink of disaster and created an organizational structure which could operate in the media era. He was not, however, the right person to lead the LPGA in a period of sustained growth. By mutual agreement between the players and Volpe, he stepped down in the early eighties. He was replaced by John Laupheimer, a corporate insider, able to keep both civic groups and corporate sponsors happy. Laupheimer guided the LPGA on a path of steady growth throughout the eighties.[38]

In the late eighties and the early nineties there were signs of player discontent with the structure and growth of the tour. First, the membership worked to remove manager John Laupheimer. They chose in his place a marketing expert, Bill Blue, in an attempt to reap some of the benefits of the recreational golfing boom. Players almost immediately disliked Blue's headstrong style, which alienated longtime supporters of the tour. Blue was replaced by Charles Mechem, a former LPGA championship tournament director, U.S. Shoe executive, and media specialist.

The players also approved a new constitution that changed the nature and structure of the advisory board. The players abandoned Volpe's cohort representation. Now all members would be voted on at large in an attempt to get the most experienced and recognizable players involved. Players were encouraging the higher-ranking players to get involved in the management of the tour, as they were perceived to have more weight when dealing with outside interests. These changes in structure and leadership point to a subtle increase in player management and control in the post-Volpe era.

This recent flexing of player strength is hardly enough to reshape the basic structure of the tour. As professional women's golf enters its sixth decade, control of the tour rests squarely on the shoulders of the corporate elite. Volpe's successful push for the investment of corporations in the tour has transformed the management of the LPGA.

Tournament sponsors are increasingly bank presidents and corporate CEOs. The tour is increasingly under the protection and control of the ruling elite.[39]

CONCLUSION

The tension between sport and business runs throughout the fifty-year history of women's professional golf. The struggle for control of the tour between the corporate power elite on one side and the players on the other seems to have been won. Struggles similar to those of the forties and fifties seem unlikely. Although contemporary players exert a certain amount of control, it is limited, and the tour is ultimately beholden to its corporate sponsors.

The early players could afford to be far more radical than today's golfers. Comments like those made by Hicks in 1954 which introduce this chapter, are far too feisty and critical for the contemporary tour player. Early professionals were not financially invested so much as they were politically invested. Tournament golf was rarely their sole source of income or their primary source of income. First and foremost, the tour provided them the opportunity to play in high-level competition and an alternative to clerical or domestic drudgery. They played tournament golf for the love of it and they were protective of it.

Today's players have a vested interest in the corporate sponsorship system. The guiding principle of most players when interacting with the press is to be non-controversial.

Although the tour became increasingly shaped by corporate interests, the legacy of the sport-focused ideology of the early players lingers just beneath the surface. This undercurrent to the dominant operation of the tour can be found in moments of crisis, such as the 1953 sit-down strike, the 1954 transition of power, and the Blalock affair. But even in relatively stable eras, it can also be found in the players' tinkering with the constitution and restructuring the organization. Like their sisters of yesteryear, today's players remain something of an anomaly within the business world and the country club. While no longer radicals within the power elite, they are not completely incorporated either. Nomadic, independent, yet strangely dependent, players are necessary intruders in a community celebration. Like carnival workers at a county fair, today's professional women golfers simultaneously attract and repulse their patrons, simultaneously affirm and disrupt the comfort of the status quo.

CHAPTER 4

GETTING IN AND STAYING OUT

O n the day before a tournament begins, two social worlds collide at a pro-am tournament. The contrast is extreme: the amateurs are predominantly men and the women are professionals. The amateurs are usually businessmen, sometimes politicians or entertainers. They range in age from just prior to mid-life crisis to the other side of retirement. Their flawed backswings and awkward follow-throughs seem misplaced inside the ropes and juvenile in comparison to the effortless and graceful swings of the professionals. Ironically, the amateurs' pro-am participation symbolizes power, security, and wealth within the social world of golf. The amateurs' secure and stable lives contrast with the uncertainty that characterizes the professional's career, and the pro-am is a reminder of the LPGA's dependency on corporate support.

But the amateur golfer and the professional share more than a golf course for a day. Within their respective worlds, they have "made it." For the businessmen, the pro-am is proof. The players wear their proof on their belts; a brass belt clip embossed with the LPGA logo, which the players call their "card." The clip is recognized throughout the golfing world as proof of professional status.

The process of earning a "card" shapes the contemporary golfer and how she views her world. The path to the pro ranks is something all players share, a rite of passage to an arduous life. The social life of the professional golfer and her subworld are incomprehensible without an understanding of how she got "out here" and how she stays "out here."

For golfers, "making it" means earning a LPGA membership. It is a Herculian task. Each year, six hundred women start the process of "trying out" for the tour by entering regional tournaments. Of these,

55

less than one hundred will be invited to the LPGA qualifying tournament. About twenty will be invited to join the LPGA. As difficult as joining might seem, staying on tour proves to be equally arduous for many golfers. The majority of each years' new crop of professionals will play less than three years on the LPGA tour.

INTRODUCTION TO GOLF

The process of becoming a successful professional tour player starts long before the qualifying tournament. Most professional golfers have childhood memories of golf. They are introduced to the game by their parents or a relative at a fairly early age. Players remember golf being a family activity, a recreational option, during childhood. Most players talk about other athletic activities in addition to golf when discussing their development. While golf was indirectly part of their lives, most professionals locate the beginning of their passion for golf in their early to mid teens. These quotes typify the pre-professional experience.

> My father introduced me to the game. I'd watch him hit balls at night at the driving range after work, and he'd drag me around on the pull cart every once in a while. To be honest, I didn't care for it that much when I was four or five until the age of twelve. I liked softball and I had other interests. I liked just being a kid. To go out and chase a ball around into a hole just seemed absolutely stupid to me. *(laughs)*
> I really picked up the game to please my father. He wanted me to do it so badly, so I thought, "I can go out and play nine holes with Dad for two hours and he'll be happy." Well, I got hooked. (Pauline)

> I always wanted to be a professional athlete. For women you have either golf or tennis. I never really played tennis, so that narrowed it down real quick. My parents both played golf. My mother was real good when she was young, about a four handicapper. (Roslynn)

> My dad and my grandfather played a lot. I was really introduced to golf when I was 6 or 8. I got a golf set for Christmas or something. I'd hit balls in the back yard. I didn't really pick it up and play until I was 15. I always liked the players. I liked to follow Dad and my grandfather around, and drive the golf cart. (Pam)

Of the players interviewed, only two had non-golf-playing parents. Both learned to play during college. One taught herself to play while she was working as a physical education instructor. The other was a scholarship athlete in basketball. She took up golf after an injury in her freshmen year prevented her from playing basketball.

In most cases, the family life and work life of a future professional revolved around the sport of golf.[1] During childhood, golf was not just one of many recreational activities, but *the* family activity.

> My father is a member of the PGA and my two older brothers used to be golf pros, so I grew up in a family of golfers. I wanted to learn to play when I was six years old. I asked my dad and he said I would have to wait two years. That seemed like an eternity to me.
>
> That's pretty much how I got started. I kept watching them go off on weekends and things like that and finally, when I became eight years old, [my father] taught me how to play. By the time I was thirteen I knew I wanted to be a professional golfer. (Molly)

> Well, my father was a television repair man, which was the family business. That was basically how he made a living, working in the shop. But he would also teach. He is funny, he just loves to teach golf.
>
> Both mom and dad played. I learned when I was four. I always knew that golf would be a part of my life. The older I got the more I realized I wanted to make a living at it. (Doris)

While parents were most frequently given credit for introducing the golf professionals to the sport, parental pressure to pursue golf was minimal. Professional golfers seemed to pick the sport of golf on their own. Helen's experience is typical.

> Well, I think my parents were always good in making everything available. They never forced us into anything. They were never "You're gonna be a golfer and you're gonna be . . ." y'know.
>
> They sort of just opened all the doors, which was great. We had the availability and exposure to almost anything. It was nice. It was up to us to decide. They've always sort of encouraged us, no matter what we did. They said "That's great, go ahead." They never said "Don't do that." (Helen)

For the most part players described their parents and family as supportive and caring. Val's socialization into golf typifies many players' experience.

> They knew it was a good thing for me to get into if I enjoyed it. They never pushed it. They just said, "You will enjoy doing this so why don't you go ahead and play." (Val)

Only one player interviewed described a family member as pushy. Nora's father required her to practice daily and pushed her into competitive golf. His demanding approach frequently reduced her to tears. Although in some ways she is grateful to her father, she laments over a lost childhood and blames his rigorous training for her lack of social skills.

> I think the isolation stems a little bit from the way I was brought up. My father was my instructor. Going through school and stuff like that, I had maybe two friends that I thought were really good friends, other than that I spent my time at the practice range. It was fifty or seventy-five yards away from the pool. Everybody I went to school with was at the pool all summer long and I was out on the practice range.
>
> And then during school, I just went to school and just said hi to everybody and just went off to the golf course in the evenings. I never spent the nights with girls. Very few. Not until recently did I spend maybe a night with a girlfriend or have a girlfriend over. I did not go to any parties.
>
> I did attend a ah—the big deal at the end of the year— prom. God, it still eludes me! I left my date at the party because I felt so out of place. I wasn't used to socializing with people my own age. Going to the country club and having dinner and that kind of thing, that was fine.
>
> I don't regret any of it, but my father, he kind of isolated me a little bit. And I think a little bit of that is still in me. And I have a very hard time getting close to people or letting myself get close. (Nora)

TEACHERS

The players are often accompanied by a teacher or mentor along their journey into the LPGA. Many golfers mention the local pro as a significant parental/mentoring figure in their development. The players who discuss their coach-athlete relationship positively generally had local coaches who were readily available to them. The nature of their relationship was usually not based on some sort of financial exchange but a shared commitment to the sport. While the relationship was founded on a commitment to golf, the relationship that developed was much more complex. June introduced me to her "old pro" at the same moment she introduced me to her family. He was, she said, "like part of the family." Holly was so grief-stricken when her teacher passed away that she took six months off and considered retiring from the sport.[2] Helen's detailed discussion of her relationship with her coach, Hank, is instructive.

> [My] mentor in terms of my golfing stuff was Hank. He's a pro from home who I've worked with since I was 10. He's sort of— he's neat, I spent a lot of time with him. Hitting balls and playing and stuff.
>
> On the course we talked about everything. The whole world. Solved the world's problems on the driving range. I still see him every time I go home.
>
> He comes out to the US Open or comes out to the Curtis Cup where we played in England last year as an amateur. Came over to England to watch. It's neat that he's gotten to see the big tournaments. He's great. (Helen)

Roslynn's experience with her coach is different than Helen's but the essence of the relationship is similiar.

> I was real fortunate, I had a guy who was the pro at our course for years, I think he retired after 30-some years. He and his son were like pro and assistant pro. I started six lessons with his son and his dad kind of took over and he told my parents that "if she's really serious about this, I'll work with her."
>
> I got to play with him a lot and I learned a lot of little things that I kind of take for granted now. But people who are new to the game I just assume that they know this stuff and they don't.
>
> He built a net in his backyard, because we didn't have a driving range at our course, so I hit a lot of balls into the net. This is when I'm 13, 14, 15. (Roslynn)

For both Helen and Roslynn, and numerous other tour players, the relationship with a coach during adolescence guided their development. The relationships were characterized by a friendly commitment on the part of the coach. Usually the commitment extended beyond the game of golf to the development of the person. In Helen's case, the sagely Hank shared his wisdom about the world as he taught her about golf. The fact that Roslynn practiced in her coach's backyard indicates that their relationship was not strictly instructional. Building a screen and allowing Roslynn into his backyard to use it is fundamentally different than giving an hour lesson.

ACCESS

By far the single most common component to becoming a professional golfer is liberal access to golfing facilities. It is not surprising that golf is associated with the upper classes. Participation in this sport is primarily limited by its costs, financial and temporal. Only a small percentage of the societal population enjoys enough access to the sport of golf to produce high-caliber golfers. In 1974, Nancy Theberge (1977) found that two-thirds of women professional golfers had received individual private lessons and a similar percentage had enjoyed membership privileges in a private country club in their youth. Fifteen years later, most of the athletes on tour enjoyed similar training facilities.

> I grew up on a country club course. A small nine-hole country club; small town. To tell you the truth, I started playing when Lopez was a rookie. I was 16. I played like once or twice a summer up until then. (Cathy)

> My parents played. I was a country club brat when I grew up. I played all the sports. I did the swim team and tennis. Golf was the last one that I really learned how to do. I guess I was eleven when I first really had instruction. We had a great junior program there. The head pro would give us lessons—free lessons on Mondays and we would get to go out and play. . . . My mom drove me all over the place in the summer. I was fortunate that I had a place to go play. It kind of evolved from there. (Cara)

Nonetheless some players, particularly players over the age of thirty, come from a working-class/public course background. They also had liberal access to a golf course while growing up.

> I got started when I was nine. [Lessons] were co-sponsored by the Department of Recreation and the local newspaper. We

lived close to the public golf course and my dad played. I used to caddy for him. The local pro at the local public course had a series of like six lessons. They were massive group lessons. They must've had fifty to a hundred kids in each group. But we were schooled in the fundamentals of golf. I did that for six years. . . . I just played everyday [in the summer] on the public golf course. (Tara)

[I] grew up across the street from a golf course, public course, and just always kind of played. (Nat)

While the younger players were family members of a golf or country club, working-class players tend to recall their childhood golf as being part of the pro shop or caddy shack. These are working-class enclaves within a middle- and upper-class sport and provide the working-class player with a supportive environment to learn the game. One of the most poignant illustrations of the working-class community was Toni's story of her relationship with the local public course pro. Toni's family rented a farm in rural Ohio near a public course. Her relationship with the professional began when she lost control of a colt on a riding trail near the local public golf course. The colt ran across the course and caused damage to some greens. As a way of making up for the damage, Toni agreed to give the local teaching professional's children a ride on her horse.

At the same time my older brother would go to the golf course and caddy. My family did not have much money. My brother used to bring home money, you know. I needed money to feed my horse, so I went over there and asked if I could caddy. So I saw the golf pro again.

"Oh, you again", sort of thing, "No, sorry, girls can't caddy." Which really disappointed me. But then he said "You've been so nice to my kids I'll give you a lesson." I don't have any golf clubs. So he gives me a club and we go do it right there.

I hit some, and he said, "You should try this game."

I says, "How much does it cost."

He said, "I will let you play and practice free." So the following year in school I took golf instead of tennis as my individual sport—went to the state finals in golf. Now there was about four girls that could play. I won the tournament—shot a hundred (*laughs*).

I got the bug and kept practicing. The pro was really nice to me, gave equipment to me and balls. (Toni)

As is the case for Toni, for the working-class player, liberal access to a golf course is often gained through the benevolence of a local professional.

GETTING FROM THERE TO HERE

Between ten and twenty new players join the tournament circuit each year. Joining the LPGA tour is, at the very least, challenging, and for some, painful. The qualifying process, often referred to as "qualifying school," is considered by many professionals to be the most stressful and difficult of all tournaments. So much rides on one tournament. There is only a single chance each year to prove oneself worthy of an LPGA card.[3] One hundred and fifty women, selected from regional tournaments, compete with each other for slots on the LPGA tour. Of these women, only about fifteen new players will be invited to join the tour.

The preparation necessary to become a tour member has changed dramatically as a result of increasingly difficult standards. Tara, on the tour for over twenty-five years, discussed the metamorphosis of the rookie in our interview.

> The difference I see is that they [younger players] are more prepared to come out here now. There are alot more junior programs, alot more college programs, alot more tournaments that women can play in now. When I came out, there were no tournaments except city and state tournaments. I bet a woman amateur could play in a tournament every week if they wanted. When they do come out here they are more competitive. They are ready to play.
>
> When I came out here I got my schooling on the golf course. I think younger players today already know that.

The survey I conducted confirmed Tara's observations. Rigorous practice during adolescence has increased dramatically. Of the players joining the tour prior to 1975, about half (46%) remembered practicing every day or almost every day between ages 14 and 17. For those joining the tour after 1983, 86 percent played or practiced daily during these teenage years.

The increased intensity of young golfers is driven in part by LPGA entrance requirements. To even apply to compete in the regional tournaments which open the door to the qualifying school, a golfer must have achieved a USGA handicap of three or less. Weekend golf enthusiasts and local club champions need not apply. The regional qualifying tournaments are made up of an elite core of women golfers, a small fraction of the approximately one million serious women golfers in the United States.

A player must also be 18 years of age or older. Absent from the tour are the teenagers (brat packs) and their parents who seem to populate the world of professional women's tennis. On the women's golf tour, rookies average 24 years of age. Although there are a few 18- and 19-year-olds on the tour, by and large the path to the LPGA runs through collegiate golf.

With the passage of Title IX federal legislation in 1972, collegiate women's golf programs sprouted up at many major universities. The better collegiate golfers spend each fall and spring competing in NCAA competition and in the summer they play in amateur competitions. High-quality year-round competition seasons collegiate golfers for the profesional tour.

In addition to collegiate golf, professional women's minor league tournament circuits have developed over the last two decades. These tours operate in a similar fashion to the LPGA but on a smaller scale. The prize money is quite small (about one-tenth) in comparison to the LPGA's $450,000 minimum purse. The mini tours give players the opportunity to hone their skills in professional tournament play. Former collegiate golfers often play on a mini tour during the summer between graduation and the fall qualifying tournament.

> If you play well you can make expenses plus some. It's mainly a learning process out there that you need for out here. In other words, you have to go to school sometime and with the mini tour you're playing every week, that's what we do out here. You have to get used to that. (Pauline)

Many other golfers would agree that the mini tour is a necessary rite of passage for future professionals.

TWO-TIER TOUR

Exactly how many new players join the LPGA is determined by how many existing players get invited to stay. Active players are divided according to their past accomplishments between exempt status and non-exempt. Players with exempt status have first choice on the tournaments they wish to enter. They can enter as many or as few as they like. But a player must play in ten or more tournaments each year to get credit for playing a full season. Exempt status allows players some control over their careers. Between 142 and 150 players[4] enjoy an exempt status. Exempt status is awarded to a player for the following achievements:

1. Exempt status is awarded to all players currently ranked in the top forty of the all-time earnings.
2. One-year exemptions are awarded to players finishing the season ranked in the top ninety.
3. Two-year exemptions are awarded to players finishing the season ranked in the top sixty.
4. Five-year exemptions are awarded to players winning a tournament.
5. Six-year exemptions are awarded to players winning three tournaments in one year.
6. Seven-year exemptions are awarded to any player winning a major tournament.
7. Seven-year exemptions are awarded to players winning five tournaments in two years.

Of the 142 exempt slots, less than half are held by players with multiple-year exemptions. Another forty or so will earn one- or two-year exemptions based on their finishes in the annual rankings each year. On the average, between 100 and 110 players earn exempt status. The remaining 30 to 40 slots are awarded to the highest finishers at the annual qualifying tournament.

For a majority of the players, retaining or gaining exempt status is a primary concern. At every tournament, the members of the LPGA compete for more than prize money. They play for security and future opportunities. They are in competition with each other for control over their own lives.

An equal number of active LPGA players are non-exempt or conditional players. These players fill the playing field at tournaments when exempt players take a week off or become injured. Non-exempt players usually find out they will play in a specific tournament one week in advance. Players with this status are entered into tournaments based on their position in the following scheme:

1. Players finishing 91 to 125 on the money list the previous year.
2. Winners of official events, according to the number of wins, with ties broken by position on the career earnings list.

3. Players finishing in the 20 places (plus ties) behind those receiving exempt status at the qualifying tournament.
4. Players finishing higher than 125 in the annual rankings, inactive members, and teaching pros.

Since tour professionals usually take time off every four to five weeks, non-exempt players can expect between 35 and 50 spots to open up in most tournaments.[5] Conditional players gaining entry to tournaments as a result of the first three standards listed above can participate in 15 to 25 tournaments a year depending on rank and willingness. High-ranking non-exempt players can expect to play a full season of golf sans the major tournaments.

The rules can dramatically distinguish players whose performances are essentially identical. A player finishing 126th in the annual rankings will have difficulty playing a full schedule. In contrast, the player finishing 124th, only fractionally better, can play a full schedule. Getting back into the top 125 is almost impossible with an abbreviated schedule.

Tour players who lose their exempt status may enter the rookie qualifying tournament and attempt to reclaim their exempt status. These players decrease the possibility of a rookie entering the tour. About 150 women compete in the LPGA Annual Qualifying Tournament, often called "qualifying school" within the golfing world. The field is made up of the best collegiate and mini-tour players as determined by regional competition and non-exempt professionals. In 1989, thirty players gained exempt status through the qualifying tournament. However, fourteen of those had previously been on tour and had returned to the qualifying tournament to regain their playing status. In 1988, forty-four LPGA exempt-status cards were awarded via the qualifying tournament, and twenty-seven of these went to players with LPGA experience. In other words, only about fifteen new players join the tour as exempt players each year.

It is very rare for a young player to qualify for the tour on her first attempt.

> It took me four times to get my card in qualifying school. I was pretty frustrated and ready to give up. I said I was going to [give up] if I didn't get my card the fourth time because it wasn't meant to be. I could live with that. But I got it and ended up Rookie of the Year that year. (Fran)

For many professional-caliber players the pressure of getting in weighs heavily and affects their play. One mistake can force her to wait another year for a chance to break in. Another year of "schleping" on the mini tour. Fran's story of failing three times only to become rookie of the year is not unusual. Some good players never get beyond qualifying school.

Just as frequently, players who do not expect to make the tour finish quite well at the qualifying tournament. For Cara the mini tour and qualifying school were just a way to bide time between graduation and graduate school.

> It took me five years to graduate and I was really burned out on school. I never really aspired to be an LPGA pro, or the tour was never my goal. I did play collegiate golf and when I graduated I played the mini tour that first summer and the qualifying schools in October. I thought if I don't make it, I'll play the futures tour for a year and maybe try again next year or maybe by then I'll figure out if I want to go back to school. What happened was I made it through the qualifying rounds and then I got on tour. I didn't have any pressure on me. I mean that is the worst thing in your life as far as golf is concerned. I went in there saying, "Hey, if I make it, great. If not, no big deal." (Cara)

Hattie was so unprepared for success at the qualifying tournament she didn't know what to do once she qualified for the tour.

> Everybody says qualifying school is the hardest thing. I go only for the experience. I made it. I didn't know what to do, so I went home for a month (*laughs*).

In these cases, becoming a professional golfer was not so much a choice or even the next step, but an accident.

Gone are the days when going out on tour merely meant a lifestyle choice. But so are the days of women making a conscious choice to be professional golfers. Today's players do not choose a career in professional golf so much as they drift into it. Whether it just seems like the next step or an accident, joining the tour is left somewhat up to fate. But the final step to making the tour is preceded by a life that is far more predictable—a golfing family or parent, family membership in a country club or some other liberal access to golf, almost daily practice, junior tournaments, a college scholarship, the mini tour, qualifying school, and finally, if they are lucky enough to make it this far, maybe the tour. While this does not describe every player on the tour, it does describe the majority of the players turning pro today.

STAYING OUT

Once on the tour, staying "out here" can be just as difficult for a young player. It is not based solely on performance, but also on a player's financial resources and personal fortitude. One hundred and forty-four players can enter a tournament. Less than half will win enough money to cover their costs. Most of these 144 will lose money. Contests generally last four days, although some tournaments operate on a three-day format. In a four-day tournament, after the second day, the tournament field is "cut" to the top seventy (plus ties). Only these seventy-plus golfers compete for prize money.

Even if a player "makes the cut" there is no guarantee that they will make a profit. In the early 1990s, tournament purses ranged from a minimum of $400,000 to $1,200,000. Most tournaments' total purses are between $450,000 and $550,000. Although this sounds like a healthy reward, after the prize is broken down the lower-scoring players may not win enough to cover their costs. The prize money breakdown for a $450,000 tournament is shown in table 4.1.

Given the costs of travel, entry fees, and caddies, only the top fifty finishers out of the original 144 entrants break even or make money. Most players entered in a tournament will lose money that week. An average player may "make the cut" once every two or three weeks. Many players never score higher than 30th all year. As a result, some players go into debt playing the tour. On the positive side, just one top-ten finish at a major tournament can cover a player's annual costs.

There is very little charity for the struggling player at the tournament. Like the rules of golf and the rules governing playing status, the

TABLE 4.1
Prize Money Breakdown for $450,000

Place	Winnings
1	$67,500
2	41,891
3	30,569
10	9,510
20	5,208
30	3,577
40	2,422
50	1,494
60	837
70	543

tournament format only rewards success. As noted above, players are ranked according to how much money they have won during the year. The top 70 players entered in a tournament play in the LPGA pro-am. This gives the top seventy an extra day on the championship course. The higher-ranked players also receive more favorable tee times. Tee times begin as early as 7:30 am or as late as 1:40 pm on the first two days of a tournament. Low-ranking players will play early one day and late the next, whereas the top golfers' tee-off times remain fairly stable. On the final two days, players receive tee times according to their standing in the tournament. The leading players go last. Again, performance is rewarded. A player in the last group has the advantage of knowing all the other competitors' final scores enabling her to make strategic choices on the last few holes.[6]

Players who struggle to "make the cut" often find themselves in increasingly difficult situations. Few of the non-exempt rookies last beyond the first few years and only about half (about 8 or 10) of the exempt rookies will play ten or more years. But before they decide to leave the tour, many players will go tens of thousands of dollars into debt.

THE COSTS OF PLAYING PROFESSIONAL GOLF

The average professional golfer makes $30,000 to $35,000 a season in prize winnings. This income is usually matched by expenses. Players estimate that each event costs them between $500 and $1,500 depending upon their lifestyle. Travel, food, housing, caddy fees, and entry fees are their major expenses. Table 4.2 outlines the typical annual expenses of an average LPGA tour player playing in 25 tournaments in 1994.

Although it is difficult to calculate expenses given the array of living styles on the tour, this budget matches data collected in interviews. Most players thought they needed to finish in between 80 and 90 on the annual earnings sheet to earn the $30,000 to $40,000 in LPGA earnings needed to break even for the year. If we consider LPGA earnings alone, only about half the approximately 200 active players playing in tournaments meet expenses each year.

> The opportunity for financial gain is great. The opportunity is there, but there is no guarantee. You can go broke—absolutely stone-cold broke doing this. There are so few of us that are doing well financially—very very few. Most people are barely hanging in there or they are going down the tubes. (Gerta)

TABLE 4.2
Players' Estimated Expenses

LPGA dues	$ 159
Tournament fees	2,500
Caddy	11,250
Air travel	4,000
Lodging*	6,125
Food/Entertainment	6,250
Clothing	4,000
Dry Cleaning	750
Health/disability insurance	2,000
Total estimated expenses	$ 36,284

*Assumes half of lodging is private housing.

To make a living off prize money alone—that is, to cover tour expenses and the expense of a mortgage or rent, food, and entertainment during the off-season, tour players have to finish in the top fifty or sixty.

It depends on how you play. That is the big if. It is fine when you've just won eighty-two thousand dollars. But for alot of these people out here who are making twenty to thirty thousand a year, they are spending pretty close to that in expenses. It is hard to save money. But you keep hoping that you are going to cash in—be a top player and make two or three hundred thousand in one year. (Cara)

Making ends meet financially is a major factor in a player's decision to leave the tour. For example, when Val was asked by a reporter, "How come you are playing so badly?", she responded,

Hey, I'm not playing that badly, I'm just not making any money. . . . If I don't start making some money I'm going to look for a real job. I'm not going to do this any more. You can only stay out here so long and beat your head against the wall.

Val's response to the question illustrates both the level of competition and the difficulty of making a living on the tour. There is a difference between playing well and making money. A player can feel that she is hitting the ball well for herself, yet not getting the breaks necessary to make the cut.

The financial crisis which results from failing to make the cut week after week can be compounded by the sacrifices a player feels she is making in other areas of her life. As the following exchange illustrates, choosing to leave the tour is rarely based solely on financial reasoning.

Q: How long do you think you will do this (stay out on tour)?

It depends how much money I make. I am serious. If I keep improving and win and make a lot of money out here, it is worth it to stay out here. But just to make enough to get by . . . well, it is just not *that* much fun. I mean if I still feel that I have the potential to get big out here, which, if I do, then it is worth it [just to get by].

It is worth it for the fun of it for a few years. It is worth it if you are making money after that. It is worth it right now just for the experience; the traveling, going to places I've never been, meeting people. But after a few years the novelty of it wears off. It is not worth it if you are just scraping to get by. It is too much pressure for that. But if you are making a good living, then it is great. (Cathy)

INTANGIBLE COSTS

Cathy's quote above underscores the difficulty of tour life. Far and away the two most common complaints the tour players have about their life are constant travel and boredom. The following quote captures both the reality of being on the road and the hostility players harbor towards travel.

A young player, with a few exceptions, gets tested the first few years: her dedication, her persistence, how much she wants to succeed. You live for a few years like a damn gypsy—making not too much money. A damn gypsy, it's true. Have you ever seen my van. I have everything in there. (June)

Boredom, in some measure, is a product of being on the road.

People kind of get the wrong idea that it is the life of glamor. It is a great life if you love golf. But it is a rat race. You travel from city to city week after week, playing six days out of seven. You get tired. Not to mention you don't get to do a lot except play golf and practice. If you slip away and do something, it is a big treat. People always say to me, "Gosh, you've got the best life in the world, you get to travel all over the country and see this and that." Well, all I see is golf courses, hotels, and restaurants. I really don't see a whole heck of a lot. I eat, sleep, and drink golf out here. You don't have time to do much else out here. (Sue)

Although golf is an exciting annual event for each community in which the tour plays, it is a rather repetitive and mundane[7] activity for the players. While out on tour, LPGA members play or practice golf six days a week and travel on the seventh. For many, tour life becomes monotonous.

The lackluster quality of tour life was apparent at a bible study meeting I observed. The bible study leader began the session by asking everyone to share with the group one exciting thing that had happened to them since they had last met, three weeks earlier. There was a moment of uncomfortable silence and then collective laughter from the players. The minister, realizing her mistake, quickly asked people to just share something from their lives, it didn't have to be exciting.

Even players, like Lynn, who claim to enjoy their life on the tour, long for a "normal" life.

I miss Bar-B-Que in my back yard. . . . It is just the things that are real commonplace to everybody else, like having a garage, or cleaning the pool or cutting the lawn. We don't do normal things like that. We just pack up, pick up, and go. Those things are kind of appealing now and then. (Lynn)

Lynn expresses a common complaint among the tour players. They miss the simple pleasures of staying put.

THE FINANCIAL BENEFITS

While life is difficult for the mid- to low-ranking player, players who survive three or four years on tour usually find a way to make ends meet for ten years. Of the approximately 200 players active in 1989, 61 had left the tour by 1993. Of these sixty players, most had either been on the tour more than ten years by 1993 (37) or less than four years in 1988 (16). That is, if a player makes it past three years, they usually find a way to stay on tour long enough to qualify for the LPGA pension. For example, of the 22 players retiring between the 1988 and 1989 seasons, 12 had been on tour for ten or more years, 8 had been on tour for four years or less. Only two players retired between their fifth and ninth year of play. As indicated above, many of these players are not making ends meet. It would seem, then, that the financial and personal costs of being on tour are outweighed by other benefits tour life offers.

Most mid- to low-ranking LPGA participants rely on other sources of income and/or support in order to remain on tour. The most common way to boost income is by playing in private pro-ams. Like an LPGA event, the proceeds of these mock tournaments go to charity. Unlike the LPGA pro-am, professionals receive an appearance fee, usually between $500 and $1,500, depending on their popularity. These private pro-ams usually take place on the Monday prior to a tournament at the tournament site or within a half-day's drive of the tournament site. Participants are selected by the pro-am organizer (often a player on tour) and therefore the older, more recognizable players are likely to be selected. Most players (36 out of 50) indicated that private pro-am and appearance fees account for less than 20 percent of their income. But private pro-ams can account for as much as 90% of the player's earnings with the lowest-ranking players relying on these monies almost exclusively.[8]

Many of the younger players find personal sponsors to help defray expenses. These players enter into agreements with wealthy golf enthusiasts or investors in which they exchange a share of their winnings for guaranteed coverage of their expenses. While this arrangement may cut into some players' profits, more often than not it acts as a safety net for younger players before they establish themselves on tour.[9] Once a player has the confidence to make it on her own financially, she usually does so. Forty-one out of fifty-six players surveyed (or 73%) indicated that they received sponsorship at some time in their careers. Of the fifty players surveyed that itemized their income sources, eight (16%) claimed income from sponsors (money received for expenses but not repaid) in the previous year.

The top-ranked golfers, and some average but photogenic golfers, can substantially increase their annual earnings through commercial endorsements and corporate sponsorship. A well-known tour regular often has agreements with non-golf-related corporations in which she will display the corporate logo or product logo on her clothing or bag in exchange for income. Earnings from endorsements can surpass LPGA earnings. For example, one player returning the questionnaire claimed to have averaged $20-30,000 in prize money over the past three years, which accounted for only 10% of her income. Almost 90% ($225,000) of her annual income came from commercial endorsements. But this is the exception. I suspect that this player used her status as a professional golfer to launch a modeling career.

For most players, these commercial agreements make up a small fraction of their total annual income and are worth between a few thousand dollars and $10,000.[10] The most common commercial endorsements are agreements between the players and golf manufacturers. Even the lower-ranked regular players on tour can enter into one of these agreements. These usually involve free equipment and cash bonuses, based on finishes in each tournament, in exchange for their use of the manufacturer's product and display of the manufacturer's logo.

Professionals can also find ways to make money during the off-season. Some enter into agreements with golf resorts, exchanging lessons for room and board for the winter. Some younger players will return home and work in the local pro shop for wages and an exemption from greens fees. Still others will accompany recreational golfers on luxury golf vacations or take winter jobs as teaching pros.

Players who can't count on golf to pay the bills will find ways to cut expenses. Struggling players often avail themselves of free housing arranged by the tournament in private homes of local golf fans or by camping. They travel and room together. Using friends, family members, or lovers as caddies reduces one of the major expenses a player on tour faces, paying the caddy. In addition, players feel secure and trusting of a caddy that not only has a financial stake but an emotional stake in the player's performance.

Finally, a significant number of players have long-term relationships with partners who contribute a stable income or help defray costs by caddying for the player. This player who had struggled for a number of years on tour as a single woman had recently married; the change in her standard of living was noticeable.

> Well, basically I couldn't afford to have a house, which we have, with my tour income. I'd still be living with my parents or my sister. I put a little bit of money away, but basically I make enough that I can stay out here—make expenses and put a little away. Last year was my best year ever and I put a lot away. (Hattie)

In their first few years, either by cutting expenses, playing pro-ams, sponsorship, endorsements, or winnings, the players who remain on tour figure out how to make ends meet. Half of the players surveyed claim to have taken more than one year to meet their expenses.

Only six players claimed to have taken more than three years to make ends meet. Presumably players who repeatedly fail to meet expenses after three or more years leave the tour to look for other work. Nonetheless, it is not unusual to see players who consistently finish between 90 and 150 on the money list return for ten years.

It is a common belief on the tour that players have to give professional golf at least three years to be fair to themselves. In those first couple of years, most players are simply struggling with the lifestyle and the grind of being on tour. The players' records corroborate this belief. Most professional women golfers don't begin to play their best golf until age twenty-eight.

After a couple of years of eking out a living on the tour, players develop ways of getting by. They cut costs by living in private housing, using friends to caddy, and supplementing their winnings with private pro-ams. Even if a player never makes it big, she can manage to stay on tour.

Roslynn is a classic example of a long-time low-ranking player. At the time of the interview she had yet to make more that $20,000 in prize winnings. She was in her tenth year and had just qualified for a pension. Her comments are revealing:

> This is my tenth year and I have this pension plan and early in the year a lot of thoughts run through your head like this might be the last time I ever come back to this tournament. And then I start getting mad like, "I don't want it to be the last time." I want to play golf, I wouldn't be happy just staying somewhere all the time and just teaching or whatever. I want to play. (Roslynn)

Four years later, in 1993, Roslynn was still active on tour, eking out a living. Roslynn speaks of a primary motivating force behind the players: the desire to play and to play well. Indeed, few players talk about golf solely as a way of making a living. Most rationalized their desire to stay on tour by citing either their sense that they were getting better and/or that they could win, or the intangible benefits of the tour life.

INTANGIBLE BENEFITS

For all the players' gripes about tour life, they expressed much more satisfaction with tour life than with life off the tour. Despite the low income and the sacrifice of a "normal" life, many players chose to stay on tour. For example, Pauline, the primary breadwinner in a family of three (a husband caddy and an infant child), would have made more by staying home and working for a minimum wage. But for Pauline and her husband, their current income is secondary to the status and opportunity.

I'm lucky because my husband realizes that it is the chance of a lifetime. Not very many people have the opportunity to be out here. And you've got to think of the money also, there is a chance to win $45,000 in a week.

Far more common than status were the players' favorable comments concerning the conditions of their work. Most of the women on tour enjoy what they do.

I am doing something that I love to do. That's just golf. I just love it. I went out and played today on my day off. (Pam)

The options available to women off the tour are not nearly as attractive as remaining on the tour.

Sometimes I think "If I'm not out here playing what would I be doing? Would I be more comfortable doing that than this?" I have thought about it and there is no way. (Beth)

Players have difficulty imagining a type of work off the tour that would come close to the experience of being a professional golfer.

I've been talking to all my friends who just graduated and are in their first jobs. They're talking about vacation days and not being able to do anything. It's kind of funny cause I'm having fun. They can't believe it. (Sara)

[Golf] really offers a good freedom of choice. In this job you're not locked into something, working for somebody else. Now that would be very hard, that's what I'm very frightened about in leaving this tour.

The thought of working for someone else just scares me to death. (Fran)

Clearly, the occupation of professional golf offers these women something that is lacking in other occupations. Even in the case below, where Hattie went into business for herself, the loss of control over life was acutely felt.

> Originally I was going to quit two years ago when my sister got pregnant. We had started a business together. I got a good taste of what I would do at an 8-to-5 job after a month of working at it. Good thing she had her baby and could come back. Golf is easy compared to that.
>
> On my day off I would play thirty-six holes. I didn't realize how much I'd miss golf. I came back with a whole different attitude.
>
> Compared to that work, this has been a party (*jokingly*). I tell everybody that I am retired now and I am going around the country playing golf and having a good time. When I am older I am going to stop and work for the rest of my life (*laughs*). (Hattie)

Although Hattie spends as many hours working on golf while on the tour as she did in the shop she co-owned with her sister, she finds playing on the tour much more to her liking.

One of the motivating factors for players to stay on tour is the lack of options for women off the tour. The players' working conditions differ from women they come in contact with off the tour. Players often indicated that a major contrast between professional golf and the "real world" was their ability to control their lives.

> Well, it is really a fantasy world out here. It is something that you dream about doing. You are your own boss. Especially being a woman, I can't think of another place where you do exactly what you want to. I really never felt like I was harassed by the opposite sex in our world. I never felt like I was competing with men. In the corporate world it is a little bit different. (Tara)

> I choose to do things, see that's the beauty of it. . . . I choose to do what I'm very good at and I choose to make the decision when I quit. And women don't choose too many things on the outside world. They really don't choose. (Gerri)

The occupation of professional golfer affords the player an amount of control working women rarely enjoy. As such, some players have difficulty imagining entering the work force off the tour.

> I don't know if I could go back and work for someone. I could, but it would be really hard to go work for someone. Hope I don't have to do that.

Out here you're your own boss, call all the shots. You can take time off whenever you want. You can work however many weeks straight. I think that's the biggest plus, you don't have anybody telling you what to do. There are not too many women who can say that. (Dorothy)

In this kind of occupation you call the shots. You get spoiled doing it. If there was a time when I couldn't play golf, I don't know what I would do. (Beth)

Players are reluctant to leave the tour not so much because they are afraid to leave the protected and insulated comforts of the LPGA, but because they fear the rewards and control the tour offers them cannot be replicated in the real world.

CONCLUSION

While many of the young players succumb to the pressures of an uncertain life, many players remain on tour long after it is financially beneficial. The decision to leave or stay on the tour is rarely a simple financial one.[11] A player's decision to stay "out here" is influenced by her tolerance for travel, boredom, and a dislocated life combined with her ability to cope with the frustration of playing poorly, missing the cut, and living hand-to-mouth or, in the case of sponsorship, "hand-out-to-mouth." Players weigh these detrimental attributes of tour life against the freedom and independence of tour life, the potential for financial gain, the opportunity to compete at the highest level, and a chance to win. Many players find the occupational rewards and culture so appealing that going tens of thousands of dollars in debt seems a small price to pay.

PART II

INSIDE THE SUBWORLD

CHAPTER 5

DOING GENDER AND THE PROWESS ETHIC

[People say], "Who is this women trying to be an athlete?" I mean athlete is almost a masculine noun.

—Tara

I hit like a woman and she hits like a man.

—Bob Hope, comparing himself to "Babe" Didrikson Zaharias

The two quotes above speak to a conflict professional women golfers face. It is a symbolic conflict. That is not to say the conflict is imaginary or can be dismissed as insignificant. The conflict is very real, at times experienced by the players on tour as wrenching, even heart-breaking. By symbolic I mean to move the discussion of the LPGA to the level of social interpretation—how the women on tour understand their position in the world and how the world understands them. Up until this point, the discussion of women's golf has focused on the material world of women's golf, its economic and political history and the material reality of being a professional golfer. In this chapter, the focus shifts to how players, fans, and others make sense of the social position of professional woman golfer.

Although we would like to believe that we arrange our world according to our ideas, the opposite is more often the case. Shared meanings and ideologies arise out of a process of making sense of social life within a particular social terrain.[1] People sharing similar lives tend to understand the world in a similar fashion. For much of Western society, the notion of women as athletes seems conflictual on a symbolic level. The meanings associated with the concept of the athlete and those associated with woman do not seem to mesh within our collective consciousness. The athletic woman upsets taken for granted assumptions about the world. In order to understand the conflict the members of the LPGA face, we need to unpack those assumptions.

The athlete is a heroic figure in contemporary society: a symbol of success. It is a success perceived as justly deserved, won through one's own efforts, achieved through strength, aggression, and physical prowess—masculine traits. In a world arranged such that men are the primary competitors in the business and political world, we should not be surprised that symbols of success be associated with masculinity and masculine traits. Seeing the athlete as heroic and masculine confirms the social arrangement. Internalizing the heroic as masculine helps us to make sense of a world in which men control a majority of resources. To be a woman and an athlete disrupts our unspoken assumptions about who wins in our society. It conflicts with how we make sense of our world.

HISTORICAL ROOTS OF SPORT AS A GENDER MARKER

Numerous sport historians and sociologists agree that sport is an institution in which men display masculinity.[2] The development of sport as a resource through which masculinity can be displayed coincided with the development of modern society[3]—the radical transformation of work, increasingly democratic political systems, and the development of market economic systems. Out of these new social arrangements arose an ideology of equality. Notions of human equality which undercut aristocratic hierarchies also undercut gender and ethnic orders. Therefore, new ways of making sense of inequalities like slavery[4] and patriarchy[5] arose during early industrial capitalism.

Justifications of material inequalities in spite of our egalitarian ideals most often focus on biological differences.[6] During the later half of the 19th century, science, medicine, education, and the judicial system,[7] helped to prop up the shaken traditional gender order by accentuating biological differences between men and women. Organized sport also highlighted these differences. By the turn of the century, the notion of sport as a masculine enterprise and symbol had solidified in Western culture.[8] Since the masculine meanings associated with sport confirm men's position in the world, women's meaningful participation in sport would subvert its gendered social meaning. For almost a century, cultural expectations and social structures have denied women entry into the institution of sport in any significant manner. A number of pseudo-scientific biological propositions (i.e., "You'll hurt your reproductive organs")[9] were concocted to discourage women from competing in physical activities. Indeed, the connection between sport and masculinity became so strong in the first half of this century that women's participation in sport came to be seen as unnatural.

Although some women gained entry into sport in the first half of the century despite the social prohibitions, they were often stigmatized as deviant.[10] Their excellence in sport could have called into question both the institutional constraints on women and sport's ties to masculinity. Instead, it was the female athlete's character that was brought into question. In the last two decades, girls' participation in sport has dramatically increased and there is a growing cultural expectation that girls will participate in sports. Yet women athletes still receive a mixed reception.

THE NOTION OF GENDER

In any discussion of gender, it is important to make clear the distinction between sex and gender. By sex we mean the biological distinctions between men and women. Gender is the public expression of a sex. We give public hints of our biological sex in our dress, our style, our movements, and our occupations. Sex and gender behavior, however, are not causally connected. Indeed, it is not that difficult to convincingly represent oneself as a sex other than one's biological sex.

Further, a person's membership in a sex need not be the same as their biological makeup. There are plenty of cases, for example, of men claiming to be women trapped in a man's body. Sociologists Candice West and Don Zimmerman suggest three interactive levels of a gendered self; sex, sex category, and gender. Within this triad of biological sex, membership in a sex group, and the management of behavior in light of normative expectations associated with a sex category, the latter is the most important for understanding women's golf.[11]

"Doing gender" is a continual social process. We are always doing gender whether we are conscious of it or not, and we are constantly reading how others are doing gender. In any social interaction, sex catagory approaches "omnirelevance."[12] Upon meeting someone for the first time, for example, we immediately assess their membership to a sex through their gender acts. We respond based on our understanding of gender. Through gender assessment, for example, we know to greet someone with a kiss or a handshake. If they are doing gender in an unambiguous fashion, we are released from any doubts as to their membership in a sex category. We are disturbed when we are in doubt about someone's sex and offended when someone fails to read our gender signals properly.

Doing gender well involves following established, albeit fluid, patterns of appropriate behavior for men or women (i.e., blue for a boy, pink for a girl). Once gender distinctions become institutionalized, they support the "naturalness" of gender behavior that is specific to each sex. So pervasive and embedded are gender behaviors that we have trouble distinguishing between the social and the biological. For example, it is not unusual to hear someone make the statement, "Girls are naturally inclined to like dance, while boys are naturally inclined to like sports." Underlying this statement is the assumption that this difference has a biological basis. In fact, the inclinations of boys and girls toward different activities are socially constructed.[13]

GENDER AND THE PLAYERS

Because sport is a resource for men to do gender, it would seem that a tension might arise for women athletes as a result of a conflict between the thinking sport requires of athletes and the thinking conventional culture encourages of women. The women who participate in professional golf, however, successfully manage the conflict. Most players expressed little difficulty maintaining their perception of themselves as women in light of their athletic skill.[14] For example Ethel saw no conflict between being a women and being an athlete:

> I don't think you have to compromise femininity for competitiveness. I don't think you have to do that.

Ethel's comment seems to capture most of the players sense of themselves as both athletes and women. This general sentiment supports the sociological notion that although dominant ideals of masculinity and femininity may exert a powerful inluence, they do not simply determine individual behavior. Individuals and groups develop varied ways to accommodate, reinterpret, and resist conventional culture.[15]

There were some exceptions on tour. Nancy Lopez, for example, well known on the tour for her traditional femininity and excellent play, discussed at length her feminine upbringing and traits at a news conference. She capped off this discussion with the press by claiming not to be herself when she struck the golf ball.

> When I stand over the ball, something clicks in and I become like a machine.

For Lopez, being feminine and moving athletically remains conflictual. Only by disassociating her feminine self from golf can she maintain her "natural" feminine identity. This resolution of the conflict between sport and gender unfortunately denies her feminine side any credit for her physical prowess.

Acknowledged in the comments above is that athletic competitiveness is often considered unfeminine behavior. For Ethel, and most of the players on the tour, being competitive does not affect the way they see themselves as a woman. Many athletes credit early childhood experiences for their ability to retain their sense of identity as athletes and as women. The golfers often described their families or communities as "safe places" to be athletic children, which encouraged them to continue their athletic endeavors.[16] The following quote from Cathy is not unusual.

> It is really funny, because where I grew up that is just what we did. We were no different than the boys—maybe I was just at the turning point (in history). Maybe my town is ahead of a lot of the other towns. I grew up where girls played softball and the boys played baseball. The girls played volleyball and the boys played volleyball. You know it wasn't unusual to play together.
>
> I have just realized in the last five or ten years it wasn't like that for everybody. So I really didn't think anything strange about this when I was growing up. I think it is a really good way to grow up because the guys don't see—don't expect—are not surprised that women are athletes. They don't look down on it or think it is strange.

She understands that the world outside her hometown country club is somewhat hesitant to accept her for who she is—a woman and an athlete. Jane expressed similar sentiments.

> We are athletes, but we are ladies. . . . I am a woman, I love being a woman, I love being feminine and being able to go out to dinner and wear a nice dress and fit into society that way. (Jane)

The notion of "fitting into society" as a woman speaks to the relational aspect of doing gender and at the same time hinting at the conflict the broader society has with women athletes. Thus Jane fits into society in two ways: as an athlete and as a woman. Being a woman is something Jane does after she finishes her round. While golfers may have little difficulty reconciling their athletic prowess with their sex, they recognize that the public may question their womanliness.

> We have been brought up for a long period of time to think that a woman athlete is just a little bit less than a woman. (Gerri)

Implicit in Gerri's comment is an acknowledgment that the meaning of womanhood is a social construct. We are "brought up," that is, socialized, to know and act in accordance with gender norms. In interviews, however, the players repeatedly framed the conflict in social terms. It is less of a problem to manage the personal identity of woman golfer than it is to manage the social interpretation of woman golfer. Women golfers are stigmatized by those outside their subworld as a result of their failure to do gender in an unambiguous manner. To complicate matters further, their golfing prowess is suspect within the social world of golf as a result of their membership in the female sex catagory.[17]

PROWESS, MOVEMENT, APPEARANCE, AND GENDER

Physical activity is integral to sport and a cause of the tension surrounding women's sport participation. Brownmiller,[18] in her exploration of femininity, noted that clothing that restricts movement, high heels for example, is frequently considered sexy.[19] Although fashions change, restrictiveness seems to be relatively constant. She went on to observe that feminine movements are often movements which are less than a full extension of the body's capacity. Restricted feminine movements like the shortened strides necessitated by high heels or tight skirts are learned movements, not a natural expression of biology. Constricted movement is a way of doing gender. For Brownmiller, it is not just sport that acts as a gender boundary, but restricted and unrestricted movement in general. Athletics, if nothing else, involves a wide range of full-body movements.

Holly speaks directly to the conflict between athletic movement and a feminine image in golf.

Take someone like Stephenson [a player noted for her feminine beauty]. You couldn't try any more than that [to be feminine]. But she is going to make all the other moves too. It is like her dress and makeup and hair have to overcome getting dirty, making big golf swings, and whatever else doesn't look feminine.

The very act of swinging the club is an unfeminine movement. The activity that is the least conflicted with the societal understandings of femininity is putting. It requires insight, thoughtfulness, and in many ways mimics the restricted movements defined as feminine. When viewed in this light, it is not surprising that excellence in women's golf has been explained within the golf community as the result of women's "natural" ability to putt better than men. While I was in the field, it was revealed that the PGA membership had significantly better putting percentages than the LPGA. Most LPGA players took the news as an attempt to discredit their abilities. Some LPGA players publicly blamed the disparity on the quality of the putting surfaces that the women are forced to play on. By discrediting the comparison, they could maintain their claim to doing the "little things" well in accordance with societial standards of femininity. The women were equally interested in maintaining an explanation of their success that fits with societal understandings of gender. If women whose golfing excellence cannot be denied are less proficient at putting than men, they must be very good at some other aspect of the game, like driving. This fact went unmentioned.

Doing gender well most often involves appearance or presentation of self. Most women golfers do not fit the image associated with the ideal typical woman (whatever it might be at the time). Their dress for the game is colorful yet practical. The ribbons, lace, and frills often associated with women's clothing and which interfere with movement are absent from the tour. Most players wear shorts, displaying legs thickened by a daily regimen of walking five miles in golf shoes. Their shoulders are broad from driving hundreds if not thousands of balls a day. As Jane observed,

> [T]here are some players that are very very masculine looking, and I think that scares a lot of people. But, I think, if people were not so closed-minded and were open enough to receive that person on another level, they will find out they are ladylike, feminine, and a total woman, too. . . .
>
> But I think it has been hard for women's sports that way—getting over the stigma—we struggle with that all the time. (Jane)

To counter the social assumptions regarding the femininity of women who display athletic prowess, female athletes are encouraged to engage in compensatory gender actions. For example, sociologists Eitzen and Zinn have noted that many collegiate programs feminize the names of their women's teams (e.g., Lady Vols, Tigerettes).[20] In the world of golf, country-club rules often segregate men's and women's playing times and require that women wear skirts while playing golf at the club. These rules ensure that women don't become "one of the boys" and that they continue to do gender appropriate to their sex category in spite of their athletic participation. The public is much more willing to accept a woman athlete if they do gender well. The long finger nails, lace tights, and makeup worn by the powerful sprinter Florence Griffin Joyner ("FloJo") in the 1988 Olympic Games and the consistent bubbly appearance of Chris Evert are just two examples of women doing gender well despite their athletic prowess.[21]

The most discussed compensatory action among the players is dress. Players feel considerable peer and organizational pressure to portray a heterosexual image with clothing and hair styles. The LPGA retains a beauty consultant on staff who travels with the tour to assist and advise players about their image. This feminine public presentation of self is euphemistically referred to as a "professional image." Dorothy was both highly critical of some of her counterparts, yet complimentary of the improvement of their presentation of self as womanly.

> [Our image] is a problem because these girls don't look like girls. They look like guys. . . . I wish they could be more feminine. . . . But compared to, like, three years ago, it's a lot better. I think the girls really care about how they look, how they dress. (Dorothy)

For many women on the tour, dressing like a "girl" is an attempt to meet mainstream expectations. Feminine haircuts, makeup, and dress all help to soothe the public's discomfort with the female athlete. It is OK for a woman to be an athlete as long as she attempts to be feminine.

However, people around Nora have difficulty resolving their stereotypical image of a woman athlete in light of her striking natural beauty. Beautiful women, be they natural or created, are not usually associated with competitive athletics. This conflict between social expectations is acutely felt by Nora.

> I've even gone through times out here when I thought, "I wish I wasn't so pretty." Because sometimes being pretty I felt like I

couldn't be a really good athlete or good player.
Sometimes maybe because you're so pretty you're not
tough. People put that in your mind.
Even my father would say "Aw, you're too pretty to play
golf." I never knew if he meant that as a joke because he has
such a dry sense of humor. But he's always very proud of me
and the way I look because he has all my fashion pictures in his
office. But during the times of not playing so good, he would
make jokes like, "Why don't you gain a few pounds and chop
your hair off and you might start playing good?" Those are
very cold thoughts. I didn't know whether he was joking or
serious.
I even had other people say "You're just too nice Nora" or
"You're just too pretty." People say funny things, you can
either take it to heart or let it go in one ear and out the other.

Nora's confusion and pain are obvious. Nora's father encouraged
her to develop her athletic skills and complimented her on her looks.
Nonetheless, Nora's presentation of herself as both feminine and athletic confounds her father. The values and expectations of mainstream
society, represented in Nora's father's comments, illustrate the belief
that achievement in athletics is masculine and in direct conflict with
his expectations about feminine beauty.
One of the sharpest examples of the conflict between professional
golf and the social expectation of femininity came from Roslynn. At
the time of her interview, she was dealing with the realization that professional golf was not simply something she was going to try for a few
years, but was actually her career. Involved with this realization was
coming to terms with the tensions between her family's expectations of
her as a woman (working on marriage and a family) and the demands
of professional golf.

I am tired of being a "normal, physically attractive women." It
is difficult. I am trying not to do that now, and not be influenced by other people who think I should be leading a more
"normal" life. Well, this is normal for me (*gesturing to indicate
that she means the tournament taking place around her*).
And I like it. I would rather be doing this than anything
else, for the time being, at least.

For Roslynn the demands of being a career golfer on the tour are so
great and the simultaneous compensatory act of "being normal" so

daunting that she must make a choice. She chooses to surrender to the demands of the sport. From this perspective of doing golf, doing femininity is a poor expenditure of energy.

AMBITION AND GENDER CONFLICT

In addition to the physical requirements of the game, the drive necessary for success on the tour conflicts with mainstream definitions of womanhood. The tour demands that players be both ambitious and independent, characteristics that are difficult for many in mainstream society to accept in women.[22]

> I don't think the tour is like society as a whole. Society can't understand but we can. We are so independent and goal-minded. We just do our own thing. (June)

The conflict players experience between the demands of the tour and mainstream expectations is reflected in their perceived possibilities of marriage. Marriage also illustrates the interactive aspects of doing gender because the way a person does gender reflects on their partner. Doing gender for men includes maintaining the image that they are in control of their partner. Similarly, for women, doing gender includes not challenging the impression that her partner is in control. "Henpecked" and "she wears the pants in that family" are common derogatory expressions in which the relationship between a couple fails to contribute positively to one's social membership in a sex.

In the following two quotes, the tension between the social expectations of marriage and the requirements of professional golf is evident.

> It is hard to keep up with the marriages and divorces. And there are plenty of both. Three years is probably the average for marriages. If the husband is traveling with the wife, they have a lot better chance of making it. It takes a special kind of guy to do that, and it seems most of them are back home. Pretty soon they want the wife to be home and the wife wants to be playing golf and he wants her home etc. . . . It doesn't make for a real happy arrangement. She will be home for one week maybe two—gone four, maybe five, or six. It just doesn't work.
> It seems to me that a gal just has to make a decision. Either she is going to play golf or she is going to be married. It

is pretty difficult to do it. Can't do both one hundred percent. You're either going to be a poor wife or a poor golfer or both. (Gerta)

Men who are interested in us would have to like strong women who make decisions and usually don't need someone to tell them what to do. So that is a real limiting thing for men. And as far as men go, if we find men to match our strength, they are probably not going to be interested in going out on tour. They have their own thing somewhere else, and you are glad that they do. So that is a difficulty. (Holly)

Holly and Gerta acknowledge both the necessity of ambition for the professional golfer and conventional expectations of women in hetero-sexual relationships. Because men are expected to be the leaders in rela-tionships and women golfers are strong, the likelihood of finding a husband are slim. Even players who find "special men" with whom they can create relationships suited to tour life have difficulties. Such was the case with Nora's first marriage.

We had a husband-wife, player-caddy type relationship on tour.

We started finishing in the top twenty and the top ten. I won in July of '82 on probably one of the best courses the tour has every played. The following day we were whisked off to New York City and the *Today Show, People* magazine, and *CBS Sunday Morning.* All these interviews, this and that.

The sad part about the whole thing is that they did not look at it or ask questions in a positive way. It was more like "Andy, how do you feel following in the footsteps and shad-ows of your wife/player?"

Looking back on it now, it was sad because the press destroyed our self-confidence in each other. The more press we got, the worse he felt. It upset me and it depressed him. His depression led to some other problems, and eventually the strain of it all was the downfall of the marriage.

Conventional notions about how to do gender were shaken by Andy and Nora's unconventional relationship. Nora and Andy were most concerned with professional golf and less concerned with doing gender properly, at least while they were on the course. What is normal in the professional golf world is perceived as unusual, deviant, and at times unnatural within mainstream culture. In particular, the press was troubled by Andy's subservient relationship to his wife in the work setting. Andy's problem was not that he was a professional caddy, but that he caddied for a woman. The situation was made worse in that the woman was also his wife. Acting as an agent of social control, the press brought Andy's masculinity into question, and by inference, the relationship between Nora and Andy.

Possibly the most notorious example of the tension between professional women golfers' ambition and the gender order took place in 1950. In a Corcoran-engineered publicity stunt, the top six woman professionals of the day took on six former Walker Cup players (top male amateurs) from England. Apparently the English men did not think much of the American professional women or Corcoran's boastful representation of the young tour. They sent him away with a challenge that got Didrikson's dander up. Didrikson led a group of professionals to a 6-0 victory in match play over the all-male English squad. Not only did she win her match, but she out-drove her competition on each hole. Corcoran writes that after the tournament, he was the most hated man in all of England. He had taken his publicity stunt too far.[23] Men, attracted to the novelty of women athletes, feel threatened by excellent ones. Any woman superior in sport to accomplished male athletes represents a threat to all men.

In less dramtic ways the LPGA chips away men's sense of themselves as the guardians of sport. Players regularly correct pontificating reporters and club members' yardage figures, and fire caddies for giving them too much advice. My favorite clash occurred in 1993 in Boston. On the second day of the tournament, I was following three players, Shipman, Chellimi, and Bretz, all three struggling to make the cut. They were about three holes from finishing 18 and were approaching a par three, a potential birdie hole. Between the green and the tee, Shipman was approached by a young man, obviously drunk.

"Do me a favor, will you do me a favor. I am a greens keeper here, will you do me a favor."

"OK, what is it?," Shipman replied walking to the tee box, trying to escape.

"All the girls are using sevens and coming up short. Do me a favor and use a six. You'll be pin high. I've been watching all day. Just do me a favor, OK?"

Shipman walked into the tee box and the young man returned to his seat in the grass with another couple and his date, who I suspect dared him to share his wisdom with a professional. Although short and slight, Shipman has broad shoulders and a wide stance, pound for pound one of the longest hitters on the tour. Earlier in the day Shipman had hit a drive that caught the back side of a hill and rolled past the 300 yard marker, something she would brag about later even though she failed to make the cut. Her club selection is usually one higher than the other professionals'.

She ignored the greenskeeper's suggestion and used an eight. Shipman hit her shot past the pin but on the green. A good shot, but it left her a long birdie putt. She was not happy with herself as she left the tee box, and furious when the greenskeeper approached her anticipating gratitude.

"An eight, I used an eight," she sneered. Then quickly soothed the dumbfounded greenskeeper by explaining, "I hit it a lot further than most of the girls out here."

THE IMAGE PROBLEM

When a golfer's performance makes it obvious that she is superb athlete, some men make comments questioning the golfer's sex. "They're not real women" and "Some of them got more testosterone than I do" were two comments I heard from male spectators watching the LPGA. More often, however, it is the players' sexuality that is questioned. In her interview, Gerri tore into the common image of the tour without prompting.

> The gay situation, I will get right into that. I don't think that we are given a fair shake. We are not jocks. We have no desire to be jocks. We are women. We were never given a fair shake when we came out forty years ago. We are an exceptional group of women, that were born with a little bit better muscle structure. On the whole, you don't see any of these women being petite. We got a muscle structure that is just a little bit different than the normal woman. But that doesn't make us any less of a woman.

On some level, Gerri understands the connection between doing gender and the public presentation of sexuality. The implication is that real women are heterosexual. Being lesbian is associated with being "less of a woman." On the LPGA tour, the issue of the player's sexuality is politely referred to as the "image problem."

The questioning of the players' sexual preference is an extension of their failure to do gender in an unambiguous manner. Social expressions of sexuality and gender are intertwined.[24] The primary way to appear heterosexual in our society is to repeatedly produce clear and emphatic indicators of one's sex.[25] Most heterosexuals, and those who want to be perceived as heterosexual, promote that assumption through appearance and actions which are perceived as uniquely masculine or feminine. Conversely, a person's heterosexuality is questioned by others when that person engages in behavior that does not match the social expectations of one's sex.

Women's participation in sport can be viewed as a "gender ambiguity." The label "tomboy,"[26] because it is so widely held, may encourage girls' physical prowess. However, "tomboy" also sends a message that continued participation in sport into adulthood is less acceptable. Doing gender properly becomes increasingly important in adolescence when secondary sex characteristics develop. Athletic participation by women creates gender confusion for others. This confusion is often expressed through an interest of others in the sexuality of women athletes.

The questioning of a person's sexuality is often employed as a means to discredit a person's accomplishments.[27] Because sport is a resource for men to do gender, women's excellence in sport is often felt as a threat to masculine identity.[28] One way to maintain sport as a masculine preserve is to undercut women's athletic prowess.[29] Women athletes frequently face questions regarding their sexuality which are intended to discredit their athletic skill.[30]

While most amateurs restrict their questions and suspicions about LPGA players to private conversation, they do at times have an impact on the players. Often the comfortable setting of the pro-am reduces the inhibition of some amateurs and they question their professional teammates about the sexual preference of tour players. The following are two examples of amateurs questioning the tour's membership and the player's response.

> Some of the amateurs say, "Hey, gimme the real scoop about the tour." I just tell them that I never had any experiences [with lesbianism]. I really don't know. (Pam)

> It is difficult trying to guess how people view us from the outside. Well, you can see it in the press and on the pro-am. Like one guy said to me, "I hear some really weird things about your tour."
> "Well, what do you hear?"
> I think that he wanted to say the "lesbian thing," but he didn't say that. He said "this born again thing."

(*Laughing*) I laughed. The guy was too chicken to even confront it. So I said, "OK, lets talk about that." I said "I am a Christian, and I am happy to be a Christian. What is wrong with that?"

Well, now he is really embarrassed and confused. So I say, "OK let me ask you a question, have you ever read the *National Enquirer*? Well, how much of that do you believe?" (Lynn)

Along with the amatuers, the press and the caddies seem to have a need to question the sexual preference of the players. I will deal with these groups in a later chapter. For now, what is important to understand is that the players feel an undue amount of interest in their sexuality in response to their athletic prowess.

THE PROWESS ETHIC

In contrast to conventional culture, the women on the tour want their athletic prowess to be understood as separate from and unrelated to their sex, gender, and sexuality. The constant attention to sexuality is frustrating for them. Cara's sentiments are typical.

It is my feeling that sexuality is not an issue. We are basically here to do one thing, and that is to play golf. Why would anyone want to cover anything that did not effect golf? I don't think [a player's sexuality] has any effect on golf or golf has any effect on [a player's sexuality]. I mean we are really tired of the issue. It is boring.

Players are clearly frustrated by the image problem which haunts the tour. It is the sort of frustration that arises from incomprehension. In their world, whether a player is straight or gay, a drunk or a holy roller, is immaterial. In their world, income is based on merit and status is based on performance. Their social position, employment, security, future are tied to how well they play golf. LPGA members don't understand why everyone cares so much about their sex and particularly their sexuality. To them, golf is not a gendered activity. The strong association of golf with masculinity is a consequence of history and its application to their tour is an error in logic or a cultural lag.

Yet they also understand themselves to be different from other women. The differences are not just material; they are ideological.

Holly, for example, had retired from the sport once, and was pondering a second retirement when she was interviewed. She was thinking about the world away from the tour and felt an acute gap between herself and her non-athlete peers.

> Well, I know that most of us are different than the typical married lady with a house full of kids in what we think about and do. Talking to them sometimes I think, "I don't get it!" Even golfers with kids would be different than those mothers.

What Holly does not "get" are the cultural rules and expectations of the "typical married lady" and how she rationalizes them to herself. How one gets ahead in the conventional culture and how one gets ahead on the tour are quite different. As such, how they make sense of their respective worlds is also quite different.

On the LPGA tour what matters is how far and straight a player can hit a small white ball. It requires a way of thinking that is different from what is expected of most women in mainstream society.

> It is hard, we are out here, we are supposed to be athletes. We are supposed to be aggressive and we are attacking—male traits. We are more aggressive than the average woman. And unfortunately people see that and look at that while we are trying to do our work and label it as manly. But you got to be [aggressive] to survive out here. You have got to get yourself into a state of being aggressive and focused and nothing else matters. (Jane)

To survive on the tour, professional golfers have to develop an obsessive concern with details.

> I can't handle doing something mediocre. I have to give it 100% or I don't even attempt. (Molly)

For Molly doing a sport "just for fun" seems an alien concept. On the professional level, golf is something to be mastered and to be fully engaged in. Indeed, to do it on a recreational level would not seem like fun for most of these professional golfers. As such, sport demands a player's entire mental and physical energies. The seemingly impossible struggle to master the game is what she finds rewarding.

> Golf is a really fickle game. It can lead you to commit suicide and drinking and drugs and everything like that, and then again the most rewarding thing I've ever done—having a hole in one—it's an experience like none other. (*Laughing*) I mean better than sex and everything, seriously. (Molly)

Ann finds the demands of golf well-suited to her need to give one hundred percent. She sees golf as an impossible challenge and thus an outlet for her competitive drive.

> Golf has always been something that has motivated me. I got bored with other sports. I played everything. I played tennis as a kid, I played basketball. I was into everything, track and field.
>
> But, I mean, the ultimate round of golf would be to go out and never have to putt. Every par three you knock it in the hole. Every par four you would knock it in the hole in two and the par fives you knock it in the hole in three. The chances of someone attaining that are so difficult that it probably will never happen.
>
> But that is the whole motivation in golf—to try and attain the ultimate. Like in bowling, the ultimate is to have a strike every time, to have a three hundred game. But lots of people have attained that. It's not as difficult to do that as it is in golf. You have so many outside factors in golf. It is not a perfect game. Whereas, bowling, which is indoors, is more of a perfect game. You are playing a ball which is yours, it is made for you, the alley is the same every shot. It is much more of a perfect environment to try to attain the perfect game—where golf is not. It changes constantly.
>
> Most people are totally turned off by it. A lot of people can't stand golf. I think it probably attracts a certain type of person. The game is almost masochistic. You are never going to achieve the ultimate, yet you keep striving for it. (Ann)

The golfers find the difficulty of the sport attractive. Every shot, every tournament, every season presents new challenges, none of which will be met with the desired perfection. It is the ultimate proving ground of prowess.

> To be able to make a golf ball go high or low, curve under trees or around trees or over trees and then be able to roll it over the

ground into a hole or out of the sand. It's just fascinating, really. There are so many facets and you have to be proficient in so many different areas that it's just hard. (Fran)

A drive to accomplish the impossible seems endemic to the profession. June sees this drive to accomplish something difficult as a primary factor in distinguishing herself from women off the tour.

What interests me is trying to figure out what makes me think differently than my childhood friends. I don't think any of them would want to do what I do. They look at me and say that it's great, she's rich and she is doing what she wants, but that is not what I want.

Sometimes I think about some people who wake up and do whatever. They hang out or go to work, live their lives, some make cash, some don't. But everyday I live, there is always something that I have to do, something that I have to be aware of, something I need to think about, something that I need to make me stronger. I am always looking forward to that thing. It makes me think that other people are so lazy.

I've kind of come to realize that they are not lazy, they are just not trying to do great things. They are not trying to win a marathon, win the U.S. Open. (June)

Drive is also viewed as an element that separates great golfers from good ones.

Golf can be learned, you get a decent instructor you can learn this and that. There are some chicks out there that can get to a certain level, but to get to a next level, the big time, I think that you have to understand what you want and where you are going and how much it takes to get there. (June)

The players on the tour do not deny talent as a factor in success, but the emphasis is on drive and determination. One is not born successful, but rather born with the potential to become successful.[31] This sense of talent is expressed by Jane.

I mean I feel like the cream rises to the top. I mean that is the way things seem to go.

It is like our qualifying school—going into qualifying school [each year] you hear of two or three players that are strong. Once in a while they will miss the cut. But they always come back. If they missed it one year, there was a reason they missed it. And they come back stronger. For instance, Betty won the amateur three years in a row, and missed the qualifier. That happens, but if they are a great player, good enough to be out here, they will be here. (Jane)

For the tour players, talent, by itself, is not enough to get on tour. Failure to get a card, for example, is seen as a sign that a player lacks some inner strength; this highlights the perceived importance of drive. Talent necessarily must be mixed with drive to achieve success. I refer to the belief in the combination of talent and the drive to achieve success as "prowess."

Prowess, at least this particular expression of it, is at the core of the LPGA subworld. The belief that prowess is and should be the path to success shapes the values, mores, and worldview of the players. Because it is believed that individual drive, hard work, and inner strength mix with natural talent to achieve success, success is perceived as earned.

According to the players, the tour allows for golfers to be judged on the basis of their prowess and thus represents an almost perfect meritocracy. Nat framed it this way:

Golf is probably capitalism at its barest form. If you do well, if you do the best, you get paid the best. If you don't, you may make thousands or you may make nothing. You don't get paid for showing up. You don't get paid for sitting on the bench. You get paid for your performance. That's what makes it interesting. It can make it very rewarding. (Nat)

This distinction between the economy of golf from the economy of other work settings is very real to the LPGA golfers. Nat clearly sees golf as being different from, and better than, the real world, where favoritism, gender, race, and arbitrary decisions affect success. These sentiments are crassly yet powerfully articulated by Denise:

Nobody plays favorites. You can't suck the sponsor's dick to get a 68, so to speak. There isn't any way—through favoritism, or favors, or anything like that—to get something out here. (Denise)

Fellatio is more than a metaphor with which to illuminate the meritocracy of the tour. It speaks to how Denise sees gender operating in the
broader culture. Beauty, sexual favors, marrying the boss, flirting, and a
whole assortment of other avenues to enhance material gain which
women are socialized to know and forced to pursue in a sexist society,
carry far less weight on the tour.

Victory or superior play is an unambiguous expression of
prowess. The distribution of rewards to the players on the tour is based
solely on performance. Rewards based solely on outward displays of
prowess are seen as just. This view that one should be respected and
rewarded according to the outward expressions of prowess I call the
prowess ethic.

Players find the unambigiousness of the game attractive and the
individualism inherent in the sport appealing.

> I've always enjoyed team sports and did them well, y'know
> basketball and soccer and stuff, but I think in the individual
> ones it's all you out there and you can't blame the quarter-
> back—that's just a figure of speech. But its 100% on your shoul-
> ders. Four hours you're out there and it is only you. It's amaz-
> ing when you're playing well, it's great, and when you're
> playing badly, it's mind-boggling because you can't blame any-
> one. (Helen)

> I started playing when I was about 12. They had a rule at our
> club that you couldn't start playing until you were 12. I liked it
> right away. I liked the individuality of the sport. I found out I'm
> not a team sport player after playing basketball and stuff like
> that in high school. 'Cause if I'd do my personal best in a game
> and the team loses by 40 points, I didn't feel bad. I like the indi-
> vidual part [of golf] the best. (Roslynn)

Golf is not merely an individual sport, but a solitary one. While
people play in pairs or in small groups, they compete in relative silence.
Etiquette requires that players not to stand close to each other. Players
will be penalized if they confer with another player about their game
(for example, what club to use) while on the course.

One's success and failure is determined solely by one's playing
ability. Golfers do not compete against or with each other directly as in
tennis. They compete against and with themselves. If there is an opponent, it is nature. But even the environment (wind, rain, altitude) is part
of the game and not an element to be controlled and factored out (as in

wind-aided track events and/or altitude swimming). The individuality of golf enables a player's performance to be a clean demonstration of their prowess.

WINNING AND LOSING

The ultimate expression of prowess, victory, is the prime motivation of the players.

> First of all, the only thing that keeps me out here after 13 years, is that I still feel I can win. (Ethel)

Winning is placed above the material rewards the players might gain from playing well.

> I don't know if that is what I'm out here for, to make a lot of money. I know that it comes with it, but I think I'm out here to win tournaments. I don't really care about the money. If the money comes with it, fine. I think I'm out here just to get personal gratification from playing golf and the money is . . . I don't think I really even worry about it. (Karen)

> It's really not the money. That wasn't my goal to come out here. My goal was to come out here and be a good player. Be respected as one of the top players. Have certain wins. I won my rookie year like I said, but once, that's nothing. I want to win more. I don't really worry that much about money. I have a really good sponsor and everything. I just wanted to establish myself as a good player. Be regarded as one of the best. I don't think you can really survive if you're out here living like you have to make $1,000 this week. You can't really think that way. (Beth)

When players talk about personal gratification and the respect of others gained through excellent play, they are also discussing feelings of self-worth. A sense of self-worth is gained through our perception of how others view us. In the context of a social world steeped in the prowess ethic, winning is proof of talent and tenacity. These are personal attributes. Performance, then, is an indication of self-worth.

Within the LPGA subworld, prowess becomes an expression of individual self-worth. The psychological benefits of being able to create oneself through hard work at a difficult task makes the tour a potentially gratifying form of employment for those with a strong prowess ethic. In the quote above, June spoke of her struggle to understand how people could lead satisfying lives without trying to achieve recognizable accomplishments. Similarly, Cara reflected on her personal growth on the tour in terms of her achievements.

> You can chart my growth on the money list. That is just one—kind of a—almost a materialist way to do it, but personally each year I have felt more comfortable out here. I have worked very hard at my game. I always worked hard, trying to improve. Improve some of my weaknesses. I still have a lot of weak spots, and always do. Something is always off that you need to work on.
>
> But I can feel within myself—especially last year—it started out (and I don't know why) sometime in July or August, I just had a good tournament. I felt the confidence click in and then I had another good tournament, two more good tournaments towards the end of the year and it kind of felt like it was starting to come around. . . . I felt like "Boy, things are going to go my way." It has really been fun to see my own progress. (Cara)

At first the tie between self, accomplishment, and ranking is bothersome to Cara ("almost a materialist way to do it"), but she quickly justifies this by placing her accomplishments in the context of hard work. Cara's sense of self is tied to her movement up the rankings, which, for her, illustrate personal growth.

Ann's unfortunate two-year slump in the ranking gave her unique insights into how achievement is tied to self-worth.

> One of the problems with our tour is that what you are on the money list is what you are. I saw a little bit more of that when I had those few years when I played very badly. . . . But then again, it is a performance-oriented sport. The numbers you put on the board are the only thing that counts. It doesn't matter how you did it, you just got to do it. (Ann)

Like Ann above, Jane expresses the downside of connecting accomplishments to self-worth. The difference here is her internalization of this notion.

Golf can just totally diminish your self-esteem too. I mean you might, the amateurs out there might be thinking you are doing great, but as a professional, you know you are not hitting your shot and you don't feel good about yourself. It is very hard, when you don't feel good about yourself, [to continue to perform well].

The prowess ethic is a predominant value on the tour. It shapes the players' worldview, including their sense of self, their perception of justice, their esteem of others, and their notion of what is noble and what is worth striving for. The dominance of the prowess ethic is illustrated by Tara's assumption of universality.

Don't we all choose something we can excel in so other people can recognize us for our skill?

She has internalized the ethos of the tour and applied it to explain basic human motivation.

There are a few, however, who quietly question the logic of the prowess ethic or admit to being somewhat less driven.

Well, I feel kind of, well my goal is to make a decent living. . . .
I feel almost guilty. Although I am trying to do the best that I can, I don't really have an aspiration to be the best golfer on tour. Like Betsy King is driven. I mean I can see it in her. She is driven to be the best. Nancy Lopez is the same way. Maybe someday I will feel that way too. But right now I am just trying to improve a little bit, compete, maybe be a factor on the tour every once in while. Maybe to cash a check every week is a good goal for me. (Cara)

Even Cara's admitted lack of drive is couched in a fashion that pays tribute to the dominant ethos of the tour and her feelings of guilt illustrate its power. It is a spirit that is contagious and necessary.

SUCCESS AND FAILURE ON THE TOUR

When success is framed in terms of the prowess ethic, failure can be seen in two ways: either as a lack of talent or as a lack of personal attributes. There is genuine sympathy for the player on tour who works hard but lacks talent. Players perceived as lacking talent who choose to leave the tour are viewed favorably. Players perceived to lack talent who remain on tour garner quiet sympathy. However, it is cutting to suggest a player has talent but lacks the inner strengths or drive to fully cultivate it. To suggest a player has failed to tap her true potential is to suggest a player is lacking in character. Comments like "What a waste of talent" or the less insidious "What's with so-and-so, she played so well last year," question the individual worth of a player.[32]

The downside of the prowess ethic is clearly expressed in the way players approach "slumps." Because the level of performance is understood in a way that affects the player's conception of self, poor play often shakes a player's confidence, resulting in a slump. Val, at the time of her interview, was preparing to leave the tour. Scarred and weary, she was playing in just a few tournaments this year.

> I have just had problems getting over a hill that needs to be got over to be successful in golf. . . . I probably made a mistake a couple of years ago, when I was not playing real great, I decided to stay out here and fight it out here instead of taking a month off and then trying to come back. It just started getting worse and worse mentally, dragging me down. . . .
>
> In order to do it, you have to get yourself right too. Because you have to be the person that does it. It's like taking the horse to water. . . . I have talent that people don't have, I have never really used it as well as I should out here. (Val)

Val's assessment that her poor play was the result of her attitude and that she could have, with the right attitude, improved her play is clearly internalized as self-blame. For her, the decision to leave the tour has less to do with a lack of talent than with a lack of personal fortitude.

Despite the dangers of associating self-worth with achievements, most players found the possibility of excelling and thus creating themselves exciting.

> I have an opportunity to be the best in the world at what I do. And at given times I am. And have been . . . the numbers tell you that. I'm one of a very elite group of people who are the best in the world at what they do. (Ethel)

For Ethel, a low score not only symbolizes her achievements and acts as a measure of her skill, but it also identifies her place in the world.

Within the context of the prowess ethic, the players' motivation to play well is connected to their desire to create themselves. To stand out from others, and, as such, to be admired and appreciated for what they have done signifies who they are. They are self-made.

THE SPIRIT OF THE LPGA

The prowess ethic is so dominant that it is a decisive influence on the character of the tour. The spirit that undergirds the culture of the LPGA is the single-minded pursuit of achievements in golf. Ultimately, it is the drive to prove oneself worthy of respect. It is a value that arises out of the demands of the tour.

This spirit is revealed in the players' obsessive practice routines and attention to detail. Sara, a foreign-born player, rarely practiced more than two hours a day before coming to the tour. But once on tour she adopted the ways of the LPGA.

> When you are out here you don't realize how much practice you are doing. You are out here and come out here in morning and hit balls before you play. Then, you don't just play eighteen holes of golf. You come in and grab something to eat, then you go out and practice for another two hours. It is a routine. . . . [A]round here you have got a hundred and forty people who want to do just as well as you or better than you. And when you see them out there hitting balls, it is a motivator. And you see people out there practicing all the time. (Sara)

The spirit of the LPGA is reflected in the way players manage their emotions.

> You never really have time to get too depressed. And if you are, it's just too bad—the tour will eliminate you quickly. (Lynn)

It has the power to mold a player's non-golfing life to the demands of the sport.

> I love him a lot, but like I said, it's just that golf is first. Financially, I didn't think it was feasible for us to get married. It would put a lot of strain on my golf. And I didn't want him to

become an out for my golf if I didn't succeed. I didn't want
people saying that Pam didn't have her heart or her soul in her
golf. (Pam)

And this spirit is reflected in how the players honor themselves. In 1967
the members set up a Hall of Fame to honor the very best of the LPGA.
Unlike other sports, entry into this Hall of Fame is determined by set criteria. No boards, sport writers, or academics are needed to pass judgment on the players. A player gains admittance to the Hall based solely
on her performance as it is represented by her career victories.[33]

CONCLUSION

Whether the motivation is to win, to make it on tour, or simply to "survive out here," all the energies of the LPGA players are directed toward
the single-minded pursuit of mastering the game of golf. The organization of professional golf demands a high level of attention. To paraphrase Sara and Lynn, there are 140 other people trying to play better
than you, and the tour has a way of eliminating players lacking the
appropriate spirit. The prowess ethic is the way LPGA players make
sense of this world. It informs the way they administer justice and
bestow awards. It is the ideological root of the players' understanding of
success and failure, and their frustration with people's overt concern
with their sexuality. It is an ideology that arises from the individualistic,
meritocratic, and uncertain world of the tour.

The prowess ethic is an ideology arising from within an athletic
subworld of women. It is the sort of mindset the tour demands. It is
how the women understand themselves and how they wish to be
understood. On the surface, the prowess ethic seems distinct from conventional gender expectations and an antidote to the image problem.
From this point of view, concerns about race, class, and particularly
gender and sexuality seem frivolous and stupid. But the prowess ethic
cannot be understood as distinct from the image problem. Indeed, the
insistence on the gender-neutral logic of the prowess ethic is a product
of the broader gender order.

The image problem is the fallout from a sexist world that uses
athletes as heroic symbols. It arises from the broader social terrain in
which the LPGA operates, a world in which sport means far more than
who is the fastest or the most skilled. The image problem is a product of
a world that associates athletic prowess with masculinity yet maintains
athletic opportunities for women. The unspoken assumptions many

hold about LPGA touring professionals' sexuality is a way of making sense of their excellence. In a society which strongly associates sport and masculinity, superior performances by women can only be understood as excellent if she is simultaneously discredited as a women. The athletism, ambition, and independence which the sport demands stand outside the norm for women in our society. In the daily life of the tour player, she is simultaneously rewarded and punished for her prowess. For some players the conflict is too great a price to pay.

> If I had to make the decision to become a professional golfer now, knowing what I know, I don't know if I would make the same decision of being out here, because this lifestyle goes against the grain with a lot of society. (Jane)

What male athletes must come to terms with in defeat or retirement,[34] women must deal with in victory. Former male athletes often have difficulty with their sense of masculinity after they are no longer competing and thus struggle to disassociate masculinity with athletics. Women in male identified sports must distinguish their womanhood from their athletic capabilities while they are still athletes.

In order to make athletic success her own and to have others admire her prowess, the women golfer must advocate a gender-neutral view of sport. The woman golfers' insistence on a gender-free interpretation of their skill, then, is a product of a society that masculinizes athletic prowess.

To suggest that the women of the tour can either "do golf" or "do gender," as many of the professionals indicate, is not quite accurate. Indeed, the golfers consciously do gender in light of their athletic prowess and vice versa. They are acutely aware of the difficulty they present for potential supporters. As a result, they are attuned to how to do gender in order to compensate for their athletic prowess and how to present their athletic skill in the least disruptive manner.

From the context of the tour, the players come to understand gender as a social construction, femininity as a performance. Tour life debunks the notion of gender as natural. Instead, players perceive "God-given" talent and the ability to make the most of it as natural. Their world is ordered accordingly.

CHAPTER 6

THE PROWESS ETHIC AND THE PARENT CULTURE

The previous chapter emphasized the structure of golf as the producer of the prowess ethic. Clearly, the structure of competitive golf encourages the prowess ethic. The question remains, however, where do these women come from, what sort of community prepares women to thrive in this individualistic and uncertain world?

The logic of professional women's golf seems somewhat out of step with the broader culture, but not totally alien. Players view conventional systems of stratification and status attainment as unjust. Within their world, prowess is the sole determinant of status, social position, and self-worth. This perspective informs almost every aspect of the golfers' lives. It shapes their sense of what is just and what is valuable.

Nora's discussion of what is important in life, for example, takes the logic of the prowess ethic to its rather disturbing end.

> You have to grab hold of things that are lasting, things that are real. Contracts and companies and people; these things come and go. Grab hold of it when you can, but those aren't the things that last forever. It's the wins, the victories, the hard work getting there, the top 40, 30, 20 finishes. (Nora)

Her logic paints a grim picture of her future—a retired athlete sitting alone surrounded by trophies and newspaper clippings. Although Nora's comment is extreme, her sentiments are repeated by players like

Ethel who claim "winning is the only reason she is still out here." Their logic stands in contrast to the more conventional struggles to attain material possessions and wealth or to cultivate friendships. At the same time, their notion of success is not unfamiliar. It is the logic of a meritocracy.

The norms and values of any subworld or group that sits on the fringe of a society are not completely new. They are extrapolations or mutations of the broader culture. They may be exaggerations of broadly held values, but they can nonetheless be traced to the conventional culture. For example, sociologists have argued that hippies of the sixties, although often preceived as having rejected American values completely, were genuine children of the American consumer culture which emphasizes immediate gratification. What made the sixties' youth culture unusual was their rejection of material possessions and the older American work ethic which emphasizes deferred gratification.

In conventional culture, the economic exchange system is the primary stratifier of society and significantly defines cultural norms and values. Ideally it is a meritocracy in which the best and brightest succeed. Success is demonstrated by aquiring wealth, and through wealth, power. It is not surprising that public displays of material goods (status symbols) have come to imply material well-being, class affiliation, or social position, and, by association, prowess. Status symbols, however, can be purchased or rented to give someone the image of importance or talent when in actuality he posesses little of either. Further, we also understand, although do not readily admit, that most wealthy people have inherited their wealth and status. Similarly, the conventional culture contains status orders based on ascribed attributes (i.e., sex and ethnicity). Despite a veneer of meritocracy, the broader social systems of stratification are not based on prowess. The women on the tour seem to reject, and actually relish being able to undermine (if only for an afternoon), this aspect of conventional culture.

THE PARENT CULTURES

The values and norms of the tour did not develop in a social vacuum. They are derivations of larger social orders. If traces of the values held by women professional golfers—including the prowess ethic—can be found within the cultures of the families of the players, then the case can be made that ideological dispositions (in addition to liberal access) contribute to the likely success of becoming a professional golfer.

To determine the social backgrounds of the professional golfers, I asked these players questions about their family histories. These interviews confirmed that many of these players were from affluent families. This was not surprising. Golf is an expensive sport and has for some time been associated with the wealthiest in our society. However, for reasons to be explain in detail later, the sport has become increasingly exclusive over the last fifteen years. Almost all the new players on the tour come from country club backgrounds. Fifteen years ago, only two-thirds of the new golfers came from families with memberships in country clubs.

Although the evidence indicates that the women on the tour are from an affluent background, they clearly do not seem a part of the country club world they entertain in pro-am tournaments, or even a part of the world that has come to support them. In interviews, the players make a point of distinguishing themselves from the country club community.

> The only reason my dad joined the country club is to be a social member [non-golfing member]. . . . He just used it to make business contacts. . . . My brothers didn't use it because they thought it was too—that all the stuck-up people went there because it was a country club. So they didn't want to show their faces there. (Karen)

> I got a job at the country club so I could play. We were members there for a few years until I got the job. I had the high school golf team, too. That is, I was not one of those people who grew up in the country club atmosphere all my life. (Dorothy)

In addition, players from small towns and less assuming private clubs also expressed a sense of alienation from the more affluent country club community.

> It was a workingman's country club, it wasn't a wealthy place. It had a club house and everything, but as opposed to $20,000 annual fee it was more like $2,000. More affordable. But that reflected the area we lived in. (Roslynn)

> I didn't have tons of amateur experience. I played mostly at my country club in Michigan. Rode my bike to the golf course everyday. Left my clubs at the course. I wasn't one of those elite country club players. It was just another sport that we played. (Lynn)

While Roslynn's description of her private country club as a "working-man's country club" may not be accurate, she clearly is making a class distinction and expressing class affiliation.

For a few players, like Pauline, the private country club membership was a sacrifice for the family. Again, the class distinctions are made clear in her description of her experience as young golfer.

> My dad's very strict with money, very much so. It was a big sacrifice for him to join the country club. . . . It was a nice country club, but it wasn't anything real fancy. It didn't have a lot of the social benefits, dances and all that. (Pauline)

These women golfers perceive their families' country club memberships as having primarily benefited them by giving them access to golf, rather than the leisure or conspicuous consumption aspects of country club life. This sense of utility is at the core of players' feeling that they are separate from the "fancy" country club community. These players did not resent feeling different from the community in which they grew up, but they clearly did not want to be associated with "those elite country club players." They seem proud of their outsider status within the country club community.

When is a country club kid not a country club kid? When is a member not a full member? I began to explore why these women did not feel accepted within the typical country club community. I began to ask them questions about their grandparents. They responded with powerful stories of hardship, struggle, and parents who had pulled themselves up by their bootstraps. A significant number of these golfers reported that their parents grew up in working-class families. Molly's family history, for example, is steeped in a working-class culture.

> My father's father raised ten kids and worked at everything he could in Brooklyn. He died of pneumonia washing cars at night just to keep his family in food, but before that he did a lot of different things.
>
> My father's mother just took care of everybody, she stayed at home and made babies.
>
> On my mother's side, my grandmother was a dressmaker and my grandfather was a machinist. They were from Easton. (Molly)

These players who were raised in upwardly mobile families, I have dubbed "first-generation country club." Ann's family is an example of a first-generation country club family.

My mother's father worked for the railroad and her mother was an English teacher. My father's father, I don't know what he did. I think he kind of switched around from job to job. He ended up white collar, lower-level white collar.

My dad had a terrible childhood. When he was in high school he had to work and give the money to the family. My dad just worked his way up and became extremely successful [as a medical doctor]. He gave his children the opportunities he never had and he always let us know about it (*laughs*).
Q: So you are first-generation upper class?
Yeah, yeah. (Ann)

June's description of her family history is a clear example of a first generation country club family and the transformation of a working-class family to the middle class over the period of one generation.

One grandfather was a coal miner. My other one worked in an electronics plant. Worked his ass off for nothing.

My dad's a restaurant owner. He loves it. He had a heart attack at forty. He worked hard at all his businesses. He had a lot of properties, little businesses, shit like that. Ran himself ragged and had a heart attack. He sold a lot of things. Now at fifty-one, we have a ball with my dad. . . .

My dad loves being his own boss. We have some cash. I mean we are not real well off, but good enough so that he does not have to be on somebody's time clock.

While this sort of rags to riches story is not in every player's family history, it was repeated with astounding regularity. In twenty-one interviews, I asked the player about her family history. Sixteen, more than 75%, indicated dramatic upward mobility or working-class roots. Survey questions were formulated to confirm this pattern.

In the surveys, players were asked questions which helped to locate the player's socio-economic class while she was a child. First, players were asked about the type of training facilities, public or private, that were available to them during the developmental stages of their training. Second, players were asked to describe the primary occupations of their parents while they were growing up, and their grandparent's occupations while their parents were children. The results were coded and ranked on an occupational scale.[1] These results were categorized in three broad occupational groupings: working-class, middle-class, and upper-class.

Third, players were asked to define their parents' and grandparents' socio-economic level. Responses were divided between working class, middle class, and upper class. However, some players added their own categories of upper-middle and lower-middle. As expected, most players placed themselves in the middle class. Self-definition of class is obviously not the most accurate tool for determining class. I was more interested, however, in whether or not a player indicated a change in economic level between generations.

Fifty-one of the players surveyed gave clear information regarding family class history. Forty (78%) reported that they received training at a private facility as a child. Of these forty golfers, twenty-seven indicated that their fathers were in occupations significantly higher on the occupational scale than their paternal grandfathers. In addition, two players indicated a significant increase in income between generations despite a lack of significant change in occupational status. The survey data mirrors the interview data. Approximately 75 percent, 29 of 40, of the professional golfers claiming private country clubs as a childhood training facility were from upwardly mobile families. Further, twice as many players claimed to have paternal grandfathers with working-class occupations than claimed to have a paternal grandfathers with professional occupations.[2]

Despite spending much of their childhood at the country club, players from upwardly mobile families feel themselves to be different from the recreational golf world.

CLASS-BASED DISTINCTIONS IN THE MEANING OF SPORT

In American society, the influence of class cultures on the socialization process is extremely difficult to assess. The mixing of class cultures through marriage and social mobility, both intergenerational and intragenerational, makes it hard to discern class-based attitudes and expectations. Determining the influence of class, outside of the effect of economic advantages and disadvantages, is difficult. Nonetheless, the theme of upward mobility in the family histories of the players suggests that there is a shared background that encourages athletic success.

Golfing excellence is highest among players raised in upwardly mobile families, and these players feel somewhat outside the country club mainstream. The remainder of the chapter is devoted to both isolating the attitudes and ideologies of LPGA golfers that promote excellent play which can be traced to values, and the ideologies and beliefs of upper-class families with working-class roots.

In his study of social taste, French sociologist, Pierre Bourdieu found considerable class differences in the meaning of sport. For instance, a high percentage (71%) of senior executives and professionals placed considerable emphasis on improving physical education but only a third wanted their children to be national champions. For manual workers, those percentages were almost reversed: 48% wanted physical education improved, and 61% wanted their children to be sports champions. Men in middle-class occupations, craftsmen and junior executives, fell between these two extremes. These findings indicate contrasting approaches to sport and point to considerable variation in its meaning to the participants.[3]

A further sign of class-based attitudes toward sport can be found in David Karen's study of students accepted to Harvard as undergraduates. Following Bourdieu's notion of culture and class divisions, Karen divided applicants according to their parents' occupations. As might have been expected, applicants with parents in occupations requiring graduate school (upper class/culture) accounted for over half of all the accepted students. One notable deviation were students designated as potential varsity athletes. Most of these students came from families headed by parents in occupations requiring college education (middle class/culture). Upper class/culture applicants accounted for only one-third of these admits.[4]

One of the most penetrating discussions of the place of sport in upper-class culture can be found in the work by Nelson W. Aldrich Jr.[5] Aldrich, himself a product of "old money," explores the meaning of inherited wealth and newly earned wealth. According to Aldrich, the defining ethic of sport for the social elite is not prowess but sportsmanship. Sportsmanship represents old money's claim to stand out from the working and entrepreneurial classes.[6]

> Nothing so becomes an upper class aesthetically and morally as the control of its aggression, and that's what a sporting code is for. The best example of this is the relative apportionment of luck and merit by and to the winners and losers of any contest.
> Sportsmanship calls for victors always to credit their good luck and their opponents' bad luck for the way things turned out, while it demands the reverse of losers; that they take responsibility for the outcome—"no, no, I played badly, that's all there is to it." In this way, winners are prevented from forcibly depriving losers of more than was at stake in the competition (such as their pride), while losers are prevented from violently taking back what they've lost. And within the game, sportsmanship demands the same self-restraint—no dirty fight-

ing, no cheating, no "taking advantage." It's a question of fine manners curbing the powers of a class while adorning its presence.[7]

Far less important than success is the manner in which the game is played. For the upper class, there is no need to transcend or create themselves anew, rather the struggle is to prove themselves worthy of their inherited position.

The drive to prove oneself stands in sharp contrast to the patrician manners of amateur golf. Indeed, the traditional send-off to "have fun out there" seems incongruous with the players' hard work and earnest determination to prove themselves through golf. Golf as a social pastime, a hobby in which the outcome is far less important than the taking part, has little need for attributes like hard work, drive, struggle, and "being tough" which are so valued by the LPGA membership. The preponderance of players from the working class, or one generation removed from the working class, suggests that the disposition and worldview necessary for success on the tour is promoted by working-class culture and/or by upwardly mobile class culture.

Prowess, a combination of talent and hard work, as the basis of success is more readily found among the working class. In Bourdieu's (1984) study of class disparities in social taste, he found that the working class emphasized hard work and talent, while the upper classes emphasized social background, education, and intelligence as the keys to success.[8] One of the most illuminating looks into the ideology of success among the working class is Sennett and Cobb's *The Hidden Injuries of Class* (1973). Their study also found a working-class emphasis on persistence, hard work, and talent as the path to success.

The empowering aspect of this philosophy is that individuals, by virtue of their ability and hard work, have the potential to transcend their social origins. Symbols of accomplishment (i.e., a college degree, a promotion, or athletic accomplishments), are symbols of a person's talents, hard work, and personal fortitude. Sennett and Cobb refer to these symbols of success as "badges of ability." The injurious side of this perspective is that the individuals are held responsible when they fail to improve their lot in life.[9] This is true even when it is understood that there are limited chances for success. This notion of success (victory) and failure (the slump) is mirrored by the attitudes of the players on the LPGA tour.

In addition to individual's limited chances for success in our world, the odds do not increase on the basis of talent, but of class. Those born into families with more cultural, financial, or political capital have an easier time attaining badges of ability. While the working class understands on some level that badges of ability (college degrees, financial stability, a second home) come more easily to the upper classes, these accomplishments still come to symbolize talent and hard work. Those people able to acquire symbols of success command respect from those unable to attain them for whatever reason. This all works to maintain the current structure of society.

The lives of their upwardly mobile parents reinforce the golfers' belief that hard work pays off. On the tour, once LPGA membership has been attained, each week every player has the chance to improve her position, to create herself anew. As Nat put it earlier, the tour is the barest form of capitalism.

THE CLASH OF CLASS CULTURES

Given golf's historical roots in the power elite, it is not surprising that vestiges of "old money" values remain embedded in the sport. For example, the traditional send-off, "have fun out there," cautions the players not to take themselves too seriously as golfers. The handicap is another example of "old money" values. Within the social world of recreational golf, success based on physical gifts is perceived as an unfair distinction between players. A player's handicap, a mathematical average developed by the amateur branch of the sport, equalizes competition between amateur players of different abilities. The result is structural encouragement of sportsmanship. Further, handicaps make hard work and determination optional. In this system, hard work and determination may change a player's handicap. They will not, however, improve the player's chance of winning.

In some amateur golfing circles, the handicap system has been transformed by the "lower" classes into a "badge of ability." Amateurs garner status within their golfing circles according to how low a handicap they claim. The irony is that the handicap system was originally designed to equalize competition and minimize the use of golfing prowess to acquire status.

Nothing quite illustrates the spirit of the LPGA in contrast to the older aristocratic spirit of the game as when elderly USGA marshals and players confer over rulings. The "sporting thing," of course, is to nobly accept the marshal's ruling. In the 1991 U.S. Open, Jane Geddes was captured by a television mike as she tried to convince an elderly judge her ball was truly on the out of bounds line despite the unpainted grass that lay between her ball and the line. Although the discussion was cordial and out of earshot of the gallery, her persistent questioning of the marshall's understanding of her argument had all the flavor of a John MacEnroe outburst. Geddes' manner of questioning a volunteer marshal is not unusual. Rulings are frequently questioned by players in a manner that is, well, not sports(wo)man-like.

These skirmishes with marshals highlight the conflict between the old money amateur notion of "not taking advantage" and the ethos of the LPGA to "take every advantage possible." The professionals frequently get their way when they challenge a ruling, and in so doing uphold the presumed superiority of both cultures. The marshals uphold the distinctive conduct of the upper class which emphasizes control of aggression and restaint of class power. This conduct reflects an aesthetic and moral character which is proof of the appropriateness of their social position.[10] The marshals prove their moral superiority by expressing the code of sport and place it in contrast to the "entrepreneurial" player by allowing her to have her way. The player, in turn, proves the value of earnest persistence.

The attitude of taking every advantage is also seen in the players negotiation of the rules. Players with unplayable lies will purposely drop poorly three times in order to place the ball. Players, as a matter of course, will replace their ball on the green a half inch or so from their mark to improve their line. Rather than play within the spirit of the rules, professionals use the rules to their advantage.

CONCLUSION

When the turn of the century sociologist Max Weber (1864-1920) set out to explain the uneven development of capitalism, his work went beyond a structural explanation. He found that although the material conditions were present for capitalism to "break out" in many areas of Europe, as well as in Asia, it developed much more quickly in Protestant enclaves. Weber's point was not to deny the importance of material conditions but to complicate our understanding of the development of capitalism by adding another component: ideology. Weber's primary point was that early Protestant thought and the radically new capitalist mindset of the time were complimentary.[11]

This chapter has attempted to make similar points. First and foremost, certain material conditions must be present fairly early in a woman's life for her to have a reasonable chance of becoming a professional golfer. Early introduction and liberal access to the sport are crucial to the contemporary player's development. For the most recent cohort, this usually meant family membership in a private country club or golf club.

Within the segment of the population enjoying liberal access, children raised in upwardly mobile families (first-generation country club families) seem to have an advantage. The relative success of this group can be traced to the similarities between values and beliefs of their parents' culture and the spirit of the LPGA.

It is a popular conception that children with working-class backgrounds make better or hungrier athletes. Sociologists generally acknowledge that stable, supportive, working-class families produce the majority of elite athletes. Working-class and minority participation and success in athletics is most often explained on a structural level. Typically it is argued that the lack of economic opportunities for working-class and minority youth makes professional sports an attractive option for them. Further, youths facing race and class discrimination find sport one enterprise in which excellence cannot be denied. Children from more privileged and well-connected families are thought to be more likely to choose a career path that is less risky and place less emphasis on prowess.

However, the LPGA adds a wrinkle of complexity to these explanations. The single largest group of women to become professional golfers are from affluent backgrounds. Despite having access to resources which might enable them to pursue far less risky careers, these women chose to pursue a career in professional golf. A significant portion of this group, however, were raised by parents who grew up in working-class households. Women raised in working-class households or in households one generation removed from the working-class seem to have an advantage in professional women's golf. The ability to put in long hours on tedious work and to consistently pay attention to detail are rewarded in golf, albeit not immediately. I suspect that hard work and deferment of gratification are highly valued in first-generation country club homes.

Because these women obviously had other opportunities, working-class athletic prowess cannot be reduced to the structural explanation that blocked opportunity in other arenas leads to an overemphasis on sport. The "glass ceiling," sexual hassament, and a gender-segregated labor force may partially explain why a player chooses to remain on tour, but they can't explain her wherewithal to succeed at golf as a teenager. Ideological and cultural components must be taken into account when explaining the large numbers of athletes with working-class backgrounds. Notions that hard work will pay off and that sport outcomes matter are held more deeply among working people than by the upper classes. And it would seem this cultural or ideological factor remains in families one generation removed from working class conditions.

CHAPTER 7

THE IMAGE MAKERS

"I saw Lopez last night, at the mall. Had her kids with her."
"What was she buying?"
"I don't know."

—Conversation overheard between
reporters at a tournament, 1989

Man, could I tell you some stories!

—Reaction from a reporter after he found
out I was studying tour life, 1989

If there is an image problem on the LPGA tour, it is manufactured by those who cover, watch, and organize the tour. At face value, there is nothing about the LPGA's presentation of competitive golf that overtly suggests that women golfers are masculine, lesbian, or sexually available. Indeed, the players and staff spend considerable time and energy trying to present a "wholesome" image. Players are instructed by LPGA staff to be as helpful to the press as possible, to respond kindly to even the rudest fans, and to dress in a professional fashion. Rookies go through an orientation to help them deal with the press and fans in order to present a "positive image."

The tour's "image" is mediated by elements outside of the players' control. At its root, the "image problem" is the tension between traditional notions of appropriate gender behavior and golf. While most players acknowledge this tension with the broader social order, most players argue that it is blown out of proportion by the press. Indeed, the players blamed the press as the catalyst and primary promoter of the "image problem."

THE PRESS

Any press coverage (even hurtful) is better than no press, but getting good press seems to be a concern of most LPGA members. The players' suspicion of the press is complicated by the necessary relationship between the press and the tour. For the tour to be successful, the LPGA must receive media coverage. However, players view the promotion of the "image problem" as detrimental to the tour. In particular, it affects their ability to gain and maintain corporate sponsorship of tournaments.

The LPGA membership is wary of the press for a number of reasons. A commonly expressed reason is the media's astounding lack of contact with the game of golf and the golfers. Most reporters cover one or two tournaments a year. The majority of the press arrives at the course between midmorning and early afternoon. Once at the course, they rarely venture out of the press area. One sportswriter told me in hushed tones that golf was an easy sport to cover because you don't have to watch it. All the information he needed to write a story was efficiently obtained in the press tent.

The press area consists of large scoreboards which volunteers update constantly. Writers do not have to leave the tent to get an idea of what is evolving out on the course. At the end of each day, the leaders are brought into the press area. In ritual fashion, the players will recount their rounds hole by hole for the press. They highlight important holes, tough shots, good putts—the players all but write the body of the article for the reporters. The LPGA media staff produces summaries of each interview. One LPGA staff member admitted that some reporters don't show up until the end of the day. These reporters pick up the transcriptions of the player interviews, look over the scoreboard, and construct a story.

This lack of contact with the people that cover their sport does not go unnoticed by the players.

> It is kind of strange that we never see them. Tournament people, staff, caddies, you're always running into them somewhere. But the press you never see. They don't even come out to watch the tournament. They are in the press room watching the leader boards and getting reports via walkie talkies and such. (Cara)

The lack of contact with the sport was particularly evident in the players' interactions with television coverage. Out of all the press and media people, only camera operators are allowed inside the ropes. The close-ups viewers find appealing and producers desire require camera operators to stand within a few feet of players while they hit. Players find the noise, movement, and closeness of camera operators distracting. While in the field, I observed a number of confrontations stemming from a camera operator's interference with a players swing. In one instance, a player was so angered by a camerman's intrusion that she cussed him out. In each instance, the camera operator seemed unaware of his violation of golfing norms.

In addition to the lack of contact, players dislike the way the print media behaves when they do interact with the players. In press briefings, I was struck by the propensity of reporters to lecture players about golf, make suggestions, and offer guidance on managing the LPGA. When I asked Ann about this observation she became quite animated. The following is a sample of her comments on the press.

> Most of these guys are frustrated athletes and that is why they are sportswriters. I mean they really are. They played athletics in high school or something and could not quite make it, so they became a writer. They don't all fall into that category, but a lot of them do.
>
> They are always trying to tell you something. . . . You get it a lot. "I can't believe you hit a five iron there when you know you're not supposed to be above the hole." You make mistakes in this game, but it is like they are looking for something you did wrong. . . . The majority of the writers don't want to write about the positive side of what you did. (Ann)

The players recognize rather quickly that freedom of the press means that their own voice will not be heard in the reports. From the players' perspective, the newspaper stories are not made on the golf course. They are created in the press tent.

> I think reporters do this: they already have it in their mind the story they want to write. They have their questions and they keep asking it until they get the answer they want to hear. Instead of reporting the facts of what is happening, they are going in there and formulating a story, and putting it down just the way they want to write it. (Jane)

Sometimes I read an article about someone, and I know the truth and then I read what someone else wrote. It is like this person you know isn't like the person in the paper, or doesn't do what he says she does. (Nat)

[The press] makes you or breaks you. They make you the person you are or they make you the person you're not. One bad swing with the press can cost you an awful lot. I don't think that the press tells the truth all the time. I know in my case I've been misquoted numerous times. (Gerri)

The press is just looking for a story, creating a little of this here and a little of this there. (Pam)

In defense of the press, there are structural constraints to the job that encourage formulation of a story prior to talking to the players. The leaders in a tournament usually come in from the final hole in late afternoon, when deadlines for both newsprint and television are fast approaching. If the reporters were to wait and write a story based on information from the players, most would miss their deadlines. Just as Jane suspects, many pieces about the players on the tour are formulated by the writer in advance of an interview. The players' view of reporters as fiction writers, whose work is only loosely based on the tour, is not far from reality.

The lack of contact, the suspect reporting, and their lack of control of the institution most responsible for creating and sustaining the tour's image make most players wary of the press. But what most disturbs the players is the press' continual fascination with the sexual preference of the players on tour.

When people get into an interview situation, you get some guys that are just going to dig and stir it up because we are women. If they did that with men, they would get flattened. I am talking about the gay lifestyle. Out here it seems to be that is all we hear about. . . . And the press loves it. Boy, do they love it. They ask about it and you say to yourself, "What do I do now?"
Q: The press asks you questions like that?
All over the place. Yeah, we were told in rookie orientation to be prepared for it. I am glad I was. I don't know what I would have said if it had not been up front and told "We know you are going to get this sort of question."
Q: And when they ask you, do they say it is "off the record?"

(*Nods an affirmation*) But you get some that must have had a bad day and they just ask you point blank. But most of the time it is more of a one-on-one situation. They say "Doris, how is it . . ." It is kind of sad, and the girls are fed up with it. But we can't escape it, unfortunately. (Doris)

The propensity of the press to push for information about the private lives of the players can be explained on two levels. The first has to do with how the press gains status among their colleagues. Peer status is measured by a press corps member's ability to gain intimate knowledge about the players. Casual conversations in the press tent revolved around trading stories about the off-course behavior of athletes or what the top-ranking players are "really" like. Comments like "and Sheehan was up there dancing," or the comment which heads this chapter, "I saw Lopez last night . . . at the mall" are common among the press corps. There is a "Can you top this" atmosphere in the press tent. Indeed, the vast majority of the comments made by press corps members about players on the tour had nothing to do with their golfing abilities. Rather than discussing fine points like swing speed, tempo, or stance, the press concerned themselves with personality, attractiveness, and off-course behavior. The more bold or intimate the details a member of the press could share with his colleagues, the longer he held the attention of others and thus the higher his status.

The gossip swapping of the press tent stands in sharp contrast to most player/press interactions. Players are cordial but guarded with the press. Few have any contact with the press outside the official context of the press tent or an interview. Indeed, seeing Lopez at the mall was hot gossip, a rare peek into the private life of a professional athlete. In contrast to the mundane tidbits that get tossed around the press tent, most reporters retain, but rarely print, titillating stories about players on tour. These stories are rarely confirmable and almost always secondhand. The few that I listened to had all the credibility of fish-that-got-away stories.

A second explanation for the press' constant fascination with the players' private lives can be understood best as a combined desire to discredit the tour and at the same time to sell stories about it. The idea that gossip sells is fairly easy to fathom. Even harsh criticism of athletes in sports can be understood as an attempt to attract readers or viewers. But among the LPGA membership, there is an added sentiment that the media industry attempts to undermine the tour.

I think that [the image] is created by a lot of jealousy and envy. I think men, well, I don't know if this is really the case, but you know, I think men have a little problem with seeing women that make a couple hundred thousand more than they do a year. So maybe they want to blow things out of proportion and make it more than what it is. (Fran)

Questioning the sex or sexuality of women athletes is a way of discrediting their performance.[1] It is as if to say, "you're a good woman athlete only because you are not a real woman."

It is easy to see that the curiosity about the players' sexuality stems from assumptions about the essence of athletic prowess, independence, and ambition. Since these are taken to be essentially male traits, an explanation is sought for why some women display these attributes.

The questioning of the legitimacy of the players' claim to the female sex category may in fact not be intended to discredit the players' talents but to explain them. However, the result is the same. The questioning of one's membership in a sex category has often been used to discredit people's accomplishments in many fields in order to defend the dominant social order from a preceived threat of deviance.[2] Thus when a female athlete's actions cannot be ignored, trivialized, or sexualized,[3] subtle suggestions of lesbianism, and the highlighting of masculine traits or ambiguous gender behavior are often used to discredit the player's prowess. All things being equal, a more logical line of questioning would be to question the essential maleness of excellence in sport. However, that could undercut sport as a resource for doing gender, and therefore status of all men involved, whether participants, reporters, or spectators.

On the surface, the desire of the press to discredit the tour is hard to understand, given the relationship of the media industry and the sports industry. As is often pointed out, the two industries have a mutually beneficial relationship.[4] Sports news sells papers and attracts viewers; in turn, the coverage of sports increases the public's interest in sports. Increased interest attracts readers or viewership to the news industry that covers the sport event best. The sports entertainment industry and the media industry feed each other. If undermining the tour is indeed the strategy of the press, it seems very much like shooting oneself in the foot. However, if we add to the equation the notion of "doing gender," the undermining of the tour becomes understandable. The pursuit of stories about lesbians on the tour serves to preserve golf as a "naturally" manly pursuit. This sort of coverage ensures the comfort of the sports media's primary market—men. The media industry has a stake in maintaining the image of sport as a resource for doing masculinity. It sells.

Part of [the image problem] has been media induced. . . . It makes good copy. It seems to happen once a year or so. Somebody will rehash it, just dig it up. (Cara)

The media's common defense is that they are merely giving the readers or viewers what they want. To justify the questioning of the players' sexuality, however, on the basis of public taste is a bit disingenuous. There is far more questioning "off the record" than on, which would hardly be the case if the reporters were only motivated by a desire to fulfil a public demand. Indeed, as Ethel notes below, the hostility is less a reflection of the public's sentiments than a creation of the press.

Undermining the success of the association (LPGA) happens a lot. People would prefer to talk about something that is not founded and not factual because the facts are very boring, most of them. I think it is an attitude. An attitude towards women a lot of times. I don't find that attitude is in the general public as much as I do from the press at times. (Ethel)

Although it is difficult to prove Ethel's assertion, it does seem logical. On a personal level, members of the press have a stake in maintaining sport as a masculine preserve and a masculine symbol. Within the news business, the content of the story a reporter covers contains a gender element. We need only to make a cursory comparison of the sex of war reporters, sportscasters, weather reporters, and TV movie critics to see how gender operates in the production of news. The symbolic gender status of sport rubs off on those who report on it. It is not surprising, then, that the field of sports reporting is predominantly male. Sportswriters and reporters have a personal stake in maintaining sport as a "manly" institution and may have difficulty reconciling the existence of superb women athletes with their beliefs.

THE IMAGE PROBLEM AND LESBIAN FANS

If the press is on some level threatened by the LPGA, the lesbian community celebrates the tour. Just as many Dominican baseball fans will only follow American professional teams with Dominican players, and many Catholics will root for Notre Dame, lesbian fans will often follow players they believe to be lesbian. The LPGA is a source of pride for many in the lesbian community.[5] In some cases the golfers become stars of the lesbian community. Some players, however, find this sort of support problematic. Ann's response to her celebrity status was typical.

> (*Laughing*) It is so true. I mean athletes are going to be symbols for certain groups, just like celebrities. People have a tendency to put us up on a pedestal. Not that we deserve it, but that is the way society treats us.
>
> At certain tournaments you can get a pretty large gay following. I mean sometimes it feels like a convention.

The belief that there are "a lot" of lesbians, albeit closeted lesbians, on the tour, increases the interest of the lesbian community in the tour. The interest of the lesbian community in the LPGA is further heightened by the conventional culture's reluctance to fully embrace the tour. Lesbian support, in turn, feeds the perception of an "image problem" within the straight community.

The players do not necessarily want the support of the lesbian community. While most lesbian players do not keep there sexual identities secret from their friends and family, they would prefer to be admired for what they do on the course rather than for their sexual preference. Some view the support of lesbian fans as potentially harmful to their careers. For example one lesbian identified player referred to the lesbian community's support as "embarrassing" and potentially harmful to her ability to attract sponsors. Some players consciously avoid interacting with female-only spectator groups, regardless of the player's sexual preference, for fear of contributing to the tour's "image problem."[6] The lesbian fans' interest in the players they identify as lesbian is not, however, intended to be voyeuristic or harmful. They are merely attempting to support "one of their own."

Not surprisingly, the unwillingness of women on the tour to be open about their sexuality can make it difficult for lesbians to determine who on the tour is lesbian. The gender ambiguity of the tour presents the broader lesbian community with the same problems it presents to the straight community: amid so much gender ambiguity it is difficult to tell who is straight and who is lesbian. For example, I observed four women who were following Lynn as she played. They were cheering loudly with each shot, despite Lynn's rather mediocre performance and failure to make the cut. It was not unreasonable to assume from their dress and style that they were lesbians. When I asked Lynn (who identified herself as heterosexual at the time of the interview) about the foursome she responded.

I didn't know them. These girls were sitting on the 18th hole, I just made the turn. They're sitting like right there watching people walk through [the ropes]. It always cracks me up [when this happens] because they can't quite get inside the ropes but they'll do anything they can to get as close as they can. So just as a gift, I say "Hi" and darn if on the next hole they're not following me.

I have this energy about me that people are attracted to. I attract all kinds of people. I attract very nice looking men and women who are just gay women. There is this neutrality about me that cracks me up. I really get a kick out of it.

The everyday life of the player is often in conflict with heterosexual/feminine norms. Players pay far more attention to their golf game than to heterosexual/feminine gender norms. As a sociologist in a world obsessed with sexuality, I found the players suspended (or fluid) sexuality refreshing. However, most people find this lack of expressed sexual identity disconcerting. Somewhat ironically, it is the players' lack of unambiguous displays of gender/sexuality which results in the public's preoccupation with their sexuality.

COMPENSATORY ACTS AND THE COMPANY LINE

The demands of the sport, the conventional meanings of sport and gender, the actions of the press, the male-centered golfing community, and the interest of the lesbian community all work together to heighten tensions surrounding the presentation of gender on the tour. In an attempt to make the tour palatable to the mass market (which tends to be both homophobic and heterosexual), the LPGA and the players actively engage in actions to neutralize the gender ambiguity (or as Lynn puts it, "neutrality") that women's professional golf presents to the public.

The tour attempts to present its members as professionals and positive role models. Women's golf, the LPGA media and promotion staff insist, is wholesome family fun. As part of the effort to be unobjectionable, the LPGA actively works to counter the "image problem." Compensatory actions on the part of the LPGA staff take two forms: emphasized heterosexuality and promotion of good works.

The tour's promotion of itself is very similar to that of the annual Miss America contest—a simultaneous promotion of wholesomeness and sexuality, of Puritan sensibilities and the legitimation of men's entitlement to use women's bodies for their sexual gratification. The tour promotes the golfers as being squeaky clean (players may, for instance, be fined $100 for cursing while on the course). The LPGA media staff also promote the work players do for local charities and junior golf programs. Simultaneously, it produces swimsuit pictorials, encourages titillating interactions with pro-am partners, and consistently promotes the tour's most attractive players to the media and the general public. Married players and mothers on the tour are listed in the media guides. The LPGA staff frequently produce articles that discuss the dilemmas faced by the mothers/wives on tour. The combination of these two approaches gives the tour an overtly wholesome theme with a sexual subtext.

By subtly supporting and promoting the (hetero)sexualization of the players, the tour plays to their male patrons' sexual fantasies.[7] The following quote by a male amateur speaks to the appeal this approach carries.

> Some of them, when you make a birdie, the pro just runs up and hugs and kisses the guys. I want to know what they do with an eagle (*laughs*). I haven't played with them yet, but I am waiting.

There are just enough examples of caddies or pro-am partners meeting, dating, and/or marrying professional golfers to maintain a colorful folklore about the women on tour.

Pro-am parties, where players are matched with amateur teams, are a further indication of the male sexual interest in the golfers that lies just below the surface. The evening is more often than not peppered with comments about the attractiveness and reputation of players. The lottery system of matching players with teams has all the trappings of computer-matched dating. The amateurs, having paid a high price to spend the afternoon with this woman, feel sexually entitled.

Although players are invited to these functions, they rarely attend.[8] The contradictory message of being nice and sexy are irreconcilable for the players at these private, mostly male events.

> Like when I try [to act feminine], there is the flip side. I used to have really long hair. I used to get really dressed up for the pro-am parties, trying to look nice and sexy. Then the men start coming on to you. But that gets sickening. That is why a lot of girls get turned off [and don't go to those parties]. Here I am trying to be nice and promote the LPGA (*laughs*) and guys are being assholes—and they are all married. (Roslynn)

The undercurrent of male sexual entitlement (fermented within the security of the male-centered country club) is so strong that fending off advances by pro-am partners is a weekly event for some players.

> I am twenty-five, and I am not exactly physically attracted to a bunch of sixty-five-year-old men. I mean, they are nice guys, and I respect them for what they have done business-wise and just as people. But you know, I don't appreciate all the time, week after week, that they think I would be interested in joining them for dinner or going out.
>
> I am not saying it is bad. I think it is normal. Guys like to be guys, and they like to hit on women, or just try. I just kind of nicely tell them I have plans or something like that. It's kind of funny, it happens week after week. (June)

While it is impossible to know why all these men try to pick up women golfers, it is clear that the players understand the come-ons as being within the sphere of doing gender. Picking up women is a resource for men to do gender ("guys like to be guys").

In golf, driving the ball a long distance, is also a resource for doing gender. For many pro-am participants, outdriving the women professionals is a symbol of their manhood. This phenomena is not lost on the players.

> The male ego is interesting. They get up there and they try to bust it by you. They can't stand it when a 125-pound women hits it by them. It is fun to watch them struggle with their egos for a little bit. (Hattie)

> Occasionally you get . . . well, I would say a lot of the times you have problems with the long hitters. When we outdrive these guys, they can't handle it. Sometimes they are trying so hard they come out of their shoes [a golfing expression for trying too hard] or they make excuses. (Ann)

The discomfort and tension the men feel, and the women sense, each week in the tee box at pro-am tournaments is a consistent reminder that sport is a proving ground for men. While the experience of outdriving men has the potential to challenge the association between sport and masculinity, some golfers choose to defuse the situation by playing up the masculine displays of the amateurs.

Sometimes you play with guys whose big thing is to hit it good and outdrive you. Then I try to make them feel good. "God, that was a great drive. Boy, you really ripped that one." I go up and squeeze their muscle or something like that. Then, hopefully they will break out of that macho type feeling and understand I am not like that. (Nora)

What Nora means to say through her actions is that she is not going to threaten their masculinity even if she does outdrive them. Through her overt admiration of masculine gender displays, she hopes to evoke a sense of security in the male amateurs. She is "not like that"—not a threat to masculine hegemony of the country club. Once this is established, she hopes the amateurs will be able to settle down and play golf and have an enjoyable afternoon.

The overtly heterosexualized atmosphere of the tour, and particularly at the pro-am, enables the women to display their athletic prowess in a minimally threatening fashion. Players engage in compensatory actions in order that their golfing skills be palatable to golf fans and patrons. In the context of the pro-am, the "come-ons" the players face from their pro-am partners can also be seen as compensatory acts. Men whose masculinity has been threatened or damaged on the course by the play of women professionals may feel compelled to conquer a player in the bedroom or steal a kiss at the end of the round in an attempt to reclaim a sense of masculinity.

CONCLUSION

Despite the golfers' "fantasy world," they still operate within a gendered world. Although it is rarely acknowledged, our social interactions are directed by our ability to accurately assess the sex of others. As mentioned in the previous chapter, we are disturbed when we can not determine someone's sex and angry when someone gets our's wrong. Knowing someone's sex takes on an omnirelevance. As such, we have developed normative gender displays to facilitate our continual assessment of sex. Almost every aspect of our society is gendered, from beverages to backpacks, from work to window curtains. Our world is arranged, marketed, and sold according to gender norms. This is not to suggest that gender norms are completely rigid, but they are fairly stable and of constant concern.

The "image problem" of professional women's golf has far less to do with the sexual identity of the players on tour than it does with the fact that the country club, golf, and the sport milieus have been appropriated as avenues to express masculinity. Women's excellence in golf threatens the accepted meaning of golf. In a society which associates masculinity with youth, golf is one place older men could do masculinity.

Although some experiences of the LPGA players raise the possibility that golf can be disassociated from traditional notions of gender, women's golf continues to operate within a minefield of contradictory images: women golfers as deviant women, countered with the equally damaging image of women golfers as male heterosexual fantasy girls or nonthreatening feminine women. Neither image fits comfortably within the prowess ethic. But then, if the image of the tour were reduced to the prowess ethic—simply women playing excellent golf—it may very well lack the social significance to attract an audience in our world.

CHAPTER 8

INTERPERSONAL RELATIONS ON THE TOUR

If relations with those surounding the subworld of women's golf are defined by gender, relations between the players are defined by the prowess ethic. This exaggerated meritocracy permeates all aspects of the players' everyday life on tour. For the average player—who only rarely engages with the press, fans, pro-am partners, or sponsors—gender issues are a minor nuisance compared to the isolation and loneliness of life on tour.

Indeed, my saddest discovery has been that within this struggle for respect in a male-dominated sport, there is very little community among the women. No one referred to the LPGA as "family," or even said that they could rely on each other for support. Just the opposite was the case. Players intentionally avoided emotional connections with each other. To understand why this is the case, we have to understand the consequences of the prowess ethic on the players sense of self in the world.

STRUCTURED IDENTITY AND INTERPLAYER RELATIONS

In the broadest context, the players define their social position in terms of athletic prowess (athlete or non-athlete, professional or recreational). Even the relations between players within the subworld are in part defined by prowess. While some players saw this as positive and freeing, others found it somewhat disturbing.

One of the problems with our tour is that what you are on the money list is what you are. I saw a little bit of that when I had those few years when I played very badly. (Ann)

Something I catch a glimpse of every once in a while are attitudes towards different levels of players. We are almost a little bit more respectful of the top players. They are little more revered than the lesser players. (Hattie)

To have qualified for the tour is a display of extraordinary prowess. As such, the players share a mutual respect for each other.

I think there is a lot of respect one player to another out here. . . . You feel like you have the respect of your peers. (Tara)

Outside of mutual respect, however, the players on tour have few ties that bond them together as a group. The game of golf has little about it that encourages interaction between players. Golf is a solitary game. As Gerri points out, golf lacks the bonding attributes associated with other sports.

It is not a team sport. I mean you look at the comradeship in baseball and football. These guys are hyped for one another. Now come on, I am not hyped that I get beat by a shot in a play-off. I am not excited about it at all. I am not excited that I shot 68 and somebody shot 67. I don't hate her for it, but it is going to be very difficult for me to say, "Betsy, let's have dinner. I want to talk to you about how you shot sixty-six." I really give a shit. I don't care how she did it. I just want to find out that I can do it. (Gerri)

For the younger players coming out of college programs, the sense of aloneness is often acute. Sara's quote is illustrative of the loneliness some younger players feel.

It is different, because you are out here by yourself. That was the great thing about college. Unfortunately you never appreciate it until it isn't there. When you are playing a college tournament, coming down eighteen, there were five other people waiting for you to come in and who want to know your score and hoped you played well. Out here you are out here by yourself. Nobody cares whether you hit 70 or 81, you are here by yourself. I am sure the people back home care, but they are not out here with you. So that part is hard. (Sara)

To be comfortable being alone with oneself seems a necessary and acquired skill for many of the golfers. More experienced players seem to have discovered a way of handling the isolation and even seek it out. For example, they tend to find private housing and roommates an added distraction or burden. Given an opportunity to do otherwise, they would rather not have to deal with people.

I basically stay alone. I am basically a loner. I like that because then you don't have to . . . you do your own thing. You don't have to make sure you don't have to wake somebody up and all that jazz. I am very fortunate to be in a situation where I can pick and choose when I want a roommate. (Doris)

In fact, many players perceive themselves as loners.

I find that I am a loner, I spend more time with myself than hanging with people. . . . When I was in high school I was a loner and imagined my life as a loner. (Denise)

I think the majority of the people out here are a little bit on their own path. (Jane)

Even in winning, players find themselves alone. After the initial roar of the crowd and the personal congratulations from peers and friends, the victor is whisked off to the press room. By the time she has finished answering questions and is making her way back to the locker room, the fans have left the club, and the tents and scoreboards are being dismantled. The locker room is empty. The other players have cleaned out their lockers and are headed to the next tournament or out to dinner with friends.[1] The tournament has an almost eerie, ghost-town ambiance.

The interpersonal relations between players can be broadly defined as respectful yet detached. Lynn captured this ambiguity when she described her relationship to other players as "close but not *close* close."

INTERPLAYER RELATIONS AND EMOTION MANAGEMENT

This is not to say that the tour is cold and that relations between players are generally strained. There is an ambiance of playfulness on the tour.

Joking and good natured ribbing permeate the tour and the relations between players. Humorous stories and unusual or remarkably good shots are passed along a sort of tour gossip circuit. The putting green and the driving range are the most common sites for passing along tour gossip, which seems to be a diversion from the routine and/or stress of a player's everyday life. Some players contend that because the competition is not directly against an opponent, as it is in other individual sports like tennis, golf allows for a certain amount of pleasantries.

> It's a one-man sport. I'm not competing against Jan or Sue today, even though I'm playing against them and they might be winning the golf tournament. I'm not competing against them, I'm competing against the golf course. I can either screw up totally or I can have a great day. And I think that is why we can go out and have fun with each other and joke around. (Beth)

Too much joking around, however, is not conducive to good play.

> But then we have to settle down and concentrate and play a good shot. There are a lot of players who come out and just decide to come out and have fun every week. But I don't think they are the ones who are succeeding. The people who are at the top, day in and day out, they concentrate more on the golf. I'm not saying they never have a good time, you have to, you'd go crazy if you didn't. When they have a week or two off they can go have fun, that's what I do now. (Beth)

This often-repeated, almost puritanical attitude is tied to the emotion management[2] required by the sport. It is a long, slow game in which slight changes in a player's emotional state can dramatically influence her performance. The tour players actively work on their ability to conjure up a sense of calm and maintain it regardless of how they are playing. So integral is this aspect of the game that the better players on tour are admired as much for their emotional control as their golf swings.

The players' struggle to "settle down" and retain an appropriate focus on golf, affects relations between players. For example, June spoke of the necessity of maintaining distance from other players as part of her process of emotion management:

> When I talk about an environment, I mean, as good as you think you are, you just have to be smart. You have to put yourself in

the right places. You have to put yourself with the right people. I try to do all my main preparation before I get in a tournament away from the tournament site. Once I get there, it is just a little bit of loosening up and going. It is just that sometimes . . . [the other players] are your friends and your competitors, you know. I practically live with them. It is hard to stand right next to them [on the driving range or practice green] and not B.S. a little bit. I mean any normal person likes to do that. It is hard, while you are doing that, to have your mind where it needs to be. So if I go where I can be alone, there I do what I need to do much better.

If a player is unable to focus fully on golf, she is not likely to do well on tour. The professionals, therefore, interact with each other at some emotional distance. Interactions tend to be cordial but superficial and non-controversial. The rookie Sara described this phenomena most succinctly:

I have not met anyone that has been rude or anything. I mean everybody keeps pretty much to themselves.

THE CAMARADERIE OF THE RECENT PAST

The respectful, yet distant relations between players are a rather recent development. The older players (on tour prior to 1970) speak longingly of the old barnstorming days, when players were closer and more supportive of each other, and the tour was more fun. One player recounted that at a recent reunion of early professionals they laughed the entire evening, exchanging "on the road" stories of the first three decades of the professional golf tour. Tara's comments reflect this fondness for the early days of golf as well as a heavy sense of loss.

When I came out, there were only twenty-five of us. So most of us were around the same age. We loved golf. We kind of took care of each other. It was a small organization. I have no idea who half the rookies are out here. Because I never get to play with them, I don't get to see them that much. So we don't socialize, unless we are going to a scheduled meeting or an annual meeting, that is not really socializing.

It has changed, it used to be that we kind of helped each other out here. I am out of touch with the younger players.

Even Ann, who would not be considered an older player, notes a historical transformation in the relations between players.

> When I first came out on tour, the tour probably was a little bit closer, because it was smaller and you knew everyone. Now, I mean there are people I do not know. I played golf today, and a girl asked me if she could join me on the last hole. She had cut over. I said sure, I had never met her. So we introduced ourselves. Here it is June, it is the first time I met this girl.
>   When I first came out, in 1979, we pretty much had a ninety-player field. So you pretty much knew everybody, so it was a little bit closer that way. It was more relaxed then. (Ann)

At the core of this lost camaraderie of the old tour was the players' understanding of their place within their community. In the first three decades of professional women's golf (early forties to the early seventies)[3] players saw themselves as active members of a group that was creating women's professional golf. In addition to the familiarity facilitated by the tour's smaller size, solidarity arose out of the players' shared responsibility for the LPGA's existence. LPGA rules required all players to attend pro-ams and sponsor parties. Each player had to participate in some form of event management. Failure to fulfill these obligations cost a player her right to participate in the tournament.

These constraints provided a nexus of fairly reliable social connections that helped build trust between the players. Not only did players know each other, they knew what to expect from each other. The LPGA rules guiding behavior institutionalized loyalty between players, which in turn was a catalyst for comradeship.

THE CONTEMPORARY TOUR

Today's player views herself less as a member of a group creating the tour and more as an independent operator within the organization of professional women's golf and the larger golf community.

> Everything out here is individual. Everything, right down to your air ticket. Nothing you do is a group. I mean nothing. Everybody is on their own. That is one of the reasons I love it, because that is the way it is. (Ethel)

This transformation can be explained in part by the transformation of the tour. Since the early eighties, women's professional golf has been marked by considerable growth in the number of players, an increase in the turnover rate of players, and the development of a complex bureaucracy which administers the tour. Today, only a small minority of the players take an active role in the governance of the tour. The players are no longer responsible for such aspects of the tour as event management, pin placement, or press releases. All these tasks are now performed by people with whom players rarely come in contact. Where once players depended on a reliable, stable, familiar community for the maintenance of the tour, they now rely on impersonal relations. Each week, the players place their faith in a bureaucracy made up of hundreds of people that ensures every tournament will be set up just like the last one. The players have faith that tournament committees will find sponsors to fund tournaments for them, find volunteers to house them, transport them, and provide services for them.

Who actually manages, watches, or plays in the tournament is of little consequence to the individual player as long as there is someone filling the positions. Trust in this type of organization does not depend on personal connections within the community, but on faith in a management system. The players experience each tournament as both familiar and impersonal, much the same way we experience fast-food restaurants. As a result of this sort of management, tour members enjoy a certain level of freedom from responsibility and comfort yet at a cost of connectedness with other players and the golfing community.

EXCESSIVE INDIVIDUALISM AND EMOTIONAL SUPPORT

The tour has all the attributes of an excessively individualistic society.[4] The spirit of the LPGA is powered by the players' drive to create themselves according to their own abilities. Each player is solely responsible for her play and thus for her tour ranking. Her identity is tied to her tour ranking. As Ann put it "the numbers you put on the board is who you are." Although one player may dominate for a while, the tour rankings are rarely constant. Players' positions are never secure. They are involved in a continual process of creating themselves. Each tournament, then, represents both the chance of transcendence of self[5] and the risk of losing face. This aspect of the tour contributes to the uncertainty[6] that permeates the players' lives.

One dilemma inherent in an excessively individualistic and uncertain society is the struggle to find support. A society in which individuals are solely responsible for the creation of themselves, and in competition with each other to do so, has limited mechanisms for mutual nurturing. Because an individuals' social position and the relationships between individuals are not clearly defined in this type of social arrangment, finding supportive relationships becomes an individual project.[7] As illustrated by June in the following quote, the players on the LPGA are earnestly in search of emotional support.

> No matter what, no matter how tough and strong you think you are, you need a hug, a boost sometime. It is not fun being by yourself all the time. Out here you fail a lot and you don't have your loved ones with you. It is tough. You come out here and play against the best lady golfers in the world. There is a lot of setbacks and knocks and nobody is there when you have them. I mean you drink off a few bad losses, jog off a few others, but shit, you need people! You need to talk to people.

One of sociologist Emile Durkheim's most salient points regarding individualistic societies is that bonding can take place nonetheless. Within small social groupings, he argued, there is the possibility of "a constant interchange of ideas and feelings from all to each and each to all." Out of which "something like a mutual support" can develop, "which instead of throwing the individual on his own resources, leads him to share in the collective energy and support his own when exhausted."[8] Durkheim's argument, in conjunction with studies that document women's skills in the area of interpersonal relations, would lead us to expect to find groups of players on tour which have formed in order to deal with common issues and extend support to each other. This, however, does not seem to be the case.

Cara's response to questions concerning peer support is typical of the tour players.

> Q: *If you were having a problem and you need [support] right away, and your husband was not available would there be someone [for you on tour]?*
>
> I don't know if there would be somebody on tour or not. I doubt it. I doubt it. (Cara)

Indeed, to rely on other professional golfers for emotional support is perceived by many golfers as poor emotion management and a risky strategy. As Holly suggests below, expending emotional energies comforting other golfers is wasteful and taking on an unnecessary burden.

Q: Do you think this competition gets in the way of having a friendship [out here]?

Look, if I shoot eighty and I want to talk to someone, I am not going to do it, probably. Not more than a few sentences. I don't want to load them down with what is happening to me. Now to me, with close friends you can do that. (Holly)

Q: So is it very isolated on the tour?

So you call somebody back home. (Holly)

Holly articulates the widespread feeling that other players are poor prospects for friendship. Holly understands the demands and the uncertainty of professional golf and thus how little she can afford to give to other players in the form of emotional support. She does not burden other players with her problems because she is unwilling to reciprocate.

Val shares Holly's distrust of other players' ability to reciprocate emotional support, but her solution is qualitatively different.

It is hard. We lead the type of life that you need good friends out here. I have a lot of friends out here. They are good friends but I try not to put too much weight on them. They are going to fall too. It is a tough life. It is hard to have anybody holding you up. But, [pause] and this is my biggest thing out here. I would probably say that my biggest support system is [pause] I am a Christian, and I have a very strong spiritual life. And that is probably my biggest support system out here.

I have learned that you cannot put a lot of faith in the people. You can, but sooner or later they will probably let you down. I mean, like, it is not that they always will, but if you put that faith in people they are going to let you down sometime. That is how a lot of people get hurt out here in relationships. It's because they don't have the Lord to lean on, you know we all have to have somebody to lean on. I lean on the Lord, that is just the way I am. That is my faith, that is where I am coming from. But, [pause] that is what I believe in.

A lot of people don't believe in that, that is fine, [pause] but, I see a lot of them getting real hurt too, people that lean on people out here. (Val)

Ann expresses similar sentiments, but has a different solution than Val or Holly.

Q: Do you actively invest your time, your emotion, energy into other players?

Well, I have gone through some stuff with some players when they were going through some personal problems, emotional problems, or something like that. And I have gone through that with them, and talked to them, tried to help them out that way. Or, I have tried to help people who ask me to look at their golf swing or look at their bunker play. But the thing is, you can't invest a lot of time in them, cause you have got to put so much time into yourself. So it is really pretty selfish.

Q: So who was there when you had trouble?

(*Pausing*) I felt like no one was there to help. I had to do it myself. (*Visibly upset*) But I did it myself (*recovers composure*).

TRUST BUILDING AND EMOTIONAL SUPPORT

Anthony Giddens' work on friendship in contemporary society enlarges upon Durkheim's analysis of mutual nurturing in an individualistic society. Like Durkheim, Giddens notes that due to the complex structure of contemporary society, interpersonal relationships are not built into the social fabric. As a result, there is a great psychological need to develop interpersonal relationships.[9]

However, the basis of interpersonal relations is, according to Giddens, trust, and not, as Durkheim maintained, shared values, problems, and lifestyles. Where trust in others is not institutionalized or structured by social obligations (as it was in the early years of the LPGA tour), trust between individuals must be won. In contemporary society, trust becomes a project, something to be worked on. A good friend, according to Giddens, is someone whose charity is reliably forthcoming even in difficult times.[10]

As illustrated in the quotes above, golfers understand the demands of the game and they understand that they cannot trust each other to be there for them in times of need. It is this lack of trust that prohibits the solidarity among players which Durkheim predicted would arise in small groups within an individualistic community.

More often than not, players seek and find a system of support off the tour. Here is a sampling of the players' comments.

Q: Do you have a support system?

Sort of, it used to be my teacher, she was older and she died about a year and a half ago. So I really fell apart. I think the lucky players are the ones that have it [support] away from here in some form. It doesn't matter [what form]. (Holly)

I tend to keep my circle of friends at home. My circle is mostly my family. (Jane)

My best friends are people I became friendly with in amateur golf and the friendships continued on into professional golf. You had more time for socializing then. And you could make those kind of relationships.

I don't like hanging around the locker room and listening to a lot of complaining or join in any form of socializing out here. I don't find it stimulating at all. So I do most of my socializing away from the course, away from work. (Ethel)

By and large, players seek out supportive relationships in which emotional support is forthcoming but not expected to be returned. Family or people off the tour who posess an understanding of the demands of golf are the most prevalent sources of support. Or to frame it slightly differently, where the gender order cannot be counted on to provide emotion work, and where the occupational demands preclude support from peers, emotion work is sought from outsiders with intimate knowledge of the individual or the occupation.

PLAYER/CADDY RELATIONS

Subordinates can also be a source of emotional support. Many of the women on the tour expect their caddies to perform emotional labor for them. Almost without fail, players define the primary responsibility of a caddy as "positive supporter."

Well he should always be in your corner always. "Nice shot! Way to go!" No matter what he does, you got to remember he's always in your corner. He's rooting for you because when you make a lot of money, he makes a lot of money. (Molly)

Even players that rely heavily on their caddies for technical assistance[11] expect the caddy to be, first and foremost, an emotional laborer.

I like them to do all the technical stuff, the yardages and the wind and the pin placement, but to me the caddy is more of a supporter, a cheerleader, encourager. (Helen)

In contrast to most players' views, caddies prefer to think of themselves as having a substantive impact on a player's game. Because players generally want less input about golf and more emotional support, there is an undercurrent of tension between players and caddies. In the following quote, Chuck, a caddy, recounts being alienated from his work because "his player," Elana, was not using his skills as a golf expert. Elana, in turn became upset with Chuck's lack of emotional labor.

> I had an attitude of like: (*showing irritation*) "I'm carrying the bag and that's all." Well, she got pissed off. Like, she says I wasn't cheering and all these little things.
>
> I thought it was patronizing, but I started doing it, you know, "Great shot, Elana! Come on, you can make it!" Just pump her up all the time.
>
> I let her blow steam off on me. Like if she gets mad, she will yell at me and say I did something. I let her do it even though I know it is nothing I did.
>
> I don't know if it is 'cause I'm doing it or what, but she has made a lot money over the last five weeks.

"Pumping her up" and "letting her blow off steam" are forms of emotional labor.

The legitimacy of the emotional support a caddy offers a player is based on trust. Although a caddy's support is built into the relationship by a profit-sharing motive, trust is still won. Caddies are hired and fired on their ability to win and hold the players' trust.

> I hire a caddy on the basis of whether or not I can trust him to be there. . . . My caddy is always on time; he does not drink. I can count on him to show up sober. After two years I can say he is a good friend. I know that he will do anything to encourage me to play my best on the golf course. (Ethel)

A player who loses trust in a caddy, loses emotional support. June fired her long-time caddy because she began to question the sincerity of his support.

> I think that he was with me and pulling for me, but I think basically our sights were in different directions. I mean my number one sight is me and my performance. . . . He just spent a lot of time going out. Which is fine, but it just got to a point,

the way our relationship was, I could not count on him all the time, for him to be in there and ready to go the way I was. (June)

For the most part, the relationship between the player and the caddy is non-reciprocal. The player pays to ensure that the caddy's charity is consistently forthcoming.[12] It is primarily a business transaction. If a relationship between a caddy and a player gets complicated beyond fee for service, the player is likely to fire the caddy. Falling in love with a player or "knowing her too well" can be grounds for dismissal.

CONCLUSION

In summary, the potential for player solidarity based on shared experience and the exchange of feelings is undercut in two ways. First, the structures of the tour no longer rely on personal connections and player management, structures that used to serve to build group solidarity. Second and more importantly, the players share an understanding of the difficulties of tour life and thus view each other as risky investments for emotional energy. Because they lack the necessary trust, players are not likely to rely on fellow golfers for emotional support.

The data presented in this chapter supports the idea that the social terrain influences social relations. Given the uncertain, competitive, individualistic structure of the LPGA, the subworld's lack of community between the players is understandable. But it is nonetheless surprising because, although women tend to do the vast majority of the emotional labor and take responsibility for making interpersonal connections in contemporary society,[13] women professional golfers have not developed relational frameworks that seem unique to women. Rather, the players' relationships resemble those more often associated with men. For example, the women golfers' relations with each other on the tour resemble the bonding relationships men create with each other in the broader society.[14] Women professional golfers rely on family and non-professional golfers for emotional support in much the same way men typically rely on their wives or girlfriends for emotional support.[15] Finally, women golfers' expectations of their caddies mirror male corporate executive management of secretaries.[16] In short, due to the occupational demands and the structure of the tour, women professional golfers need and expect others to do emotion work and emotional labor for them.

This is not to say that women professional athletes have miracu-
lously escaped internalizing the gender lessons of the broader society.
There is evidence to suggest that the interpersonal practices of women
athletes may differ from their male counterparts despite the strong
influence of occupational structures. Women professional athletes may
differ from male professional athletes in two ways. First, women athletes may have less interactions with each other than men. Sportswriter
John Feinstein notes that women professional tennis players also keep to
themselves.[17] He contrasts them to the more outgoing male tennis players. This may be the result of gender socialization which grooms boys to
operate within a competitive environment and to bond through competition.[18] Girls and women are more likely to avoid competition[19] or
where competition is unavoidable, avoid each other.[20]

In addition, women athletes may be more adept and forthright in
asking subordinates to perform emotional labor. In general, women are
better skilled at paying deference to those in power by being attentive to
their emotional needs than men.[21] Although men do not specifically
demand it, they expect women to perform these emotional duties at
home and in the work force.[22] When the gender hierarchy is turned on
its head, as is case with male caddies and female professional golfers,
women may find that their male subordinates fail to live up to their
expectations with regard to emotional labor. However, given their
expertise in the area of emotion work, women may be more adept than
men at stating their expectations in these areas (as was the case with
Elana).

The experience of the women on the tour has implications within
the broader context. The position of emotional caretaker and relationship builder that women so often assume and men relinquish, is neither a
"natural" arrangement nor simply a persisting consequence of a bygone
era. Rather, it must be seen as a consequence of our current social arrangements. By implication, the everyday life of the LPGA professional supports the feminist argument that if the workplace, and thus, domestic
life, are to be transformed, it is not enough for women to simply gain
entry into male domains.[23] Intentional efforts must be made to incorporate
caring networks[24] into the paid labor system and other male domains.

CHAPTER 9

FANS, STATUS, AND THE GIFT OF GOLF

---

*It's quite something to stand behind the eighteenth green to watch
the last group approach. The gallery is thick on both sides of the fairway as they walk the last group home. The eighteenth looks like a
multicolored ribbon with a green stipe down the middle. On the
green stripe are eight dots: three players, their caddies, a marshal,
and a score keeper. As the players come closer, the gallery swal-
lows the fairway behind them. Silently the gallery engulfs me too.
The gallery now surrounds the players, the green, and the 100
yards of fairway behind the players.*

*Spectators have to watch from either side of the fairway.
They have further to go than the players, so they hurry to get into
position to see each shot. And then like a wave, stillness spreads
through the gallery just before the golfers hit.*

*With this final flight of players, the drama has reached its
height. Fans try to get to the green quickly in order to get a good
spot to see the final approach shots. In contrast, the players walk
slowly toward their balls.*

*Tension is high. It's hard to see. People are straining. I hear
complaints.*

*Then the marshals' hands go up. The crowd hushes itself
silent and strains to see where the first approach shot will land.*

—Fieldnotes, Atlantic City, 1989

One aspect of the tour that is quite
striking is the friendly relations the professionals maintain with fans. On
the LPGA tour fan/athlete interactions extend far beyond autograph

149

seeking and signing. Fan avoidance by athletes, which characterizes most other professional sports, is rare. The tour has the feel of a county fair or a neighborhood picnic. Players seem to move in and through this civic event easily.

It is not uncommon for total strangers to approach athletes they admire and engage them in conversation. While there is a limit to the cordialities—for example, fans don't engage players while they are practicing putting—any player walking to or from the clubhouse is generally open to conversation. The professional might not stop to chat, as they generally have a tight schedule, but if a fan is willing to walk with the golfer, fairly complex interactions can take place.

While the average fan does not interact with the golfers, the golfer's day is filled with interactions with fans and supporters. For most veteran golfers, each city on the tour is a homecoming in a way. Relationships with fans built on these once-a-year interactions are re-established and affirmed. In particular, the older athletes talk positively about playing in tournaments where they expect to see loyal friends and supporters whom they first met at a pro-am function or through private housing. Quite frankly, there are times when the area around the clubhouse feels more like a family reunion than a major sporting event. It is primarily these interactions that define the players' relationship with fans.

The structure of the tour necessitates that the athletes deal directly with the fans. Management of most tournaments is dependent on the volunteer labor of locals. Some golfers choose to stay in the homes of these supporters to cut down on expenses. At the tournament site, the athletes and the fans share the same spaces. There are no barriers to protect the athletes from the fans as they walk between green and tee, and between clubhouse and course. The athletes mix with the fans to such an extent that it is often difficult to distinguish the golfers from the fans.

Some might argue that friendly player-fan relations on the LPGA tour are simply a product of the physical environment of the tournament: a golf course lends itself to such interactions. If this were the full explanation, one would expect to find similar relations between fans and athletes on the men's tour. While there is no real difference in the layout of the course for men and women, the women are said to be more approachable, pleasant, and outgoing in comparison to the men. Comments like Cathy's permeate most comparisons between the men's and women's tour:

> I've heard that we are a lot friendlier than the men on the PGA tour. Amateurs enjoy the women more because men feel they should not be bothered with the pro-am. They are not all like that, but a lot of them are. (Cathy)

A common explanation for the differences in the two golf tours is that "the men don't have to be nice." Corporate sponsorship and television dollars pay for the men's tour; the LPGA's dependence on putting on good pro-am's and drawing a decent gate require the players to be friendly and accessible. Although this reasoning is highly plausible, it is a cynical explanation of the women's relationship with their fans. To reduce these interactions to a straight exchange relationship within a cash nexus fails to capture the genuineness of some of these interactions. This is not to say that every player is approachable and every interaction sincere. But clearly there is bonding and empathy between LPGA players and fans that is not replicated in other sports.

A better explanation is that the game of women's professional golf lies, at least in part, outside a system of rational exchange and within a system of reciprocity. Within the world of women's golf, the interaction between fan and athlete stems from a common prowess ethic and blooms into a complex reciprocal relationship.

RECIPROCITY

Studies of social systems based on reciprocity, or gift giving, are most often grounded in Marcel Mauss' classic essay, "The Gift" (1954). By comparing the data collected by various anthropologists, Mauss constructs the bases of "archaic" economies. He contends that, in these "primitive societies," bonds develop around the moral obligations of gift giving. Gifts and obligations are the determinants of status or social place in these societies, and define a social hierarchy. "The spirit of gift exchange," according to Mauss, "is characteristic of societies which . . . have not yet reached the stage of pure individual contract, the money market, sale proper, fixed price and weighed and coined money."[1] For Mauss, gift exchange societies are an intermediate system between tribal society and industrial capitalist society.

Gift giving, however, does not completely evaporate with the rise of free-market economics. Vestiges remain in interactions within contemporary society in such practices as inheritance, housewarming gifts, and philanthropic giving. Indeed, in contemporary society rational exchange and gift exchange seem interlaced. Diane Margolis suggests that status systems based on reciprocity play a critical role in the maintenance of social order within modern societies.[2]

Lewis Hyde's employment of Mauss' concept of reciprocity to explain the position of art in an increasingly capitalistic society is applicable to professional sport.[3] Hyde begins his discussion by arguing that artists are either talented, inspired, or both. In either case, the bases of their art come from beyond themselves. Artists are "gifted."

Hyde takes for granted that works of art exist simultaneously in two "economies," a market economy and a gift economy. Art can survive without the market, but where there is no gift there is no art. This is not to say that the market and gift giving are in conflict, nor are they wholly separate spheres. The gifted musician, for example, although hoping for commercial success, must remain true to the craft and create inspired pieces which will move her audiences.

Following from Hyde's reasoning, it can be argued that although spectator sport is increasingly being commodified, at its core, it must exist within a gift exchange economy in which gifts are given, received, and returned. Reciprocity in sport is predicated on the idea that athletes are "gifted." Athletes' prowess is generally understood as a combination of hard work, talent, and luck. While athletes tend to emphasize the hard work and fans tend to focus on the talent, the debate is one of emphasis only. Talent and inspiration are perceived by both athletes and fans to come from beyond the efforts of the athlete. Athletes, like artists, often feel that they have been given a gift, and thus feel obliged to display their talent through sport. The spectators, in turn, receive the gift of sport. In the same way that art lovers are moved by good art, and feel as if they have received a gift, fans are moved by displays of athletic prowess. With only slight revisions, the following quote from Hyde about art seems equally applicable to sport.

> The [game or match] that matters to us—which moves the heart, or revives the soul or delights the senses, or offers courage for living, however we choose to describe the experience—that [game] is received by us as a gift is received. Even if we have paid a fee at the door of the [stadium], when we are touched by [excellence in sport] something comes to us which has nothing to do with the price.[4]

GIFT AND MARKET ECONOMIES

Despite the integration of the two systems, there remain two primary distinctions between commodity exchange and gift exchange. First, in a commodity exchange system, success is measured by material gains. In systems based in reciprocity, like art, sport, or parenting, success can be measured by the increased well-being of those subject to it.[5] Success of this sort is more likely to be publicly honored than monetarily rewarded (i.e., Halls of Fame, Mother's Day). Second, a gift establishes a feeling-bond between two people, while the sale of a commodity does not neccessarily leave a connection.[6] We feel tied to those who give us gifts in a way that would seem unthinkable had we purchased the same object from them.

Social arrangements governed by the rules of reciprocity, which lie either in part or wholly outside the political and/or market systems, are status orders. The exchange of Christmas gifts within a family generally follows commonly understood rules of reciprocity which articulate family relations and affirms status within the family.[7] Fan/athlete relations can be understood as a status order.

Status orders are governed by rules of reciprocity. We learn these rules much the same way we learn the rules of grammar. And, like grammar, we are more likely to follow the rules than know and articulate them. Nonetheless, breaking the rules of grammar or reciprocity rarely goes unnoticed.[8] Infractions of the rules of reciprocity, felt as insult or offense, disrupt the status order. Infractions often generate a response which involves the loss of social standing for the perpetrator. Punishments include shaming, degradation, loss of reputation, and expulsion.[9]

When athletes fail to display their talents adequately they are often shamed by fans with the taunt, "You're a bum!" When they fail to live up to their moral obligations, they suffer a loss of reputation, as was the case with Pete Rose, barred from the Baseball Hall of Fame for gambling on baseball. In the case of cheating, possibly the most offensive act in which an athlete can engage, they may be expelled from the sport, losing their status as athletes, as was the case for Jane Blalock.[10]

On some level, sport is built upon a system of reciprocity. This is not to say that sport cannot be commodified, but if it is completely transformed into a commodity, then it is no longer sport. The relationship between fans and athletes is similar to that between artists and museum-goers. The expression of excellence in both fields moves the viewer. On the LPGA tour, bonding is brought to the fore because of the unusual amount of contact between fan and athlete and the relatively small crowds, which enable players to recognize the faces of consistent supporters.

This chapter looks at the LPGA athlete-player relations from the perspective of the reciprocity system outlined above. First, it examines how the reciprocity system works in establishing the bond between athlete and fan. This is followed by a discussion of how and where it breaks down, and how gender norms impact these relationships.

THE GIFTED ATHLETE

Like Hyde, my analysis of fan-athlete relations on the tour assumes that on some level the talents of the golfer are a gift. It is not of the player's doing; the talent to play golf well was simply there at birth. Doris captured this sense of talent in our interview.

> I feel very fortunate to have been given a talent and I can wake up everyday and hit a little white ball and make a living doing it.

This is not to say that she did not have to work. Indeed, most golfers work extremely hard to hone their talent. Talent is understood as the intangible core of all accomplishments. The athletes work hard to cultivate talent but cannot claim credit for creating it. Lynn noted this distinction between talent and effort.

> We have talent. A lot of people are golfers and they know they will never be able to do it. They will never, as much as they want to, they never will. As a group, we make it look easy.

Earlier, I defined the prowess ethic as a belief that success comes from a mix of talent and hard work. The giftedness of an athlete is only visible when it has been cultivated by years of practice.

FAN APPRECIATION

Regardless of a player's talent, it does not become a gift until it is received as such by the spectators. The gift of talent can only be received if it is presented in a fashion that is consumable. While in the field, I was repeatedly struck by the average fan's knowledge of the sport and their desire to watch it performed well. While there were a number of gawkers following the most attractive players and a few fans simply following the leaders for dramatic pleasure, the vast majority of the fans had a fairly complex understanding of the game. Without it, watching the sport, I must admit, is rather boring.

The manner in which most fans watch the sport necessitates at least a professed knowledge of the sport. Fans seemed to watch in one of two ways: they either plant themselves in one spot and watch the entire field of golfers perform one particular shot or series of shots, or they follow a particular golfer for some portion of the entire eighteen holes. In between shots, fans discuss the relative merits of a player's club selection, the lie of the ball, distance of a tee shot, a player's read of a putt, and a myriad of other details of the game.

It is really only on the last day that drama and suspense mount to the point of entertainment, and then only if the leaders have been paired together. Otherwise, spectators are resigned to watching numbers change on scoreboards posted around the course which track the running score of the leaders. These leaderboards help maintain drama, but in the absence of a through knowledge of golf, this would hardly be enough to sustain more than a passing interest.

In any discussion of sport spectating, it is essential to keep in mind the multiple levels of enjoyment. As Roone P. Arledge said about televising football, "If they don't give a damn about the game, they still might enjoy the program." It is in this spirit that Lynn made the following comment about fan motivation.

> You have no idea why people are interested. It could be the way you look, or the way you looked at them, or because you just made two birdies in a row, or because they think you have a great butt. Who knows!!

The display and appreciation of athletic prowess is not the primary motivating factor that transforms sports into spectacles for mass consumption. Suspense and drama are the stuff of mass appeal. However, talent and its cultivation are at the core of the relationship between many fans and athletes on the LPGA tour.

While the golfers understood that fans follow the tour for a variety of reasons, throughout the interviews they spoke of their belief that on some level many of the fans appreciated their golfing prowess. The comments of Fran and Doris are illustrative of how players experience fan appreciation.

> They want to come watch golf. They are purists. They don't go through the listing and say, "Yeah, I've heard so and so is . . . and this one, she's . . ."
>   They come to see golf, they say "God, look at this pairing." "Golly, what time are they playing?" "Let's do it" and "this hole is close to that one. Well, I can come from here to here and catch this pairing." (Doris)

> I was on a par three, I forget the number, this man says, "What did you hit?"
>   I said "five iron."

He just shook his head, and said "Wow!" And he goes, "I have to hit a four here. Really well done, really great shot." And he really meant it. I could tell that he just thought that was great. (Fran)

Fans openly acknowledge and appreciate talent and the hard work associated with good golf. This quote from a pro-am participant is typical.

After we had a little awards dinner she was right off to the driving range. It was a tough day, the humidity was up, and the temperature was up, and everybody was pretty tired and she had enough energy and discipline to go and practice. That is what it takes, discipline. These girls have enough to be doctors. These are world-class athletes.

Players reap psychic benefits from the spectators' reception of their prowess. The golfers' view of themselves and their belief in the prowess ethic is affirmed when they are admired by spectators. Applause, for example, is understood as an affirmation of the players' prowess.

This fan appreciation is often deeply felt by the players. Hattie displayed an emotional change when she talked about fan appreciation. This rather outgoing, effervescent player was visibly moved as she recalled the fan reaction to her finest round of golf and her only win.

Chills going all the way down my body, when they clapped for me (*speaking in a very quiet shy voice*). When I sank that putt on eighteen they clapped for me (*her voice fading to a whisper*) (Hattie).

Val's reaction to the fans is similar:

It is not that all the people are watching you, it is just that it is a good feeling to be playing good and having that amount of people really appreciating what you doing out there. That is pretty neat.

Clearly, applause has a dual purpose. It is a sign of appreciation for the gift of an excellent or moving performance and, at the same time, it is a gift given in return. There is a certain thrill in knowing that your gift, your talent, was received and appreciated, as the quotes above illustrate. Spectators understand the charge a performer receives from applause and thus heap collective praises on the performers. Cara expresses this dual function of applause in recounting a day in which she had not played particularly well.

> It is really neat coming up eighteen and having all these people around and cheering. Like yesterday I didn't play very good yesterday, and yet we got a big ovation when we walked up to the eighteenth green, which was fun. That is pretty neat that they come out and appreciate you even though you did not shoot 68 or 69 that day.

People congregating around the final hole at the end of the day applaud all the participants, honoring them and paying tribute even when the golfer has not performed outstandingly. Applause is the way the audience repays the artist, entertainer, and sportsperson in our society.

THE GIFT OF STATUS

In a system of reciprocity, the gift will eventually circle back toward its source.[11] When players are continually successful, they attract attention. As a result, they gain elevated status. Players can return the gift of status by allowing individuals to associate with them.[12]

Athletes give the gift of status in a number of ways. Giving autographs is the most obvious example. Like a photograph or a memento, the autograph is an indication of having spent time with the athlete. Golfers often throw golf balls to fans in the gallery and or hand gloves to children as a way of showing appreciation. Often golfers share their status by giving fans their time and a bit of conversation. Molly expressed her desire to reciprocate this way:

> When someone comes up and says "I loved watching you play today," I want to meet them and tell them, "Thank you for your support and we appreciate you coming out and watching us." It's just a little personal touch, but it means a lot for those people. And it comes from my heart, it's not just a lot of hot air.

The notion that her expressed thanks "comes from the heart" speaks to the level at which her motivation to respond is felt. Complete strangers who follow a player for the day are frequently thanked by the player at the end of the round. These fans are also often introduced to the player's family, friends, other loyal supporters, and caddies.

On one observation of the tour, I experienced this sort of player appreciation directly. I was following a threesome of low-ranking golfers. It was a particularly hot day. I was one of a handful of supporters and the only one not related to any of the three players. One player showed her appreciation of my support by throwing me an ice-cold bottle of water at the thirteenth tee. I was touched that this player would recognize my unbiased support for all three golfers, and take something from "inside the ropes" and share it with me.

High status in a community can be shared or traded to bolster the standing of others. This aspect of status sharing is most evident in the pro-am tournament which precedes all tournaments. Pro-am participants are generally leaders in their community. In exchange for the opportunity to play in the pro-am, community leaders give a cash gift of up to three thousand dollars. Although the money may have been earned within the market economy, it is given as a charitable gift to a golfing tournament. This gift-giving assumes a certain level of reciprocity. Tournament organizers show their gratitude by giving pro-am participants clothing, equipment, and other gifts. But as Ethel points out, it is the gift of status that most participants seek.

> I think anytime you're in a position to be considered the best in the world at something you do, people are in awe of that. As far as these CEOs [pro-am participants], I'm sure that he feels he's the best in the world at what he does. But he's not going to be able to pick up the paper and see himself listed number one at the end of the week. Golf is very finite. There are no ifs, ands, or buts. I think people appreciate that.
>
> I think they are just rubbing elbows with people they know are the best. Some people need that kind of recognition. They are use to rubbing elbows with the best. And they appreciate the work and dedication that goes into [golf]. But I think that primarily people are interested in the fact that you are the best and considered the best at what you do.

It is important to Ethel that she make the distinction between *being* the best and being *recognized* as the best. Talented people garner little social status if what they do is not recognized as being worthy of appreciation. Recognition is the clear demonstration of the golfer's talent, which, by association, bestows status on the pro-am participants and confirms their standing in the community.

LPGA pros regularly schmooze with pro-am participants, talk to fans, and give golf lessons to facilitate this status exchange. Status-sharing cultivates player support. The people with whom the professional played in the pro-am, or talked to in the gallery, or gave a clinic to at their club, tend to become supporters of that player.

Status as a bonding agent between player and fan is such a part of the everyday reality that it is often a basis of golf humor.

> I hit the shot yesterday and pulled it a little on this par 4 (*she points to the 15th hole*), and it just landed on the left side of the green. And the gallery was there (*pointing*). And it just took a big jump to the left and they separated so the ball could jump right through them off into the rough, right. And as I was walking, I said "Jeez, sometimes I wish I was Arnold Palmer, his gallery would have thrown their bodies in front of my golf ball." And they all started cracking up. (Molly)

The moral obligation to give and to receive does not end with excellent golf and the gift of applause or fan loyalty and status-sharing. This is just the beginning of the reciprocity that permeates the golfing world and, in particular, the relationship between the fan and the athlete. In addition to the numerous volunteer hours put into the preparation for the tournament and the hospitality shown every professional golfer, favored players receive gifts from fans. From sunglasses and roses to meals, I observed players receiving gifts with no strings attached other than spending a little time with the fans, sharing their status, and playing excellent golf.

Occasionally, these conversations will develop into something more than a passing of pleasantries. The relationships build from year to year, and meetings eventually take on the characteristics of a yearly reunion. On one occasion, I had the opportunity to accompany Roslynn to a dinner with one such family. The family and the player had met some years before when Roslynn was paired with the employer of the father in a pro-am. Family members had come out to see the boss play in the pro-am. Roslynn was cordial to the pro-am fans, and as a result, they became her loyal supporters throughout the tournament. This family would meet her after each round, praise her, and give her small gifts. In return, the pro spent time with these fans discussing her round.

The next year, the relationship resumed, the fans seeking out the pro, bringing her small gifts and inviting her over to the house for a meal before the tournament. This pattern had been repeated for a couple of years prior to my visit.

The player knew her way to the house by memory, and settled into the living room as if she were at home. In contrast to her casual style, the family treated her with the reverence and honor of a celebrity.

The house was modest and reflected the income of a typical blue-collar worker. The family was made up of a husband and wife and two children—a son and a daughter—and the daughter's child. The meal was labor intensive and due credit was given to the mother and daughter for all the work that went into the meal. Throughout the evening the player was fawned over and catered to. All conversation was directed to the golfer.

Prior to dinner, the player received gifts, two new golfing outfits. Not only did she graciously accept the gifts, but requested one be sent back because of the color and the other because of the size. The next day at the course the player received the outfits in her requested size and color.

The last two days of the tournament she wore the new outfits. The mother was especially pleased, admiring the clothing during and after the rounds. (Fieldnotes, Hershey, 1989)

I quizzed the family and Roslynn about their relationship separately. The fans were attracted to this player because she gave them time, talked to them, and treated them like regular people. It was not that the other players were not nice; it was that Roslynn was special.

When I asked Roslynn how she could accept all these gifts from people who could not afford many luxuries, she said "How could I not take them (*laughing, surprised that I didn't get it*)? They want me to have them." It wasn't until I was off the tour that I understood fully. Not to take the gifts would have insulted the family. By accepting and wearing the outfits, she was reciprocating their gifts. By taking time to share a meal at their home and by sharing in their daily lives, she was affirming her fans.

CELEBRITY STATUS

Fan appreciation can also take the form of fame, or celebrity status. In this media age, as athletes gain status, they gain celebrity status, which is to say, they are known. While there are a few professional women golfers that become household names and celebrities in their own right, most women golfers' celebrity status is derived from their occupation. They gain celebrity status by being known as a professional golfer.

Everybody out there that is playing that week is famous, no matter who you are. It is so weird to walk off and give kids and adults autographs. I wouldn't go anywhere and give anybody autographs, they don't know who I am. Even the fans here don't know who half of the people are, maybe more then half. I think that is one of the things that makes you feel that you are really, really special. (Karen)

Q: What does it mean to be a professional golfer?
I am going to give it to you as honestly as possible. It means recognition, sometimes unwanted. Now, I am proud of what I do, but I marvel at the way people react to what I do. It is like being a movie star. (Gerri)

To have celebrity status is to be known or recognized by a significant percentage of the general public. While such status is usually associated with talent or wealth, it not necessary to have either to achieve it.[13] Celebrity status is created and maintained by staying in the public eye. Therefore, public exposure leads to status and status generates publicity. Frequently, the managers of celebrities will produce events in which celebrities will come together for a contrived media event, which will serve the purpose of keeping their faces before the public. Celebrities can shore up their image and garner publicity by being seen with other celebrities or by being seen in exclusive locations.

Rubbing elbows with the stars or vacationing where the elite vacations improves the status of the non-celebrity. In interactions with friends, people name-drop, relate stories about eating dinner next to a famous person, and recall dancing at hot spots in New York. We have our picture taken with national politicians and frame and hang them over our desks. All of these practices are intended to give us credibility in the eyes of others. The most illuminating practice of this sort is people having their picture taken with life-size cardboard cut-out photos of famous people. This trickery is commonplace in our nation's capital, where, for a fee, a tourist can have a picture taken with cardboard cut-outs of the president and the first lady on almost every street corner. Upon returning home the traveler can impress friends and relatives, if only for a moment, with the photo and a plausible story.

Celebrities, by virtue of their being celebrities, can give status. By simply allowing individuals to associate with them, they give that person higher credibility among their peers.[14] As this amateur points out, contact with LPGA stars can enhance an amateur's respectability within golfing circles and, in turn, the fan feels a sense of loyalty to the athlete.

Let's face it though, it is an ego trip for certain people. Let's say I played with Kathy Whitworth or Amy Alcott, the name means something to a fellow golfer. I see that Sherri Turner, who I played with last year, won the LPGA, that's great. I just love to see it. You develop sort of like a "That's my gal" attitude, "That's the one I played with, and she is doing well this year." (Amateur, pro-am participant)

BENEFACTORS

Margolis notes that in occupations where the primary concern is creating humans (teachers, mothers) or human excellence (artists or athletes), compensation is rarely more than subsistence.[15] Golf is no exception. In their first few years on tour, most women golfers are doing well if they break even. Most young professionals cannot afford to go on tour. It is estimated that the tour costs players $40,000 a year. It is not unusual for a golfer to be tens of thousands of dollars in debt.

Within the social world of professional golf, there are men and women of means who act as benefactors to young players. These sponsors are to golf what a patron is to the arts: these private sponsors put up money, in advance, to support a golfer at her craft.

Private sponsorship needs to be distinguished from corporate sponsorship or speculative investments in a player. Corporate sponsorship is a business deal, in which formal obligations are spelled out in contracts in advance. In exchange for financial gain, a player displays product logos, plays in corporate golf outings, and/or agrees to use a golf manufacturer's equipment. Similarly, some investors enter into an agreement with a player in which the player trades potential prize money for up-front expenses. In these two cases, the sponsorship is a rational business deal. In contrast, private sponsorship is a gift.

There are basically two types of private sponsorship arrangements. For some players, the sponsor agrees to cover the player's expenses. In some of these cases, the support takes the form of an up-front gift, but it is more likely to be some sort of arrangement that includes the use of a lease car and an expense account. The player's winnings are often used to reimburse the sponsors for the original gift. Any winnings above and beyond the sponsor's investment are retained by the golfer. The other type of sponsorship arrangment is a cross between a gift and a business deal, in which the winnings beyond the cost of participating are shared between the player and the sponsor. This type of sponsorship does not necessarily fall within the system of reciprocity, but most arrangements of this sort assume elements of reciprocity. In either case, the motivation for giving usually arises out of a desire to give back to a sport which has given the sponsors a great deal of pleasure. These two types of sponsorship are illustrated in the cases below.

Beth's arrangement with her sponsors is an example of a successful reciprocal agreement. Sponsors put up her expense money, which she pays back, and she retains all her profits. She is comfortable with the relationship, in part because she is playing quite well. She knows that her sponsors don't lose money and that they enjoy their affiliation with her. The gift they have given her is security. The sponsor's backing acts as a safety net, in case of a slump. She does not have to worry about finances.

> I have a great sponsor. It's three guys. They give me all my expenses throughout the year. And if I make the expenses back, whatever I make up to my expenses, I give it back to them. Over and beyond my expenses, it's mine. They buy me a car and they pay for my auto insurance.
>
> Financially its all a write-off for them. I ran into some guys that really like golf. They knew I needed the help to come out on the tour and they just wanted to see me play well and not have to worry about money and that's all they wanted . . . to make me happy. I guess they're satisfied with saying "Hey, I sponsor her."

> *Q: Do you do anything else for them, do you hang a sign on your car or hand out their business cards?*
> No, I don't do anything. When I'm in Texas I play golf with them—which is no big deal—they're my friends too. I'll go out [to Texas] during the wintertime. I play with one of my sponsors a lot, he's a really good golfer. And the others I play with a few times a year. But I don't have to do anything, I don't have to . . . they're in the clothing manufacturing business. I don't even have to wear the clothes or wear the name on my visor or anything like that. I don't have to play golf with them, I just do it because I like them.

> *Q: Yeah, sounds like a great arrangement. Do they have your picture on their wall or . . . ?*
> No. They don't do anything like that. One of my sponsors, there's three guys, one of them is 73. He calls the press room about ten times a day [an obvious exaggeration], he keeps

track of me every week. And the other two guys, they're in business with this older man, they care about me and they want to see me do well. They want me to shoot the best that I can, but if I'm not playing well they don't care. (Beth)

Unlike Beth's relationship with her benefactors, Sara's relationship with her sponsors is a blend of reciprocity and capitalist speculation. Her arrangement is with the members of a country club. Given her circumstances—she is a non-exempt rookie, and the number of partners involved—profit is clearly not the primary motivating factor for them. But the chance that sponsors might make a profit introduces the notion of risk and thus limits the pressure (or obligation) for Sara. In this arrangement, the golfer who is unable to reciprocate can always dismiss the sponsors as investors.

I met a golf pro from an Atlanta country club who said if you need help to let him know. He knew I was turning pro and said let me know if you need help.

He said I know there some people around here that would like to help a pro in some way.

For the first year, it was in a contract that made it mandatory for both me and them to keep the contract. Next year if they want to back out, they can do it. And the third year I have the right too, like if I'm making a reasonable living I can terminate the contract. I think, we have met quite a few times and from what they told me, they are prepared to go three years.

[We split the prize money] seventy/thirty, after I pay them back I get seventy [% of the winnings]. I have it really good. [Most arrangements are 50/50 or 60/40.]

I don't have to do anything really. I go up there, I spend quite a bit of time up there and I have the name of the club on the bag and play with them. I help out; there is going to be a junior clinic next week, and I am going to be there and help. And I also send a newsletter. I write one letter and send it to them, and then I take photos and I got the pro to put up a bulletin board. So it helps them get a little more involved. It is difficult when you are out here. You are not home for weeks on end, so you want to get a little personal.

Q: What are they getting out of it? Is it an ego trip?

Well, I think they just want to help me. I went to a Christmas dinner and I spoke to them about qualifying school.

There were quite a few people, probably one hundred—hundred fifty people. I spoke to them about qualifying school, and I spoke about the St. Petersburg tournament, and how I felt about hitting balls next to Lopez and King and teeing it up. I think that got a lot of people interested. A lot of people just want to help. (Sara)

Despite the obvious commodification of status and the speculative investment by members of the country club, a level of reciprocity remains between the country club members and Sara. She shares her stories and goes to the trouble of putting together a newsletter of her progress in response to their gift. This integration is not always smooth.

BREAKDOWNS IN THE RECIPROCITY SYSTEM

Mixing the values and expectations of reciprocity systems within the dominant market system is not without difficulties. Confusion abounds and expectations are shattered when players and fans fail to live up to their obligations or feel that they have been let down by others. The data suggests that breakdowns in the system can occur for a variety of reasons. I will discuss only four: conflict in perception of excellence, false intimacy, inability to respond to a gift, and the confusion of market and gift relations.

Conflict in Perception of Excellence

As stated earlier, at the core of the relations between fans and athletes is the respect and appreciation of the professionals' prowess. Failures in the relations between the two groups often center on the fans' appreciation of the game. Although golf fans have a general knowledge of the sport, the majority of golf fans lack an understanding of the professional game. For the most part, players view the fans' lack of knowledge about the game with mild amusement.

I found that the fans, one of the things they like the most, clap the hardest for is when you back a ball up on the green. When you put spin on it they love it, they go nuts. The ball can back up off the green and they will go nuts. They don't care. They just like to see it spin because they can't do that.

They really appreciate good bunker play. Because most amateurs cannot play out of bunkers. So if you get the ball any-

where near the pin out of a bunker the people are going to clap.
Even though you might not think it is a good bunker shot, they
are going to clap. (Ann)

At other times, players express hostility toward the fans for their
lack of knowledge about the sport, and thus their inability to truly
appreciate the golfers' talents. The high-spirited June captures this hostility toward the fan that lacks golfing knowledge when she discussed
her reaction to fans questioning a poor performance.

> [I]t just drives me crazy when a fans says (*deepens voice*) "What
> happened out there?"
> "Oh, shut up buddy, never in your whole life have you
> done anything like this." They think it is so easy, they have no
> idea. But what do you say to that guy? "Sorry buddy, . . . " I just
> make a joke of it or I don't say anything. I don't say anything
> anymore. I mean I don't give a shit what they say.
> I mean in one respect they are your fans, and they are
> pulling for ya, but I am not playing to please this asshole in
> this town and that asshole in that town. You would go crazy.
> (June)

False Intimacy

Ann expresses similar hostility toward fans in a discussion of autographs. The asking and receiving of autographs is a form of reciprocity.
By asking for an autograph, the seeker pays tribute to the athlete. The
athlete repays the fan with an autograph, material evidence that the
fan was in the presence of the athlete.

> I was never that much of one for collecting autographs, I never
> got into that kind of stuff. So it is hard for me to understand
> why people want my autograph.
> [But] part of autograph hunting is just that you are that
> close to that person. That has got to be part of it. *It is a desire to
> get a part of that person.*
> Now if someone writes me and says I am an autograph
> collector and here is a special card, I know they are sincere. A
> lot of times when kids come up, with these little pieces of paper
> all mashed up. "Would you give me your autograph?" or
> "Would you sign my shirt?" Something like this, that is going
> to get thrown away in two weeks or something. (Italics added.)

Ann wants her autograph to be valued because it is a symbol of intimacy.

The presence of spectators does not necessarily guarantee the appreciation of the golfer's prowess. The desire to talk to or be seen with a golfer often has less to do with their appreciation of talent than it does with the desire to gain status. As a result, players approach relations with fans in a guarded fashion. Players often adopt a posture that communicates unapproachability as they walk to and from the course. They pull their visor low on their forehead and keep their eyes and head lowered to avoid eye contact. Cara explained the players actions this way.

> I think it is a fear of having people talk to you and get you into a conversation that you don't want to be in. I know with some of the players people come up to them and say, "I played golf with you in 1962, and we did this and this and don't you remember me." Those kinds of conversations are the ones players like to avoid.

What players are attempting to avoid are inappropriate demands on their sense of self, or false intimacy. Fans seeking interaction with players for the sake of interaction take without giving, forcing a personal exchange without a corresponding commitment to the golfer.

Inability to Respond to a Gift

Difficulties for the players can also arise when fans give too much and players have no way of reciprocating. If the receiver of a gift has no way to respond in a fashion commensurate with their perceived status, they will feel uncomfortable or burdened. In the following case, Lynn finds herself in situations with sponsors in which she feels uncomfortable by her inability to respond in a proper fashion.

> They gave me some money and a vehicle, and every 10,000 miles I'd get a new car. But it was something I didn't want to continue, 'cause I just didn't want to take money. There wasn't anything I had to do in return.
>
> *Q: You didn't have to do anything in return?*
> Well, I was going to pay them back but they never took the money back.
> It was three guys, who just liked to play golf with me when I came home for the summer.

I'm still really good friends with them. But it got to the point where I really didn't feel like taking their money anymore.

Q: How many years did you do that?
Three years. Once I got off the mini tour and I found myself self-sufficient, I didn't really want it. (Lynn)

Being of average talent and minimal status, Lynn is limited in her means to reciprocate. She felt that she was "just taking money." Lynn is not uncomfortable with the level of her sponsors' generosity, but rather her means to repay them. The arrangements were such that Lynn could not pay the sponsors back in any way. Getting a gift without the means to reply properly can be unsettling. In the end, she was burdened by a sense of unmet obligation, and terminated the arrangement.

Confusion of Market and Gift Economies

Like art, the commodification of sport seems relentless. Many athletes and fans view their relationship as a business contract. Fans complain that they pay good money for tickets and therefore expect to be entertained. Even the last vestiges of reciprocity between fans and athletes— the autograph and the public appearance at children's camps—have been commodified. But the commodification of sport is never complete. At the very core of sports rests a system based on reciprocity. Thus gift and market economies exist simultaneously.

Misunderstandings, however, can result from a confusion over the incongruous demands of commodity exchange and gift exchange. In the following case, Dorothy is sponsored by friends. Friendship is a status order maintained by the rules of reciprocity. In this case, the business of golf confuses their friendship.

I had some people at my club at home sponsor me for two years, I had a contract for two years and my third year was negotiable. At the beginning of the second year they said, "Well, we'll sponsor you for another year."

It was awful. I was struggling, I wasn't making any money and every time I'd go home I'd hear, "When you going to start making some money for us?"

I had played in about eight tournaments and had made about $300 and they said that the money's all run out so that's it. . . . It worked out well actually, because after I lost my sponsors I started playing a little better, so I made some money last year. (Dorothy)

The emotional ties to the sponsors combined with the pressure to make money for them was stressful. Despite not having security of a sponsor, Dorothy feels relieved of the burden of playing for others whom she might disappoint. Fending for herself, she is able to play better.

Similarly, there are tensions around interactions between players and pro-am participants. Most players understand that the pro-am is a way of showing appreciation for the participant's donation. A significant number of women, however, approach the event as another practice round or worse, an exchange of time for money: the player's time for the pro-am participant's money.

Despite an understanding that the pro-am is a thinly veiled opportunity to buy status, most pro-am participants simultaneously view their payment to the tournament as a gift. With that gift, they assume players will follow certain unwritten rules and carry certain expectations into the tournament.

> [Pros] ought to be congenial, pleasant, happy, and talk to the amateurs. I mean that is why we are there. There are a number of pros out here that I've played with where they go out and shake hands with the people and that is the last time they talk to you. Very non-communicative, they are off in sort of a shell playing golf. . . .
>
> The whole bottom line, I think some of the pros who participate on the tour should get their act together and realize that if it wasn't for events like this [pro-am] there wouldn't be an LPGA or a tournament like this. (Pro-am participant, Hershey, 1989)

The hostility of this pro-am participant arises from the players' failure to follow through with this ritual of status boosting by acting grateful. Gratitude is a way of paying deference[16] to the sponsors and thus affirming their social position by treating them as gift givers. To openly treat the pro-am participants as mere customers or the pro-am event as another practice round destroys the illusion of intimacy and reframes the event as crass status buying.

GENDER AND RECIPROCITY IN SPORT

It is refreshing to see professional athletes readily interact with fans outside of a fee-for-service relationship. Even the hostilities between the players and the fans are an outgrowth of this reciprocal bonding. It is also refreshing that the bonds arise out of appreciation of women athletes' skills. I am not the first to make these observations.

In May of 1989, for example, Thomas Boswell, a prominent sportswriter, captured similar sentiments in a column in which he compared LPGA and PGA events. He writes that the LPGA "puts on a better show" than the PGA, yet draws only a third of the fans and plays for about a fourth of the monies. He berates fans and writers for their homophobia and asks his readers to honestly compare the play of individuals on both tours. He notes that Laura Davies outhits Tom Kite off the tee and that Patty Sheehan and Beth Daniel have superior swings to those of PGA pros, Calcavecchia and Wadkins. But he also writes,

> When it comes to personality and rapport with the galleries—a greater selling point in golf than in other sports—the spunky candid women leave America's painfully bland men in arrears.

The women, Boswell implies, pay more attention to the fans than do their male counterparts. Boswell is referring to more than just the reciprocal relationships detailed above. The LPGA players actually think about the needs of the fans.

In her discussion of pro-am partners, Holly made a similar and rather revealing comment:

> Once they get over the fact that we might outhit them, we are females entertaining males in the game of golf. I feel I have a good pro-am when they start to enjoy each other. I feel that's what my job is. It's kind of a female-type job, isn't it, traditionally female anyway. Being a good host of a pro-am is sort of a women thing to do.

Clearly, Holly understands herself to be an emotional laborer. Despite her superior performance, she remains something of a cheerleader for men whose masculinity is tied to their athletic performance.

Taking care of others, Holly reminds us, is not a new role for women to play: mother, wife, social worker, nurse, teacher. In all these positions, the primary concern is with the emotional state of the client, taking care of others' needs. Women and minorities are more likely to occupy a position within status orders in which they take care of others and in an increasingly market-oriented society, women occupy positions in which clients pay them for emotional services.[17] The LPGA is part of this trend.

Regardless of Boswell's and others' insightful comments about the quality of play on the LPGA, golf remains a male province. By and large, it is men who fund the tour and coach the players. It is men who are journalists and commentators and who publicaly pass judgment on the women as athletes. And it is primarily men who cheer for women golfers from the galleries. It is, after all, their sport. Women are still guests in the world of golf; outsiders within. As much as the interchanges between athletes and fans are grounded in mutual respect, we must also recognize that gender plays a role in framing these interactions. In the end, we should not be surprised that men expect women athletes to pay deference to them for their generosity and benevolence. Nor should we be surprised that women athletes do.

PART III

THE IDEOLOGICAL STRUGGLE OVER WOMEN'S GOLF

CHAPTER 10

THE CORPORATE IMAGE

An understanding of the media and the publicity process, and how to use it effectively is essential to the success you have in your business lives and to the current and future success of the LPGA. Without constant cultivation of the media by our staff and LPGA Tour members, interest in our game would gradually fade. The result would be great losses in corporate sponsorship and prize money.

—LPGA Media Primer for New Tour Qualifiers, 1988

Since the Volpe era, the LPGA has increasingly marketed itself to corporate sponsors. The tour events, once a promoter of civic pride for the benefit of local charities, are increasingly organized according to the interests of corporations and corporate leadership. In 1978, corporate funding reached 40% of total donated dollars, up from 10% a decade earlier.[1] By 1988 corporate sponsorship, as a percentage of revenue, dropped back to pre-Volpe levels. The PGA, in contrast, is funded completely by corporate dollars.[2]

The change in focus to the corporatation has meant a change in the management of events from local golf enthusiasts to national business leaders. Since the mid-seventies, the guardians of the LPGA (the commissioner, the board members, and the tournament sponsors) have been recruited from the corporate elite. Most hold or have held positions on the boards of foundations, on corporate boards, as CEO's of corporations, or presidents of banks or large businesses. In a phrase, they are members of the power elite.

The power and extent of this network of corporate insiders, the current guardians of the sport, is revealed in a 1985 joint memo from LPGA commissioner Laupheimer and PGA commissioner Deane Beman.[3] The memo, concerning the 1986 Reagan tax reform bill, was sent to Tournament Representatives and was intended as a primer for face-to-face visits to federal legislators. The Reagan bill threatened to eliminate the business deduction for expenditures in connection with sporting events. The logic employed by the golf lobbyists was that these tournaments are primarily volunteer-run events whose profits are given to charity. The final 1986 tax reform package reduced the tax benefits for all other professional sports. But, as a result of a successful lobbying effort, the bill contained a special exclusion for golf tournaments which enables professional golf to retain its tax-exempt status. The success of the effort speaks to the sphere in which the guardians of professional golf operate and the power they possess.

There are remnants of the old community-sponsored tour. Tournaments like the Corning Classic, the Jamie Farr tournament in Toledo, and other small-city tournaments still have a hometown feel. Farr's tournament, for example, still includes an evening with the stars (TV "personalities") at a banquet for contributors and volunteers—a throwback to the Bing Crosby "Clam Bakes." Small-city tournaments that have survived have developed a sponsor group that is loyal and community support that has a momentum of its own.

It takes as many as 750 volunteers to put on a small-city tournament and about 1.5 million donated dollars. Volunteers carry a certain status in the community. Some schedule their vacations to coincide with the tournament. While most of these communities rely on a major sponsor to put up prize money (Xerox and Kodak perform this function for the, Rochester, New York tournament; Corning Glass for the Corning Classic), the vast majority of the money needed to put on a tournament is donated by local businesses. Fan support at "home-grown" tournaments tends to be strong—many outdraw the big-city, corporate tournaments.

Small-city tournament charities are local, supporting youth programs or local hospitals. Many of these tournaments use community and civic pride to promote and finance the event. In Corning, where profits go to area hospitals, hospital staff sell tickets and pro-am slots. In Rochester, where profits support a local children's camp, area Rotary Clubs compete for the honor of selling the most tickets and supplying the most volunteers. This type of LPGA event has a feeling of community celebration.

The newer, corporate tournaments feel very different. In the words of sociologist George Ritzer, tournaments have become rationalized—that is predictable, efficient, and controlled. Tournament staff is more likely to be paid and the tournament uses far fewer volunteers. Parking-lot attendants, press-room monitors, and security personnel, who volunteer at Corning, are employees in Boston. In interviews, LPGA staff members expressed a preference for paid workers over volunteers because it gave them more control, and improved the efficiency of the tournament organization.

On the negative side, the community seems less connected with the newer corporate tournament. The community has little or no personal connection with the charity or with the promotion or operation of the event. The crowds are smaller, and more likely to be made up of those who received tickets from their corporate employers, and less likely to have a direct or indirect connection with the LPGA or the organization of the tournament. Much of the fundraising for these tournaments takes place within the cloistered corporate world, as the primary sponsor drums up support from customers and suppliers. The charity is usually a noncontroversial national organization with only indirect ties to the community (i.e., March of Dimes, Special Olympics).

One obvious distinction between the older community-centered events and the newer corporate events is the stature of the pro-am players. In the small-city events, the pro-am is populated with entrepreneurs, mid-level sales executives, and presidents of small local companies. In the corporate-sponsored events presidents and CEOs of corporations from all over the country participate in the pro-am.

At a McDonald's tournament, for example, I engaged a pro-am participant in conversation. He was standing by the eighteenth green, having finished his round. He was beaming with delight. "A first-class operation", he told me. He was from the Midwest and was a president of a company which supplies products to McDonald's franchises. He indicated that his donation was part of the cost of doing business with McDonald's. "I was basically told I would contribute." He had been unenthusiastic about the event because of the two-day commitment, but was sincerely pleased he had come. It wasn't just the pro-am, he told me, but the dinners, parties, and the people involved. At these "corporate" tournaments, the feeling of celebration remains, but the "social world" which is being celebrated changes. Rather than a business commmunity connected by region, it is a community of corporate managers related by position, products, or a shared production process.

THE TOURNAMENT AS CELEBRATION OF CORPORATE LIFE

The presentation of golf at a tournament reflects corporate life. There are no signs of poverty, war, or race issues. Indeed, on the tour, the world seems to have few problems except illness (medical-related charities are preferred to those that might support social change) and inclement weather (one apparently wealthy fan actually discussed with me the difficulty he had in finding sunny weather in New England one weekend, and how he had traveled 200 miles to play golf in the sun). These tournaments celebrate a particular lifestyle.

Even the fans are a homogeneous group. Despite the variety of brightly colored golf clothing, fans look shockingly similar. At tournaments, there is a noticeable lack of diversity. In other sports, the stands hold diverse groups, although they may be segregated by section due to a variety of ticket prices. No one in the gallery comes close to resembling a "bleacher bum," or a drunken, rowdy football fan. Even the expressive behavior from fans that is common at other sporting events is absent from the LPGA tour. Fans do not take off their shirts (considered inappropriate on a golf course) or paint their faces. It is as one LPGA official explained: one of the only sporting events to which you can bring your children and not worry about being offended by other fans.

Players and tour officials are quick to point out that despite the unrealistic and self-serving atmosphere of tournaments, they are ultimately events which help the needy. Charitable monies raised through LPGA events are promoted by organizers at each tournament. In 1993, the LPGA helped raise 6.8 million dollars for various charities.

Hidden, however, is the fact that tournament sponsors contribute at least $1.5 million to put on each tournament—far more than actually goes to charity. Most tournaments give less than $25,000 to charity, a return of less than two cents on the dollar. There are notable exceptions; the McDonald's tournament raises 2 to 3 million dollars annually for it's charity (The Ronald McDonald House). Nonetheless, in total, LPGA events donate less than 10% of what they raise each year.[4]

If we view an LPGA event as a celebration of corporate community, an LPGA tournament is a typical charity. Most philanthropic giving (70% in 1991) is to the religious, social or educational, or adult recreational organizations to which the donors belong.[5] The corporate elite, guardians of upper-class culture, are in effect giving themselves a gift— a corporate outing for management and their families. From this perspective, the tournament's charity is not much more than an excuse—a cover—to put on a tax-free celebration for themselves.

At the same time, event organizers increasingly present tournaments as sales and marketing opportunities to potential sponsors. The packaging of sponsorships is specifically designed to sell exposure. Corporations donate funds in exchange for ads in programs, on pairing sheets, on signs at each tee or green, on the uniforms of the officials. Indeed, almost any flat surface or printable space is for sale at a tournament. Golf attracts an audience with expendable income and, increasingly, marketers find it advantageous to associate their products with the sport so many of their prespective customers play or watch.

The golf tournament offers the perfect background for a live commercial. The players are well-groomed, polite, and professional. They work hard to ensure that pro-am partners have a good time, that sponsors are not offended, and that sufficient deference is paid to organizers. Absent from the tour are players identifiable with marginalized groups or social issues: the poor, people of color, gays and lesbians, or any other groups that might detract from the products being sold or the lifestyle being celebrated.

In contrast to the players' prowess ethic, a view which assumes worth is continually achieved, the life blood of the tournament is its ability to affirm and celebrate class, gender, and political hierarchies. For the tour to continue, it must sell itself as a viable advertising vehicle to corporations and as an entertainment value to fans with disposable income. Put slightly differently, the unstated product the LPGA sells is the affirmation of those who have gained the most in the current system. The majority of those in this group have enjoyed numerous economic advantages, yet believe they have earned their position in the world by overcoming obstacles.

Indeed, the corporate tournament celebrates class stratification. Through status boosting, the pro-am tournament, and parties, it affirms the social position of the sponsors. Similarly, preferred parking, seating around the eighteenth green, and special parties and tents feed the notion that the sponsor is deserving of special treatment. The vast differential in earnings between the top players and the rest of the field mirrors the growing disparity between corporate executives and workers. In addition, the charitable contributions associated with the event further supports current class stratification, as philanthropy confirms for the upper classes their right to wealth and the logic of class hierarchy.[6]

THE CORPORATE DEFINITION OF GENDER

When the tour is sold as a marketing tool, image becomes increasingly important element for maintaining the tour's viability. The market encourages the presentation of the female athlete in a fashion that supports conventional notions of gender behavior and appeals to a primarily male market. The membership of the LPGA is aware, on some level, of the discomfort women athletes seem to inspire in the public at large. To lessen this discomfort, the players actively engage in actions which uphold conventional gender norms. Within the professional women's golf community, considerable energy is directed toward maintaining the dominant social order in spite of the inherently subversive quality of professional women's golf. The LPGA staff and media services relentlessly promote the image of femininity, motherhood, and heterosexuality in an attempt to counter the "image problem." While in the field, I noted that the normally unbiased LPGA media staff tends to privately cheer for the players upholding a "feminine image" and/or who have a history of positive press relations.

Not surprisingly, players exhibiting a traditional femininity and heterosexuality are often the centerpiece of LPGA promotions, television coverage, and print media. In turn, comments by television commentators that sexualize women athletes or trivialize their accomplishments are common.[7] In the print media, articles often focus on players who choose a traditional parenting role and femininity.[8] While collecting data for this study, *Fairway Magazine*, an annual publication dedicated to the promotion of the LPGA, contained a photo spread of LPGA members posing in bathing suits.

Most LPGA members engage in activities that appeal to the ideological dispositions of their mostly male benefactors. Most players support the measures taken to promote a "feminine image" to the media. When asked about the photo spread, for example, Tara expressed a pragmatic need to use sexuality and femininity to sell the tour.

> It is just the way things are today. That is what they are selling. That is not all they are selling on this tour. They are also selling golf—the girls can hit the ball. Not all of us have the looks, but we all have great golf swings. Some of us have both and they do with that what they can. It is the public that buys it. If the public didn't buy it we couldn't sell it. So I suppose it is supply and demand.
>
> I can't say that I feel that it tarnishes the tour. I would hope that we would be appreciated for our skill rather than our good looks and the cheesecake role that goes with it. I think it is a viable tool to use to promote the tour. I would have trouble with it if it were the only tool that we were using. (Tara)

Because the tour is so tied to corporate marketing, the players actively work not to offend anybody. Players police themselves as does the LPGA media staff. Players who make seemingly benign but critical comments about the condition of the course, or the management of a tournament, are often reprimanded by fellow players.

In particular, the players are discouraged from associating with anything controversial or political. Overt political acts, such as taking a public stance on the abortion debate, can be damaging to a player's career.

> I was going to put on a [private] pro-am for Planned Parenthood. My major corporate sponsor didn't want to touch it with a ten-foot pole. I got the impression from the managing director that if I went real public on this issue that I was looking at not being renewed next year. At the time I thought I will find another sponsor. A month went by and I did not play well, and then another month went by and I really played crappy and I thought the last thing I need is to start all over. (Denise)

In the end, Denise, felt the risk to her career was too great, and decided against organizing a private pro-am for Planned Parenthood.

The players may privately accept lifestyles and political beliefs that are in conflict with those widely held in the broader society. But the demands of the tour and the pressure to be non-controversial is stronger than the players' willingness to spend emotional energy on political action or risk financial loss. Because the social world of the corporate elite remains essentially a heterosexual male domain, lesbian-identified players might feel the pressure to conform most acutely. Denise's comments are illustrative:

> If sexuality could become a non-issue it would be wonderful. I don't know how to do that. I am sick and fucking tired of being in the closet out here.
>
> One of the things I'd like to do before I retire is come out in a public way—really come out. But if I came out, nine out of ten players would say "Hey that's going to hurt me if you do that." No, probably ten out of ten would say that it would hurt women's golf. It would hurt our image. (Denise)

There is something of an ironic twist to the pressure women feel to remain non-controversial. The members of the recreational male golfing community often define the women professional golfers as "dykes" or "holy rollers." In either case, the display of prowess by the women professional golfers is dismissed as deviant, an attribute of odd women. The irony is that when men define women athletes as lesbians, it diminishes the golfer's threat to masculinity; but if a women defines herself and claims a lesbian identity, she is percieved as a threat to heterosexual masculinity. Proving once again that the power of a stigma resides not so much in the name but in the naming.[9]

COPORATE IMAGE, RECIPROCITY AND DIVERSITY

In some ways, it is the LPGA's success with corporations which may subvert one of the most attractive features of the tour, the reciprocal relationship between fans and athletes. As corporations find it in their interest to promote the tour, and by association their products, players increasingly see the value of the LPGA and themselves as their ability to sell products.

As the tour becomes a media event for corporate advertisers to exploit, the connection between fan support and player worth will become increasingly tenuous. The loss of openly pleasant relations between players and fans would be tragic on one level. But the financial survival of the tour may soon depend on the ability of the LPGA and the players to play to the camera to sell products.

Status, in this context, does not entail a moral obligation to reciprocate to the public but is merely a resource to be marketed and sold. This sort of status is not acquired so much through talent as by one's ability to remain in the public eye, and or to establish a recognizable name, face, or voice—in other words, celebrity status. In this context, to borrow a phrase, image is everything.

Although corporate funding represents less than half of the LPGA's support, the impact on players' lives is evident, particularly among the younger players. Pam, a rookie, approached her entry to the tour in this fashion.

> I also solicited myself (*laughs*)—that's how I put it—to a couple businesses in Cherry Blossom City as soon as I turned pro. I did up a brochure—a pamphlet—of myself and I just sold myself to a couple businesses. The logo for the golf club I represent, Austin Creek, is on my bag. I also sold myself to Mr. Blackstone and put his logo on my golf bag and I went to the development company of Cherry Blossom City. I had those two endorsements. (Pam)

Pam's comment may be a sign of things to come. If the LPGA continues to develop in accord with its current path, relations on the tour will increasingly fall outside the gift exchange. In this context, young players needing financial support to cover the cost of playing on tour will increasingly turn to corporations. They will sell themselves as a vehicle to promote products. Those garnering corporate support will be obligated to reflect the sentiments of the corporation. As image becomes increasingly important, players are less likely to find support for their distinctiveness. This corporate financing of professional golf may discourage diversity and lead the tour down the path to homogeneity.[10]

CONCLUSION

The homespun local chamber of commerce events of the fifties, sixties, and seventies are almost history. Today's tour competes for corporate money, and sells itself as a marketing opportunity. There is pressure on the tour players to affirm the status quo and to avoid political action. It would seem the professional women's tour poses little threat to the ideologies that support the dominant gender order and class structure. The players allow their public image to be shaped by the market. The image of the tour is quite easily molded into a "corporate outing" for corporate management and their families and into a promotion for corporate products. But the image of women playing golf is not merely an image that sells consumer goods. For many women, LPGA golfers have become a symbol of a broader struggle for equal rights. It is this image of women's golf that I turn to in the next two chapters.

CHAPTER 11

PROWESS AND TRANSFORMATION

Sports philosopher William Morgan has been critical of works that reduce the meaning of sport to the dominant ideological struggles of a society. He has urged social theorists to discover the liberating potentialities within the formal autonomy of sport.[1] At the same time that symbolic meanings attached to sport radiate outward from it, the meaning of sport radiates inward on to its participants.

We come to know the world through the body. The human body, in particular, body movement, is no more or less important than thought, or sight, or touch. Body movement, like the mind, is a resource to understanding. Body knowledge is crucial for success in athletics. Coaches are forever telling athletes that "the body is smart," "don't think too much," "let yourself go," and "let it happen." In sports we privilege the body over the other senses. *Indeed, t*o be unconscious is the ultimate complement in some sports.

Each sport, with its particular rules, regulates the movement of the athlete. It is here, at this intersection between body and sport, that we can catch a glimpse of the liberating potential of sport. The interaction between the body and sport provides the athlete with ways of thinking about "self" in the world.[2] Recall the face of a child on a tricycle careening around a corner on two wheels. It is an expression of both fear and enlightenment—fear of an impending disaster, understanding of centrifugal force. If we restrict movement, we restrict our ability to know the world.

Controlling movement is an integral part of institutions whose principle task is to promote an ideology. Religions, cults, social protests, and military organizations all incorporate body movements to enforce or communicate belief systems or worldviews.

185

Sport, if it does nothing else, promotes and regulates movement. Denial of access to sport is nothing less than a denial of a resource. Restricting access to movement is not unlike restricted access to high-tech information, or restricted access to credit or capital. It hinders that group's ability to understand the world.

With the exception of James' autobiographical work[3] and a few works by feminist scholars,[4] little attention has been paid to the ideological production which arises from within sport. This intersection between movement and sport is a point of departure for understanding the professional golfer.

SPORT, IDENTITY, AND EMPOWERMENT

The primary struggle within the subworld of the LPGA is to play competitive golf. Golf is a solitary game in which the golfer constantly struggles against herself and the elements. It is consuming of both space and time. It requires a cool, balanced disposition, and hours and hours of tedious practice. The mastery of the game is an isolated, endless Sisyphian task—a challenge most professionals find attractive and empowering (see chapter 5).

The everyday life of professional golfers is so singularly focused on golf and insulated by the structure of the tour that their culture develops somewhat apart from conventional culture. Out of this insulated social terrain grows a particular set of values and expectations, the keystone of which is the prowess ethic. The logic of a prowess-based status order is encouraged by the logic of sport. In sport, accomplishments cannot be denied. Within the subworld of the LPGA, this logic is cultivated in the relative isolation of practice and play, nurtured by knowledgeable fans and reinforced by a highly individualistic merit-based system of rewards.

The values and norms of subworlds arise out of the shared interest and production of a "social object," in this case competitive golf. The values are adopted from the dominant culture, albeit in slightly deviant or exaggerated forms. Women's professional golf is no exception. Sociologists might classify the prowess ethic as an outgrowth of the Protestant ethic, the American work ethic, or the spirit of capitalism. What distinguishes the prowess ethic as a unique value in professional women's golf is its primacy. Prowess is the determinant of status, social position, and self-worth and informs almost every aspect of the golfers' lives. Out of this ethos comes the golfers' belief that they should be judged according to their abilities, represented by their accomplishments.

Because of the gender-rich meanings attributed to athletic superi-ority, the conflict between the culture of women's professional golf and the norms and expectations of conventional culture is most clearly seen in gender relations. Viewed from within the context of the prowess ethic, the conventional norms and practices of doing gender border on the absurd. The prowess ethic is further distinguished from mainstream values and beliefs by its approach to material wealth. Achieved status on the tour undercuts the status symbols which mark divisions within conventional culture. The prowess ethic asserts that status should fol-low from achievement, both in principle and fact, not the other way around. Achieved status at the exclusion of other status orders (gender, class, material wealth) defines a player's social position.

THE TRANSFORMATIVE POTENTIAL OF THE PROWESS ETHIC

While conventional culture has far more influence in shaping subworlds and subcultures of a society these smaller groups can act as agents of social change. They can be incubators, if you will, of ideologies which affect conventional culture. The relatively small subcultures of beat-niks[5] and hippies,[6] for example, had an impact on the broader culture. Willis refers to this mixing of influences as the dialectical relationship between culture and subculture, between the mainstream and the slightly offbeat.[7]

On the surface, the LPGA confirms the dominant values of main-stream culture. Players engage in activities which promote conven-tional images of femininity. But rather than seeing these actions as weakening the transformative potential of the tour, players view their actions as merely pragmatic. The general sentiment I got from most players was it did not matter so much how and why a fan was first attracted to the tour. It was far more important that a fan's interest was retained through the display of golfing skills.

One problem we have is that there is still a little bit of a gender gap. There are still some pretty strong male chauvinists out there.

For instance, two years ago I played in this pro-am in Atlantic City with a group of travel agents. It had been set up through the Trump Hotel. This one man told me after the round, "I can't tell you how much I dreaded to do this today. I was so wrong." He just thought it would be so boring, and he was so amazed by the level of the golf. Since then he came to follow me in Boston. He became a fan of the LPGA.

It is for anybody, I don't care who you are, man, woman, or kid, it is really something else. The level of play is so good out here. (Fran)

Within Fran's story lies the players' hope for social change. Despite the powerful forces that define women's golf in a fashion that is palatable to conventional culture, the players retain and, to some degree, espouse an alternative ideology. They believe that anyone who spends time with the players will be struck by the players' level of skill and that their level of play is so awe-inspiring that it can dismantle preconceived notions outsiders might have about the women on the tour. In this way, the players use golf as a structural tool for transformation of the gender order. Through their golfing prowess they challenge conventional expectations held by many in the world of recreational golf.

BOUNDARY CROSSING

The pro-ams of the LPGA resemble an aspect of childhood play sociologist Barrie Thorne calls "boundary crossing." The schoolyard is primarily a sex-segregated space. However, there are occasional boundary crossings when boys play with girls and girls with boys. Like the LPGA pro-am, successful boundary crossings for children are characterized by persistence and high skills in the play activity of the unlikely participant.

There is a liberating aspect of boundary crossings. For some, like Lynn, there is an evangelical desire to use pro-ams to transform people.

I try to give an impression to people in pro-ams or in the press to help people to understand that it is not that big of a deal to be a female athlete. I mean we are very exceptional and talented people. I don't want to minimize that. But it is not such an exception. Ever so slowly, I think they are getting used to women being athletes.

Q: Do you see that as a mission?

I think that my mission is to assist people in getting the best out of themselves. If it happens to be a way of thinking or to look at something a little differently or making them see themselves a little bit.

Q: The idea that women can be athletes is part of that?
Oh yeah. I mean, why be part of the problem? Help somebody change, or help someone see it a little bit differently.

"Getting the best out of someone" means convincing them to shed preconceived notions about themselves and others. Seen in this context, Lynn's comments are a mix of marketing the tour and promotion of the prowess ethic. Players' golfing skills can only be recognized if they are unfettered by social expectations. Unlike the men's tour, where excellence can still be associated with the current gender order, the excellent play by women jars the preconceived notions of golf fans and amateur players. The dilemma faced by the LPGA tour players is how to get the public to "turn on" to their excellent golf without being "turned off" by it.

UNDOING GENDER

Although there is a pragmatic necessity for players to stage compensatory gender acts, it seems to be a cumbersome burden for most players. Therefore, at the same time that players are attempting to soothe the public's perception of them with displays of femininity, many players try to expand conventional notions of gender in accord with their own.

The relative independence and freedom enjoyed by the professional woman golfer is, in part, a result of the membership's rejection of many of the mainstream expectations of women. The membership's escape from these expectations is based on their fundamental belief that they should be judged according to their abilities, represented by their accomplishments. Achieved status, in their minds, takes precedence over ascribed status. The spirit of the LPGA asserts that socially ascribed status (race, class, gender) can and should be transformed by one's prowess. The LPGA offers women an avenue to an extremely high level of status. The status acquired via athletic excellence is enhanced by the rejection of other status orders.

Not surprisingly, the players view the world outside of the tour somewhat critically.

I am not really a gender person, I don't look at it and say this is male and this is female. This brings up a question of discrimination of women in the world, I see it that way. But I don't know. I tend to look at everything as one gender when I am out here. When people have trouble out here, I don't see it as a man's problem or a woman's problem. I am just kind of more on a human level and not a sexual level.

It is interesting, from my own little world [the tour], I think of it as a human being and judge people not whether they are male or female. But then, given reality [outside the tour], I would say that there are definite women's issues. The whole situation is interesting because we are women dealing with large corporations that are run by men. (Jane)

What is particularly interesting about Jane's comments is her recognition of sex discrimination off the tour. Despite the contradictions between tour life and "reality," gender-related issues are not really a concern for her. The structure of the tour provides sanctuary from conventional gender expectations. For many players, gender issues seem moot as long as they remain on tour.

Not only do players reject the conventional gender order, but they believe that their merit-grounded status order takes precedence over status acquired via social position or material wealth. Players are aware and critical of these hierarchies of power. From within their "own little world" they actively work to dismantle the trappings of conventional hierarchies. I was often struck by the contrast of casually dressed golfers lounging about opulent hotel lobbies and expensive dining rooms, exchanging banter with local and national business leaders. In part, the players' behavior is intended to get these men to shed their corporate pretense so that they can enjoy themselves and the event. But it is also a way for the players to fashion the interactions with these men on the players' terms.

Lynn's comments about interactions with pro-am participants is illuminating in this regard. Like Jane, she began the discussion by dismissing gender as an organizing concept. But almost immediately she acknowledged that the tour makes this stance possible.

It's funny, because I don't think the players think of it as a man-woman thing, we think of it as a golf thing. We're not treated as women are treated.

Like, we take over the country club. We don't have any rules like your shorts are a little too short or, "I'm sorry, [because you are a woman] you can't play on Saturday mornings." We just take over. It's our club. . . . We just take over.

First the club is restructured according to the mores of women's professional golf. The conventional gender order is dismantled. Her following caveat emphasizes that the gender rules on the tour are very different than those off the tour.

> Not that I don't like being a woman. I really like being female, it's just that there are certain rules that are really stupid.

As a result, the political need for gender-identity politics is diminished because they are freed from conventional norms and expectations. From this context, Lynn asserts that the players can disassociate the pro-am players from their symbols of power.

> [When we play in a pro-am with men] we don't care how much money they have, or what car they drove up with, or where they just came from on vacation. It's up to us to just not make a big deal of it. 'Cause we really don't care. . . . There is no power play going on. There is no desk or secretary or tie to hide behind. It is not like he walked up in a suit and he had his limo driver drop him off. We don't have to go through all that junk.
>
> We've got them in golf shirts and shorts. They're so neutral, so bare, so naked in front of us.
>
> Whereas in his office, he has a big desk and a secretary and there are all those doors that make you feel intimidated before you sit down. That is what they do to people to make themselves feel like they're up on a pedestal.
>
> [Out here] they're so apart from their things. They can't hide behind anything.

For the professional golfer, her prowess and the game of golf are the great equalizers. On the golf course, the athlete and the community leader or business person meet on equal footing. For a rare moment, men and women engage in an activity in which the social norms associated with gender and class take a back seat to individual talent. Dorothy found the power gained through the structure of the sport uniquely enjoyable.

> If you play in a pro-am, you play with four men. It's the only thing that I've ever felt that I was a little bit superior, because I am a little bit better at something then those guys. I really love it. I play with four men and they'll ask me—I've got the final say on everything. You don't really have that anywhere else—they trust

> you in what kind of shot you're going to hit, which ball you
> should play. It's just fun to be that good at something. (Dorothy)

Status, trust, and respect are gained from men on the basis of prowess. Dorothy finds power and respect on the golf course that she would not enjoy off the course.

By placing these men in a situation where the trappings of status are dismantled and the skill levels equal, the power dynamics between the LPGA professionals and the male amateurs is relatively balanced. Now the pro-am participants must relate to the players on the players' terms. As Lynn points out, in this context, the players only have to deal with pro-am players' "personality and their golf."

> That is really easy to deal with. So it's great. It is not like we're in
> control, but it takes a lot of their control away. Then it is really fun.

Like for Lynn above, Thorne observed that boundary crossings "chip away at old ideologies and hold out new possibilities."[8]

On the other hand, boundary crossings do not dismantle gender boundaries. Golf remains a province of men despite professional women golfers. Professional women golfers replicate the norms of a predominately male world. They are a kind of "fictive men," whose presence in golf does "little to challenge existing arrangements."[9] The women on tour adopt men's habits and customs. For example, it is not unusual to hear an LPGA professional chastise herself for leaving a putt short with the gender-laden insult "Hit it Alice!" Indeed, the intent of the pro-am is to support the very status orders at which the players chafe.

Nonetheless, while the transformative potential of pro-am encounters may seem minimal, there are enough converts to encourage the players' continued efforts. Most players interviewed could tell stories of converts to their cause: amateurs regretting having to play golf with women who became fans as a result of their pro-am experience, fans dragged to the course by friends, expecting to be bored, drawn in by the high level of play. Minimal as it may be, it is in these encounters that the potential political power of the prowess ethic as a tool for social change is felt by the players.

THE REVOLUTIONARY IMAGE

There is another level of interaction on which players define themselves, albeit unwittingly and express the subversive qualities of the tour. Although it is mediated through the lens of a camera, television enables us a close-up view of the subworld in action. It offers a view from inside the ropes. For example, on occasion, the camera will capture the dead-eye gaze of the player as she studies the pin placement from the fairway. It is a gaze which cuts through the camera and beyond the viewer. It is a gaze that contrasts sharply with the typically passive, beckoning gaze of women presented to us in magazine and television advertisements. Television coverage of women's professional golf also provides us with images of women punctuating birdie putts with clenched and pumping fists. And then shows it again, in slow motion. And when the camera zooms in on the face of a player swearing to herself, for a moment the genteel facade of golf dissolves. Rarely do we see such an honest public expression of determination by women in popular culture.

CONCLUSION

The politics of the athletes on the LPGA resemble a version of classic liberalism. It is somewhat subversive because the extreme emphasis on merit undercuts all other status orders, including wealth, race, and gender. Their political acts are modest; uncompromising display of athleticism and brief encounters with awe-struck fans. Ironically, these small actions are surrounded by a communal celebration of the status quo which reproduces status, gender, and class hierarchies. Even the potentially powerful symbolic images of athleticism are reduced to fleeting images, squeezed in between commercials for Cadillacs and dish-washing soap, and mediated by commentators who tend to promote the most conventional images of femininity.[10] Nonetheless, on some level, the alternative culture of the LPGA comes through. And to some degree, these images and interactions reset what is possible and push the limits of what is acceptable for all of us.

CHAPTER 12

FEMINISM AND THE TOUR

Since I embarked on this study, something of a revolution has arisen in the recreational golf community. Golf has become extremely popular among women. Women are the fastest-growing segment of the golf market. Women's leagues are popping up all over the country.[1] The increase demand is transforming the country club. Women golfers are demanding that restrictions on playing times based on sex be dropped. Some women are suing private clubs over tee times.

This legal battle within the golfing community arises out of a body of civil rights law. In 1988, the U.S. Supreme Court upheld a New York City law which extended the right of equal opportunity to participate in "the business and professional life of the city" to private clubs. Because golf clubs have so often billed themselves as extensions of the boardroom, women found a legel wedge to fight for increased access. In 1992, Michigan gave women of that state an even more powerful tool. Using civil rights legislation passed in the early 1960s, women legislators pushed an antidiscrimination bill through the Michigan Legislative Assembly and State Senate which catagorizes private clubs as "places of public accommodation." As such, private organizations like country clubs are not beyond the reach of civil rights law. That means that clubs cannot deny women members equal access to facilities or deny membership on the basis of sex. In Michigan, at least, it is no longer legal to have men-only tee times or operate men's grill rooms at private country clubs.[2]

Although this struggle is essentially over access to golf, it is a part of the larger and historic struggle of women to participate in sport. By default, then, this struggle is about defining and shaping gender rela-

195

tions as a whole. The ongoing battle of women to transform the structure of sport cannot be separated from the ideological battle to define how men and women ought to "do gender."

Ideology is the descriptive vocabulary of the day-to-day existence through which people make rough sense of their lives. It is the language of consciousness that suits a particular way in which people deal with each other. Through ideologies, we make sense of our world. When the social terrain changes, ideologies are brought into question. During revolutionary times, differing ideological explanations compete for acceptance.[3]

Ideologies are not delusions. They are real. They shape and give meaning to our social relations. Although they are real and deeply felt, they are not necessarily scientifically accurate. For example, although there was ample evidence to suggest otherwise, in the 1920s and 1930s an ideology persisted that jumping was dangerous to women's reproductive organs. This ideology not only justified women's restricted access to sport but also served to discourage women and girls from challenging this restriction.[4]

Ideological justification of inequality based on biological distinctions takes a distinctive form in industrial Western society.[5] Our Western economic and poltical system is accompanied by ideological principles of equality, opportunity, and individual freedom. Nonetheless, status systems based on ascribed attributes are firmly in place.[6] The apparent conflict between persistent inequality, including a lack of liberty for some groups and strongly held principles of social equality, individuality, and freedom, are often explained away with biologically based ideologies.[7]

The notion that men of European descent are physically superior, or at the very least represent the standard of normality by which others are to be judged, has been used to justify unequal power relations between men and women, whites and people of color, and between Western and colonized people around the world throughout the modern age. By restricting the participation of women in sport, men ensured themselves an arena in which they could display their physical prowess in a fashion that reinforced an ideology of biological difference.

For ideologies to remain viable, they do not have to make sense to those outside the society or group that holds them. They only have to help insiders make sense of the things they do and see on a daily basis. When ideologies do not match the everyday life of a group, new ideologies compete for acceptance.[8]

The seventies and eighties represent a period of revolutionary change in gender relations. In addition to marked increase of women in the labor force and in politics, considerable efforts were made by women as a political group to reclaim control of their bodies. From natural childbirth and reproductive rights to self-defense and access to sports women have expanded what was considered biologically possible. In doing so, women redefine what it means to be a woman. They have also transformed themselves and their understanding of their place in the world.

Of all the changes that call into question biologically based ideologies, women's entry into sport is perhaps the most dramatic. It strikes at the most public symbol of support for biological ideologies.[9] Women's sport represents a shift in the social terrain and thus a challenge to the ideological basis of traditional gender relations.[10]

In academic circles, it has become quite popular to present sport as a site of cultural resistance and social transformation.[11] In these studies, sport is viewed as a cultural enterprise over which various social interests compete to assign meaning. Most discussions of ideological production through sport focus on broad political movements and the meanings they impose on sport. The dominate powers in a society define the central social meanings of sport. At the same time, sport is often used by socially disadvantaged groups to gain respect and power within a society.

Groups as various as school boards[12] and magazines,[13] attempt to shape the symbolic meaning of women's sports. Sociologists argue that the media and the male-centered sports establishment present the female athlete in such a way that women's participation in sport does not conflict with the conventional culture. When the athlete is presented as feminine, polite, and heterosexual, her athleticism can be more easily accepted by the mostly male market. Pro-feminist scholars highlight the contradictions between the reality of being an athlete and biology-based patriarchal ideologies—that is the social construction of sport as masculine.[14]

The temptation is to project the symbolic meanings associated with women's athletic prowess on to the woman athlete. I would be less than honest if I did not admit that I expected to find a politically inspired community of women empowered by their sporting experience. The women on tour clearly enjoy the challenge of their sport, the competition, and a sense of competence. The LPGA, by its nature, cuts across the grain of conventional culture. It is a women's organization which has managed to carve a niche for itself within a male domain. By its mere existence alone, the LPGA seems to espouse a transformative agenda. As such, I thought I would find an undercurrent of feminist principles espoused and acted upon by the professional golfers on tour.

THE TOUR AND FEMINIST IDEOLOGIES

The LPGA, however, is far from a hotbed of revolutionary activity. Its members, by and large, do not identify with feminist causes or the gay and lesbian rights movement. Clearly, part of the reason for the distance between the LPGA and political movements is the desire to stay out of controversy and the ability of mainstream society to "feminize" women's sport. The lack of political connection to the feminist movement may also have something to do with the players' isolation from women outside of the sport. Indeed, when I asked players with which group they most identified, women or athletes, all said they identified with the athletes. Here is how Toni answered this question.

> I feel I associate with all sports people. Whether it is someone who is in love with camping or horses, any kind of sport. I think I associate more with sports people. My friends that I met through my daughters, you know, the mothers of other children, it seems like I have nothing to do with and want nothing to do with the typical housewife. But if she has outside interests like swimming or whatever, I seem to be able to get closer to these people. I'd say that I am not the average old housewife who sits and gossips.

Toni has been able to enjoy her life and has avoided what Betty Freidan called the "disease with no name,"[15] from which so many of her peers suffered.

The lack of identification with women or the feminist movement may also be caused in part by players not feeling discriminated against as women.

> I have never felt a part of the women's movement. I never participated in it that much. Like I said before, I never was discriminated against. But I am sure in the corporate world they are probably discriminated against much more than I will ever know. (Tara)

Furthermore, because the golfers are in an all-women environment, the punitive sanctions for disrupting the gender order are directed at them as a whole. They therefore experience these sanctions as something that happens to them as golfers rather than as women.

Fear of controversy, limited identification with women outside the tour, and insulation from the worst consequences of a patriarchal order, can only partially explain professional golfers' aversion to feminism. Despite an apparent symbiosis between feminism and women professional golfers, there appear to be ideological differences between the tour players and the broader feminist agendas. A liberal feminist agenda of sex equality seems contradictory to the everyday life of a tour player. Unlike most occupations in contemporary society, in golf, biology matters.

> They want us to hit it like a man. There is no way. Let me be me. Don't change me and make me into a man. I don't want it and I can't do it. There are certain things a women cannot do. (Gerri)

The biological differences are reflected in performance. Although there are women who drive the ball further than professional men, on the average men outdrive the women by 30 to 40 yards. Therefore, following the logic of the prowess ethic, this disparity in performance should be similarly reflected in the rewards. With surprising regularity, women on the tour upheld this view.

> It is frustrating to think about how much the men make, how much they are getting paid to do the same job. But they are more spectacular, you have to give them that. They are. And there is a price to be paid for that. (Jane)

Toni held a similar view despite an understanding of a liberal feminist ideology.

> I know that are some people out here that think we should be playing for the same amount of money. I don't. It may sound funny, but men are better golfers. People, spectators, like to see power. They like to see strength. The men can hit the golf ball a hell of a long way. That impresses the average Joe Blow gallery person. We have fans that appreciate how far we hit the ball pound for pound. But I don't think that we put on the show that the men do. (Toni)

Despite their contention that unequal pay is fair, the players are not conservative or reactionary. Contained within their comments is a criticism of the current gender status order. While acknoweldging that men may hit the ball further and should be compensated accordingly, the current rewards are out of line with reality. Molly's comments uphold the logic of the prowess ethic and criticize the current system of rewards.

Well, this is not what society says, but personally I don't think that women . . . well . . . there is no conceivable way that we will make as much money as the men's tour. We'll never be on an equal basis with them. Okay, I do the same kind of job, but the results aren't the same. The men can hit the ball a lot father and stronger. I don't call it an unfairness or not a fair shake, it's just that's the way it is.

Now should they get paid three or four times as much? That is too much of a difference, way too much. I can see them making double or a little less than double. Not triple or quadruple. It's getting a little out of hand. (Molly)

Given the above comments, it is reasonable to suspect that a feminist ideology which focuses on transforming the structures of domination might find more affinity with the tour's members than mainstream liberal feminism. The stumbling block here is that a radical feminist perspective would include a gender critique of the structure of sport. As Catherine MacKinnon argues, contemporary sports which emphasize power, speed, and aggression are defined by men's physiology.[16] The logical conclusion of a radical feminist perspective is some sort of transformation of the structure of sport. One activist noted that "[t]his transformation will render sport as we now know it unrecognizable."[17]

Most women professional golfers do not see sport as a male construct. Golf by itself is not sex-biased. Players recognize the gendered meanings associated with golf as injected into the sport, and do not see sport or golf as a product of a patriarchal society. To the athlete, sport has within it a formal order that remains partitioned off from the broader society. As Lynn puts it, "I don't think the players think of it as a man-woman thing, we think of it as a golf thing." As such, the women on the tour seem resistant to a structural critique of the game of golf.

Historian Susan Cahn and others note a similar lack of connection between women athletes and feminism.[18] Nonetheless, women athletes has become a cultural symbol of resistance to the status quo. MacKinnon, a feminist legal scholar, refers to women athletes as pioneers. *Ms.* magazine's twentieth anniversary timeline of the women's movement is peppered with women's athletic accomplishments. Clearly, women's sport is a site of an ideological battle: on one side is the white male corporate establishment; on the other, women from all walks of life who see women's athletic prowess chipping away at patriarchal ideologies.

For the most part, the battle over the meaning of women's sport is waged outside the ropes, in the gallery, in press rooms, and in family rooms. The weapons are images and symbols. This is not to suggest that the battle over meaning of women's sport is not important—quite the contrary. As sociologist Paul Willis has noted, the ideological meaning that the newly won access to sport takes on is more fundamental to the lasting transformation of relations between men and women than the participation itself.[19]

It is important, however, to recognize the abyss between the symbolic life of the athlete and the everyday life of the athlete. There is a distinction between women's struggle to win access to athletics and the struggle of women athletes to win. The former is inherently a political act, while the latter is not.

PART IV

THE LPGA AS AN
AGENT OF
SOCIAL CHANGE

CHAPTER 13

CLASS, RACE, AND
THE INCREASING
EXCLUSIVITY
OF THE TOUR

One feature which may change . . . is the players' social status, now typically upper-middle class, [it is] likely to broaden in the future. [A]t the professional level at least, the sport will become democratized.

—Theberge

Nancy Theberge wrote this prediction in her study of women's professional golf. She was disappointed with the relatively low number of working-class athletes on tour in the mid-seventies. Her spirits were lifted, however, by the "democratization of sport" theories popular during this era. These theories speculated that golf and other upper-class sports like tennis and swimming would become increasingly egalitarian. Theberge identified the following changes which would act as catalysts for the democratization of golf: professionalization, collegiate expansion, improved quality of play, and increase in prize money.

This optimistic view contends that as a sport progresses from amateur to professional, its meanings and structures demand a change from avocation to vocation. Aristocratic obstacles dissolve as athletes can make a living by playing a sport. While the process might be slow at first, it is not long before the sport is well integrated. Illustrations of the democratization of sport are easy to come by: football's transformation from collegiate elitism to a working-class symbol being the most obvious. The recent move by the International Olympic Committee to allow professional athletes to participate is another, as it expands these contests to those who use sport to make a living rather than limiting them to those who can afford to train and compete for nothing.

All of the changes which Theberge predicted have occurred in women's professional golf, yet the democratization she anticipated has not.

CONDITIONS FOR DEMOCRATIZATION OF WOMEN'S GOLF

With the expansion of women's collegiate sports programs beginning in the seventies, collegiate golf now acts as the primary training ground for women professional golfers. As a result of the growth of golf into college athletic departments, the overall quality of women's golf has improved. This has ultimately impacted the LPGA tour. For example, in 1974, the fortieth-ranked player in the LPGA's annual rankings averaged 76.8 shots per round. In 1987, the fortieth-ranked player's average score was 73.8. In 1993, a 73.8 per round average placed a player at 120 in the annual rankings—fighting just to remain on tour. In other words, there are more good players competing for a limited number of prize-winning positions. As a result, we can suspect that only the most serious golfers remain on tour.

Further, as Therberge predicted, entry onto the tour is now determined by skill, and players must now qualify to become a member of the LPGA tour. At the time of Theberge's study, most tour members turned professional simply by declaring themselves so. Now the avenues which lead to a career as a professional golfer almost without exception lead through collegiate competition. Entry to the collegiate ranks, with their scholarship programs, is based on merit, not financial resources. This, Theberge predicted, will produce a more diverse field.

The increased competition and higher quality of play has increased interest in the sport, which in turn has resulted in increased rewards. Prize moneys have increased 1,000 percent since the mid-seventies. Financially, professional golf has become an attractive career, not just an amateur pastime.

One part of most democratic sport scenarios[1] is the appearance of a working-class sports hero—and in this case, Nancy Lopez fits the bill. Lopez, quite possibly the only household name in women's golf, comes from humble beginnings and consistently plays a leadership role in

promoting improved access to golf for youth regardless of background.
Given the presence of all these factors (an increase in status, economic rewards, tougher competition, collegiate expansion, and the existence of a working-class hero), we should, according to democratization of sport theories, see an increase in working-class and middle-class participation in women's golf, at least on the elite level.

THE WOMEN OF THE TOUR

Who are these women that become professional golfers? Where do they come from? How can we explain the lack of diversity among tour players? Gerson in her study of women's careers argues that it is important to examine life histories within the context of a cohort, because people who share similar historical options often share similar values and expectations.[2] People just don't choose their futures from an infinite set of options. The life choices people make are selected from the options history and society present to them. An examination of a person's life within a historical context highlights the enabling and constraining features of a society.

The options, obstacles, and choices women faced preparing for adult life in the seventies were quite different from those women face in the nineties. The tour and tour life have changed. Most importantly, golf itself has changed. Therefore, when examining the LPGA players' introduction to the sport, athletic development, and subsequent entry into the tour, it is crucial to locate the players' biography within a social and historical context.

This chapter explores the life histories of women professional golfers prior to their entry on the tour and the transformation of the golfing world since the mid-seventies. It focuses on players' introduction to the game, their access to the sport as children and teenagers, and the preparation they received prior to qualifying for the tour. Analyzing the women professional golfers' development within a historical and contextual framework makes it possible to locate significant social patterns and changes that affect women's participation in professional golf.

THE GENERATION AND CLASS GAP

In the interviews, players made a distinction between older players and younger players. Although, the players couched the distinctions in terms of cohorts, I found the distinction to have class undertones. Players from a public-course background seem to be from less affluent families and are more likely to be veteran players (i.e., older). Although players from public and private courses share the experience of liberal access to golf facilities, class distinctions are fairly clear-cut. Older public-course players frequently viewed the younger players as spoiled, rich, and bratty. As illustrated in this quote from Gerta, an older player, the differences are not subtle.

> I think that a lot of the players are coming out of well-to-do backgrounds. The golf scene is a country club scene. There are exceptions. I am an exception. I came from very poor parents. I picked the game up myself and I came from a fairly poor background. When you talk to the youngsters [about life on the tour] you are going to get a really different perspective [than mine].

In general, I found the older players were less likely to have had access to a private course and to college, and tended to have gotten a later start on the tour. Seventy-six percent of the US-born players surveyed in 1989 indicated that they had had access to a private club or described their families as upper-class at the time they were developing their skills. Twenty-four percent indicated that they gained their training on a public course.[3] By dividing the sample according to the number of years on the tour, we see a dramatic shift between the older and younger players (table 13.1). Eighty-six percent of the players on the tour for five or less years[4] learned the game of golf on a private course or described their parents as upper class. This is true for only 62 percent of the players who had been on the tour for six or more years. The figures of players on tour for over six years match Theberge's 1974 findings (about one-third public and two-thirds private). In a word, golf has become more exclusive over the last decade.

TABLE 13.1
Training Facilities of Professional Golfers as Youth

	Upper-class/Private	Public
1974 Theberge	66%	33%
1989 6 or more years on tour	62%	37%
1989 5 or less years on tour	86%	14%

THE TRANSFORMATION OF
JUNIOR GOLFERS' SOCIAL TERRAIN

As the survey data shows, women's professional golf became more exclusive during the years 1974-1988. More and more players on the professional tour are learning the game on country club courses and come from upper-class families. There are a number of factors that to help explain this move away from egalitarian participation on the professional level, in spite of the seemingly favorable atmosphere for democratization.

Two significant changes affected women's sport in the early seventies. In 1971, a national organizing body for collegiate sports for women was created—the Association for Intercollegiate Athletics for Women (AIAW). The AIAW helped to standardize the national sports structure and promoted collegiate sports for women. At almost the same time, the Federal government passed Title IX (1972). This assured women's collegiate sports teams comparable funding to men's sports teams. These two structures combined to create a women's sporting boom in colleges and universities.

Golf represented a practical and economical sport to start and fund as a means of complying with Title IX. Many colleges and universities already operated a college course or had arrangements with a nearby course for their men's team. The athletes usually come to school with their own clubs and bags, so equipment costs are minimal. For most schools, a golf coach was usually already employed as a physical education instructor or the men's coach. As a result of the low cost to the school, women's collegiate golf programs sprang up across country in the early seventies as a way of complying with Title IX.

The impact of Title IX on women's professional golf can be seen by comparing the survey data of the pros that came of age before and after the passage of Title IX. Only two of the thirteen older players received scholarship money for athletic prowess (15%). Of the forty-three professionals coming of age in the post-Title IX era, all but three received athletic scholarships (93%). Of the three non-scholarship players, two opted to turn pro prior to college and the other started playing the game after she graduated.

The second significant event in women's sports was the NCAA's usurpation of the AIAW in 1980-81. This was significant because the AIAW operated under a different philosophy than the NCAA. The AIAW emphasized participation in addition to performance, and aid based on need as well as athletic prowess. The NCAA supports aid based on athletic talent regardless of need. Further, the AIAW rules allowed outside institutions like country clubs and the National Golf Foundation to give athletic talent and need-based scholarships. In the NCAA, alumni abuses necessitated the elimination of such charity many years prior to its usurpation of the AIAW. The NCAA rules are shaped predominantly by men's pre-professional sports like basketball and football. Attending to issues and concerns of these sports is central to the financial and political survival of the NCAA. This has lead the NCAA to formulate rules that deal with the issues and concerns of these sports. If this has resulted in rules that do not meet the needs of women's sports and men's "minor" sports, it is viewed as unfortunate but unavoidable. In particular, NCAA rules treat all sports as pre-professional training grounds for athletes.

The hostile takeover of the AIAW by the NCAA corresponded roughly with Lopez's sensational rookie season. The media attention Lopez received spurred teenage golfers' interest and promoted professional golf as a viable career option. Thus, not only did the NCAA treat women's collegiate golf as a pre-professional sport, the players began to view it as such also.

In Table 13.2, the survey data is broken into three groups according to the age of the players: athletes 17 or older at time of the passage of Title IX, athletes entering college under the influence of the AIAW and Title IX, and athletes attending school under the influence of the NCAA.

Although the sample size is small, it is clear that the younger athletes began to play the game seriously at a younger age than the older athletes. While some might argue that professional sports are simply becoming a more acceptable vocation and, as a result, women are discovering sports sooner, I would argue that alternative routes to a professional golf career have all but evaporated since the NCAA gained

TABLE 13.2
Type and Amount of Training Professionals Received as Youth

Cohort	Pre-Title (N=13)	AIAW (N=29)	NCAA (N=15)
Received formal golf training by age 13	53%	65%	80%
Played or hit more than once a week by age 13	38%	58%	66%
Played or hit daily between ages 14 and 17	46%	72%	86%
Access to private course prior to age 21	53%	72%	80%

control of women's collegiate sports. There are six basic reasons professional golf has become more exclusive in the last decade.

Collegiate recruiting practices favor the country club athlete because she has the opportunity to become a good golfer as a teenager. NCAA recruiting rules promote the recruitment of the best teenage golfers. Junior national ranking is based on national amateur tournaments. The best collegiate programs recruit solely from these national and junior national tournaments as it is efficient to use these tournaments to view the country's best prospects. The economic need of the players is not a consideration.

For an athlete to be invited to participate in national junior amateur tournaments, she must perform well at local and regional tournaments while in high school. To play well at age 16 or 17 means, more than likely, that the athlete must have daily access to golf from age 12 or 14 on. As the chart above indicates, this was true for the current cohort of professional golfers. Supporting data can be found in National Golf Foundation (NGF) golf participation studies. Despite the fact that an overwhelming majority of junior golfers play at public and municipal courses, they are not likely to be frequent golfers, who play twenty-five or more rounds a year. NGF findings indicate that golfers are far more likely to be a frequent player if they belong to a private facility.[5]

Val's casual everyday access to the sport typifies the experience of many of the younger players.

> I learned on a country club course in Houston, Texas. My parents moved there when I was fifteen, and they moved me on the golf course. We lived right on the golf course. They kind of did that to make me want to play more. I was right there, it made it very easy for me. I just walked out my door and played. They knew it was a good thing for me to get into if I enjoyed it. They never pushed it. They just said you will enjoy doing this, so why don't you go ahead and play. So I grew up on a country club course. I played in a lot of junior golf tournaments. (Val)

Further, golf is fairly expensive. Lessons, greens fees, range balls and clubs, and most of all, travel to regional and national tournaments, are all necessary for the development of a collegiate golfer and would be a burden for most families. Families of junior golfers with the financial resources to meet these costs almost always belong to private country clubs.

In a nutshell, the current structure dictating entry into collegiate golf, which is now the stepping-stone to the professional ranks, has lowered the age at which a future professional must discover and take up the game. This favors the country club athlete, whose family can afford the costs of the sport and whose use of the club as a hub for family summer activities gives her casual daily exposure of the sport.

Another factor in the increase in the number of upper-class professional players is the higher qualifying standards and improved play of the LPGA membership. The improved play limits the possibility for non-collegiate golfers to gain entry to professional golf. Higher standards of play and the standardization of entry have increased the expense of training, and limited the possibility of "on the job training" while on the tour, thereby preventing a late blooming, independent golfer from making a career shift to golf. In the seventies, an average golfer could gain the necessary experience on the tour. Denise, one of the few non-college golfers, is one of these latecomers to the sport.

> I won't say that I really worked that hard or practiced that hard. It was probably a couple of years of being on tour before I realized that I really wanted to play championship-caliber golf. For probably about three years, I was basically a hack. [I] was out here having fun and I had just enough talent to stay on.
>
> That's something you couldn't do today. You just couldn't hack it around like I did in the first couple of years and stay here. (Denise)

Tara, a working-class golfer who worked as a high school teacher before turning to professional golf, had a similar assessment of the younger players.

> They are more prepared to be out here now. There are a lot more junior programs, a lot more college programs, a lot of tournaments that women can play in now. When I came out, there were no tournaments except the city and state tournaments and maybe a national tournament. I bet an amateur could play in a tournament every week if she wanted to, to prepare herself to come out here.
>
> When I came out, I had nothing. I had gone to college, and taught for a couple of years. I didn't play in very many amateur tournaments. When I came out here, I got my schooling on the golf course. I think younger players today already know [what I learned after I came out here]. (Tara)

Another factor that makes it harder for the non-collegiate golfer to succeed on the tour is the mini tour. The mini tour is the small professional tour which acts as a farm system for the LPGA tour. Most future professionals use the mini tour after college to fine-tune their game and prepare for the LPGA qualifying tournament. It is an expensive and risky venture without capital support. The costs are less than those of the LPGA, but so are the prize winnings. A player can get by, but she rarely turns much of a profit. Most players lose money while playing on the mini tour. Few players can enter this tour without some sort of outside financial backing, usually from family or friends. While the mini tour can be utilized by the late blooming golfer, it favors those athletes with financial support and collegiate training.

A fourth contributing factor to the decrease in the percentage of working-class, public-course golfers on the tour is the demise of working-class cultural centers within golf. The caddy shack and the pro shop were once bastions of working-class culture. In the fifties and sixties, they represented an avenue by which working-class youth could be introduced to the game. The club professional, once a working-class service position, is now often from a country club background. Thus, mentors with working-class backgrounds are disappearing from the teaching professions.

Electric carts and pull carts for bags have eliminated the need for caddies and thus the caddy shack. The primary connections between working-class youth and golf have been severed.

The fifth reason for the decrease in the number of professionals from working-class backgrounds is tied to the popularity of the sport. The golfing boom of the eighties has limited working-class children's access to municipal courses. Young single adults, who have no need for the family-centered nature of country clubs, find the public and for-fee courses more to their liking. Group lessons for children are uneconomical and have been replaced by the more financially rewarding adult lessons. Playing time for youth has been reduced by the increase in demand by paying adults. The tradition of turning over the club to youth and caddies on Mondays has all but disappeared on public courses, and with it, easy access to the sport.

Finally, the decrease in disdain for professional golf by the middle and upper classes has actually enhanced the exclusiveness of the sport. The aristocratic preference for amateur status for women was quite strong in the golfing community in the early years of the tour. Indeed, during the first two decades of the tour, many private clubs prohibited professional play by women on their courses. As a result, most of the early tournaments were played on public courses.

Prior to the passage of Title IX, many proficient golfers remained on the amateur circuit. Joanne Carner, for example, spent thirteen years (1957-1969) on the amateur circuit before turning pro. She enjoyed considerable media attention while on the amateur circuit, and her status remained quite high within the golfing community. As the stigma of professional golf waned, amateur tournaments were no longer viewed as ends in themselves. Amateur tournaments and collegiate competition are now viewed as a farm system for the professional tour for all social groups and classes. As a result of this transformation in the meaning of professional golf, affluent players, once satisfied with amateur status, now seek careers in golf.

The old division of talent between the two circuits, amateur and professional, worked in favor of late-blooming working-class public-course athletes. Limited competition allowed these public-course players to fine-tune their game on the professional tour without fear of losing their card. The diminishing stigma of professional golf for the upper class unleashed a bevy of talented players onto the LPGA tour whose skill has been honed by private lessons and liberal access to golf facilities.

In sum, despite developments in women's professional golf which would seem to lend themselves to the democratization of the sport, golf has become increasingly more exclusive. Today, children of affluent families with private golf memberships face fewer obstacles to a career in professional golf than less affluent children whose access to the sport is through the public golf course. Influential economic, structural, and social changes have changed the sport such that only the children of families with country club memberships have the degree of access to the sport that is necessary for professional success. Thus, women who have enjoyed country club privileges as children are most likely to become professionals. As a result, women's golf participation varies along class lines within cohorts. Australian-born Jan Stephenson, a veteran of the tour, may have summed up this phenomenon best when she said, "It's not often the best athlete in America that makes it in golf. It's more often the richest best athlete."[6]

THE RACIAL EXCLUSIVITY OF PROFESSIONAL GOLF

When Theberge did her research in the mid-seventies, there were two African-Americans on tour, Althea Gibson (more famous as a tennis player) and Renee Powel. Outside of a few Asian players on the tour, today's tour is almost exclusively white. This did not strike me as strange, for after all most of the players come from upper-class families with liberal access to the sport. African-Americans, I assumed, had yet to gain access to the sport in any significant fashion. Any African-Americans on tour prior to the nineties were simply an anomaly. I believed that until I met Alma Horn, at the Atlantic City Classic in 1989.

I met Ms. Horn on a trip between the press lot and the clubhouse. She was the driver of the shuttle van. I was surprised to see an older black woman volunteering at a tournament. As she pulled out of the clubhouse drive, she asked where I was from. When I told her Boston, she asked if I had ever played Ponkapoag. "No, I don't play much golf." And I still didn't think she had either—Ponk-a-pog! Right!

But, as she drove, she began to tell me of her playing days, of the country club the black community had purchased outside Baltimore and of the UGA (United Golfers Association)—the African-American competitive golf league. She also told me of the UGA's archivists, Ethel Williams of Washington, D.C., who kept the records, newspaper clippings, and memorabilia of the UGA. As a result of this conversation, I decided to pay Ms. Williams a visit.

Her apartment was laded with golf trophies and scrapbooks detailing the glory days of the UGA. With the help of her scrapbook, Williams patiently recounted for me a history that has been largely ignored. The UGA was born out of a combination of the rapid increase in public-course development of the 1920s and Jim Crow Laws. The members of the African-American Wake Robin Golf Club, a public course in Washington, D.C., formed the UGA with other similar clubs in major cities in the mid Atlantic region. From the forties through the sixties, the UGA championship served as a spring board for African-American golfers. It was through the UGA and UGA-sponsored events that the great African-American Golfers of the late sixties and seventies gained experience and support. Charlie Sifford, Lee Elder, Pete Brown, and Renee Powell all won UGA titles prior to joining the PGA or the LPGA.[7]

Why haven't there been more African-Americans in professional golf in the eighties and the nineties? The answer, I think, can be found in Ethel Williams' scrapbook. Between the newspaper clippings, and scorecards, are invitations to events, socials, and golf tournaments. They are elegant, some ostentatious. The UGA and similar African-American cultural organizations offered African-Americans an opportunity to be something other than guests. The members of the Wake Robin UGA were the hosts.

Desegregation promised to integrate African-Americans into all aspects of society. The reality is that they remain guests within a predominantly white culture. Jim Crow, for all of its evils, allowed African-Americans a space in which to develop cultural events apart from the white community. Once legal segregation ended, that space disappeared. Many of the African-American courses were reclaimed by the city and the land sold off to generate revenue. Retaining a space for African-Americans within the golf world became increasingly difficult for the UGA.

The rise and fall of the UGA mirrors baseball's Negro Leagues. The Negro Leagues were a central part of African-American culture. The annual All-Star game often outdrew the white leagues' All-Star game. But after integrating, the Negro Leagues died a slow death.[8] The African-American community's interest in baseball also faded. Currently African-Americans make up only 5 to 6 percent of the spectators attending major league baseball games.[9]

As golf became increasingly privatized and public courses became integrated, the sport has become increasingly less accessible for African-Americans. Despite the PGA's and LPGA's refusal to play official events at courses with all-white membership, such clubs still exist. Some private clubs, the primary avenue to the LPGA, still retain overt racist practices. And many that do not actively block African-American membership passively discourage it.

CONCLUSION

The argument made above is fairly simple: the structures which provided access to golf for working-class youth and African-American youth have dissolved over the last twenty years. As a result, the tour is less diverse today than in mid-seventies. Professionalization, by itself, is not the key to increasing diversity within professional sport. Indeed, the democratization of sport theory is something of a trickle-down theory, which fails to take into account grassroots development of sport and the broader sociopolitical context. Diversity in professional sports does not come about simply as the result of professionalization of amateur sport, but requires liberal access to sport for all groups as youth.

CHAPTER 14

GENDER EQUALITY AND THE LPGA

It is really a fantasy world out here . . . especially being a woman, I can't think of any other place where you can do exactly what you want to.

—Tara

If I had to make the decision to become a professional golfer now, knowing what I know, I don't know if I could make the same decision of being out here, because this lifestyle goes against the grain with a lot of society.

—Jane

Implicit in modern sport is a liberal philosophy—equality of opportunity and just rewards for hard-won success. As a result, sport is often an institution that embraces oppressed racial and ethnic groups before other mainstream institutions. Athletes affiliated with oppressed people often become symbols of liberal progress. The women of the LPGA are no exception.

Out here, women operate in a sphere in which gender discrimination seems reduced. For the players on tour, gender seems to matter less than it does in the "real world." Inside the ropes, the action is directed by the rules of the game as opposed to the gender norms of mainstream society. Women professional golfers relish the objectivity of payment for performance, and experience golf as liberating. In addition, women professional golfers debunk stereotypical notions about what is appropriate for women.

The LPGA's gender neutrality is enhanced by the tour's all-female work force—unlike other occupations to which women have recently gained access, the professional golfer's is sex segregated. Women on the tour do not compete directly with men or rely on men for career advancement.[1] But the tour also differs from the intentionally sex-segregated work of other women's organizations like rape crisis centers and battered women's organizations because LPGA members do not join the tour for the explicitly political goal of working for sex equality.[2] As such, the LPGA tour offers a window on aspects of gender that may remain hidden in more conventional sex-integrated occupations[3] or intentionally sex-segregated political organizations.

THE DOUBLE-EDGED NATURE OF THE TOUR

The two quotations that open this chapter illustrate the double-edged nature to the life of a woman professional golfer. Tara's quote suggests that LPGA members enjoy some of the same benefits enjoyed by women in sex-segregated political organizations: the tour is seen as a safe haven from an oppressive gender order. At the same time, as Jane's comment makes clear, the women of the LPGA tour also suffer some of the same social costs faced by politically active women. Politically active women expect, and in some cases, actively invite, a hostile response. The women on tour want more than anything to be accepted.

The success of the LPGA reflects progress in gender relations. It is unlikely, however, that the LPGA represents a social advancement that will help to cause a chain-reaction of enlightenment, tipping the scales in favor of a new gender order.[4] Indeed, if history is any indication of the future, more often the opposite is the case. Dominant culture adapts to accommodate what appear to be subversive transformations.[5] With each small step in the struggle for equality, new and unforeseen issues present themselves. Where access to sport was once the primary concern of women athletes, now the battle is over the meaning of women's athletics. And while the "image problem" may be the current issue for the women of the LPGA, other issues which hinder women's advancement are lurking just ahead.

Within the very transformative practices and ideologies currently employed by tour players lay future barriers to equality. Tactics now used by women athletes in their struggle for acceptance, can be turned around and used against them. I call this phenomenon "the subversion of subversion." By exposing this undercutting of the tour's transformative potential, I hope to point to the issues which women, regardless of occupation, may be facing in their struggles for equality.

The transformative potential of the tour is blunted in at least three ways. First, the notion of the gender-neutrality of sport, a rather radical notion on one level, supports the status quo on another level. Next, the prowess ethic, another potential transformative tool, is often incorporated and understood in the broader culture as deviance. Thus, the status achieved via prowess is often undercut. Finally, the sex segregation of the tour, often pointed to as a liberating structure, can also be turned around so as to justify discrimination against women athletes.

THE DOUBLE EDGE OF GENDER NEUTRALITY

In interviews, players often claimed that golf is a gender-neutral activity. By disassociating sport from gender, women golfers actively debunk golf as a male resource for doing masculinity. In some ways, this transformation of the symbolic meaning of golf expands our expectations of what is possible. But as I have argued earlier, the golfers' insistence on the gender-neutrality of golf is possibly less a political act than a response to the genderedness of sport. Because sport is symbolically masculine, the women on the tour must disassociate sporting activities from gender in order to maintain their identities as women and claim golf as their own.

The players' gender-neutrality arguments reshape somewhat the social meaning of golf. In an effort to convince people that sport is gender-neutral and an appropriate occupation for women, the current members of the tour actively deny the subversive qualities of women's participation in the sport. For example, in order to illustrate the gender-neutrality of the sport, women on the tour must convincingly present themselves as a mirror of the broader society. They work very hard to present a heterosexual and feminine front and resist amplification of any actions outside the norm. Only by reproducing the gender order can players maintain the image of gender-neutrality.

Golf as a gender-neutral activity also promotes the notion that gender discrimination is something which has been injected into golf—and therefore something which can be extracted with little or no transformation in the organizations which govern golf. Sociologist Joan Acker[6] argues convincingly that gender cannot be understood as being outside organizational processes. Gender is not something layered onto gender-neutral organizations which will dissolve with the addition of women employees. The genderedness of jobs is built into job descriptions.

Increasing access to previously male-dominated occupations by women has not significantly changed those organizations. Professional women repeatedly feel they have to choose between family and career—between a man's job and a woman's job.[7] Explicit in this contemporary dilemma is an assumption that upper-level management and professional jobs will be filled by individuals whose lives center on full-time, life-long work. Implicit in this job description is that someone else will be available to take care of the worker's personal and familial needs. Traditionally these jobs have been filled by men. Low-paying jobs, often filled by women, assume the worker has responsibilities outside work which will impact on effort and long-term commitment.

Rational, sterile job descriptions mask a taken-for-granted genderness of our society. Claims of gender-neutral organizations within a gendered society reinforce and reproduce an already gendered world. Until job descriptions take into account equality of domestic duties, parental duties, and the need to sustain a high quality of life away from work, organizations will continue to be gendered under the guise of gender-neutrality.

The organization of professional golf also assumes a gender order. Historically, the creation of modern sport coincided with men's desire to distinguish themselves from women.[8] It is impossible to think of current sports organizations as gender-neutral because the rules and the structure of sport are embedded into the historical process of creating and maintaining a particular gender order. Our current sports were created by men for men to accentuate men's biology. The criteria for a legitimate golf course, for example, is determined by distance, which amplifies the importance of strength. In a society in which gender mattered less, official courses could just as easily be determined by the difficulty of the greens, the number of hazards per hole, or the number of doglegs which require accurate tee shots.

Because the LPGA assumes the gender-neutrality of golf, they often follow the lead of the PGA tour. Like other traditionally male-identified occupations, the requirements of the tour assume that the athletes personal and familial needs will be met by someone else. For half the year the professional is away from home. While there are a few exceptional women golfers who manage to make a living and have a family by playing a limited schedule, they are the exception.

While it was possible to be a mother and a professional golfer, these women repeatedly expressed the difficulty of balancing the two roles. The LPGA, for its part, assists mothers on tour with child care. When I began this research, the LPGA provided day care through a national chain in exchange for advertising. But the day-care centers did not accommodate the player's playing and practice schedule. They were often as much as thirty minutes' drive from the course, adding as much as two hours of travel time to a golfer's day. Worst of all, they were closed on Sundays, the final day of a tournament. The wealthiest players with children travel in motor homes and employ a full-time nanny. And without exception, playing mothers unable to afford these comforts are envious of those who can. To this non-golfing sociologist, it seemed ironic that each tournament sight provides caddies—individual caretakers of the players' clubs—for all those players needing one, but did not provide similar caretakers for professional golfers' children. As of this writing the LPGA offers on-site day care. Surely, had the sport been created by women for women, child care would have been provided at each tournament site long before 1992.

While the tour is sex-segregated, the rules of the LPGA do not reflect the primary biological differences. There is no official maternity-leave policy on the LPGA. Marginally ranked players choosing to have children, risk losing their card if they are unable to compete in enough tournaments to qualify for full-time status, or if changes in her body adversely effect her performance.

Clearly, there are benefits to women's expanding career choices within the current framework of work. But women's expanded sense of what is possible, their hard-won place in previously all-male occupations, and their ongoing challenges to the symbolic meanings of cultural products have not radically transformed Western society. While these advances seem necessary steps to eradicate gender as an organizing feature of our society, real social change will not come about if women simply replicate men's lives. It is not enough to simply add women to current organizations and expect that those organizations will be transformed.

Without intentionally choosing otherwise, women in sport act very much like men (chapter 8). Because of the assumption of gender-neutrality, women golfers do not connect the distance they feel from each other with patriarchal structures. They do not see their difficulty in being mothers and golfers as connected to a history of male dominance of sport. Rather, they understand these problems as a consequence of the sport they choose to play. If a player decides not to go on tour in favor of raising a family, few are inclined to question the structure of golf. Rather, we are inclined to question the character or the talent of the athlete. The player is not "up to the challenge" or "did not want to make the sacrifice" needed to compete on the professional level. We place blame on the individual for what is actually a social-structural problem. Rather than asking (as I did in chapter 4), "What does it take to get on to the tour, and stay on tour?," a better question for those who truly care about the quality of the sport might be, "How do we insure that the best golfers (men and women) can play golf for a living and provide for their families as parents and partners?"

Judith Lorber comes to a similar conclusion in her study of women physicians. Although women medical students relied on gender-blind criteria to get into the medical profession, gender played a key role in their career development. She concluded that there is a strange paradox of women's struggle for equality in the professions: it is necessary for women to identify and organize as a group in order to "defuse gender as a discriminative status." To break down historic barriers, counter men's devaluation of women, and amplify women's contributions, women must come together as a political group. But this political identity of women is intended to create social structures and attitudes in which gender matters less and ultimately to eradicate gender as an organizing feature of society.[9]

This paradox seems to be a future dilemma for the tour. Is there a way to retain the politically powerful notion that sports are gender-neutral, while at the same time working to transform sport to reflect women's lives?

THE SUBVERSION OF THE PROWESS ETHIC

The subworld of women's professional golf represents "an alternative order of reality and reason."[10] The prowess ethic, the belief that one should be respected and rewarded according to outward expressions of prowess, shapes this alternative order.

For some players, the prowess ethic is an approach to living from which many could benefit. For these players, the pro-am represents the moment of the greatest political gain. It is an event through which players can use their high status to confront conventional culture, express and transmit the values of their subworld, and win converts.

The sad irony is that within the broader culture, participating in pro-am is a status symbol, designed to uphold the current class and political structures. The cost and/or social position necessary to become a pro-am participant limits access to a select group. The participants are overwhelmingly male and professional. Furthermore, the pro-am is laden with acts and images which affirm the conventional gender order. As has been illustrated, the women golfers are likely to act as hosts or defuse a threatened pro-am participant by shoring up his masculine identity. The structure of the pro-am event diminishes the tour's subversive qualities. As a result, the impact of LPGA golfers on social life via direct contact with pro-am participants is subverted by the broader message of the tournament event.

The subversive aspect of the prowess ethic is undercut in other, less obvious ways. The players' use of talent as an explanation for excellence dulls the radical edge of the prowess ethic. Talent, an arbitrary gift at birth, separates those considered great from the rest of us. Women professional golfers describe themselves as gifted, and are described by others as unique or special.[11] Indeed, this is a major selling point of the tour. However, a far more radical notion is that the women on the tour playing golf reflect or represent the average woman. To think of professional women tennis players and golfers, Olympic athletes, and elite collegiate sportswomen as average, yet determined and hardworking women who happen to be really excellent in sport—this challenges the notion that men are biologically superior. But to view women athletes as average yet hardworking also dulls some of the luster of the tour. Lynn's comments about the "ordinariness" of players captures this paradox.

> [I]t is not that big of a deal to be a female athlete. I mean we are very exceptional and talented people. I don't want to minimize that. But it is not such an exception. (Lynn)

An unusual aspect of the concept of "talent" is that most people are not considered talented until they have worked very hard at something and, through habitual training, become successful. Excellence probably has far less to do with talent than good habits.[12] For the athlete, excellence is the result of practicing a movement until it becomes habitual, and is incorporated into mind, body, and soul.

To reduce excellence to being the result of God-given talent makes the athlete special, outside the norm. Ultimately, it excuses our own lack of excellence.[13] That is, "if we had only been given the same gifts," we say to ourselves, "we, too, could be excellent." Talent makes for a very compelling and palatable explanation for others' success. We are less inclined, however, to adopt it when it is our own excellence being discussed. Talents reduce our sense of having earned an accomplishment.

Athletic talent has a slightly different impact when assigned to women, given the gender-laden meaning of sport in our society. For men, watching sport involves gender narcissism.[14] Male athletic excellence seems to confer upon all men (no matter how unathletic) a superiority complex. That is, male fans believe they have a small part of whatever it is that makes Larry Bird or Micheal Jordan excel. Thus, male athletic talent simultaneously excuses male fans from of being excellent in athletics and assures them as men of their rightful position in a male-dominated world.

However, when talent is used to describe women, it takes on the meaning of deviance or biological abnormality.[15] At the very least, the female athlete is understood to be outside the norm. They are not understood as being more woman than the average woman, but rather different from the average woman—deviant. Framed in this fashion, the descriptor *talented* can be used to make athletic women less of a threat to the current social order. In the case of women's golf, the emphasis on talent as an explanation of women's athletic prowess, excuses other women from playing excellent golf, confirms golf as as a masculine practice, and ensures golf will continue to be an ambigious gender behavior for women.

THE DOUBLE EDGE OF SEX-SEGREGATED SPORT

Sex-segregated settings have often been used by women as safe havens in which to do liberatory work. From consciousness-raising groups of the seventies to shelters for battered women in the nineties, all-women's groups have worked to end sex discrimination. While the tour lacks the political intent of many women's organizations, it enjoys some of the benefits. Women on the tour do not compete directly with men or rely on men for career advancement. They cannot be compared directly with men, and encourage fans to seek single-sex comparisons.

At the same time, sport invites biological comparisons between men and women. Although they do not compete against each other, the distance of the average length of drive can be compared between the men's and women's tours. Everything from putting averages to approach shots can be compared. Regardless of how small the quantitative difference, as long as the very best male golfers can outdrive women golfers, these numbers will be used to fortify social expressions of the importance of biological distinctions between men and women.

Most importantly, the minute differences in performance are accentuated by the huge disparity in prize money. This disparity in earnings exaggerates the social significance of biological differences. Such comparisons undercut the subversive qualities of the tour.

There is something of a snowball effect when the performance differences between men and women are highlighted by social constructions like earnings and TV coverage. Sports fans seem reluctant to support women's sports because women athletes are thought to be less talented, slower, and less skilled than men. Consequently, women's sports get less support, because they are less popular than men's sports.

This excuse for not wanting to support women's athletic activities denies the social meaning of sport. If it was truly skill that fans were going to see, how can we explain the lack of fan support for women's college teams that could easily handle boys' high school teams, which draw more fans. Quite simply, sports have more significance for men regardless of skill level.

The comparison between men's and women's golf is, from the start, improper. We need to understand women's sports on their own terms. Defining elite women's sports in comparison to elite men's sports is a set-up to discredit women's athletic prowess. There are differences between men and women, albeit subtle and insignificant in most activities, which, on the elite level of sport, matter. The only proper comparison of the LPGA is against other women golfers.

OUTSIDERS WITHIN

The women of the LPGA sit on the edge of conventional culture. They stand somewhat outside the broader culture, yet are a part of it. For all their skill, the LPGA professional golfers remain outsiders within the golfing community. Despite top billing, they are outsiders within an annual corporate and/or community celebration which takes place around each tournament. LPGA members are even outsiders in the ideological debate about their meaning in society. As various social groups attempt to stake a claim to women's golf, define it, and give it meaning, the women on the tour struggle for acceptance as golfers.

They are reluctant and frustrated outsiders. They want nothing more than to be accepted as golfers. At the same time, they are reminded, week after week, by pro-am partners, sponsors, fans, and management, that they do indeed operate by slightly different rules.

In their interactions, they struggle to illustrate to all who will watch that being a woman athlete is "no big deal." Despite their pragmatic marketing of themselves and the tour, which blunts the radical edge of women competing in sports, I never felt that the women of the LPGA tour "sold out" just to play the game of golf. What I felt was a powerful desire to prove themselves, to define themselves, and a fierce desire to hold onto an organization they had created in somewhat hostile territory. It would not be accurate to suggest that the emancipatory aspects of the tour are all a ruse and that the tour is nothing more than the "lap dog" of the golf industry, or that the LPGA professional is a poster woman for patriarchy. Reality is far more complicated.

The LPGA in the late eighties and early nineties represents part of an ongoing process of changing relations between men and women. While there are those around the tour attempting to define the women in ways which uphold a patriarchal order, the women on the tour are searching for alternatives. But the search is not overtly political. It arises out of a desire to play golf extremely well and to be respected for it.

The difficulty of self-definition in the public forum of professional golf is frustrating. The saddest comments came from players like Jane, whose lament opens this chapter. For her, the conflicts with social norms and the frustrations of being left outside are overwhelming. For every comment like Jane's, there were many more like Tara's. The two comments are not in conflict. They merely describe two aspects of the tour. The frustrations of being an outsider are outweighed by tournament play.

It is a thin rope that divides the gallery from the competitive course but it marks a great divide. Inside the ropes, players escape the cultural conflicts. It is, as Tara said, "a fantasy world out here." "Out here" the players enjoy a social world in which their position is in their own hands. They experience a sense of freedom, equality, and justice not found off the course. It is where the women of the LPGA are most comfortable.

> I am most at home when I am all by myself, playing golf. Not in the pro-ams, but when the tournament starts, and it is just you and your caddie. I am not expected to jump across the ropes and greet people. I can just walk, relax, and play. (June)

Quite possibly June's comment speaks to the essence of professional golf and its greatest prospects for change—the love of golf.

APPENDIX A

PLAYER PROFILES

Sport ethnography presents unusual problems with regard to maintaining the anonymity of the subjects in the study. Because sport is so public and the athletes' performances are documented and recorded with statistics, shielding the identity of the players while revealing relevant information becomes problematic.

The most relevant information a reader needs to know is where a player stands on the tour. In sociological terms, what are the players material conditions—is she making money. Rather than using statistical information in the text, which is cumbersome to both writer and reader and can be cross-referenced with a media guide, I have ranked the players alphabetically. Players with names beginning with letters coming first in the alphabet were ranked high in the standings when they were interviewed. Players like Lynn and Molly were ranked somewhere around ninety in annual earnings. These players retain their card and are breaking even financially. With one notable exception, players with names beginning with letters in the second half of the alphabet are struggling to make ends meet and to retain LPGA playing status. The exception are those players with names beginning with "T". These players are veterans of the tour, at one time highly ranked, just a bit past their prime. Although they do not generally end a season ranked in the top 100, they retain tour status as a result of lifetime earnings or tour victories.

What follows is a brief profile of each player. Each description is preceded by a word or phrase which summarizes the players ability. The meaning of these codes is explained below.

Great = a great or former great player. These players have been on the tour eight or more years. Their career earnings are in the top

100. They have won two or more tournaments and are consistently ranked in the top ten in the year end earnings when they were in their prime.

Steady = an average career player. They have been on the tour for five to ten years and consistently rank between 30 and 120.

Up and coming = a player who has been on the tour less than five years, has an exempt status due to top ninety or better finishes. These players seem to be improving and are likely to become either a great or steady players in the future.

Marginal = a player who has been on the tour for less than five years and is struggling to get and maintain an exempt status. They generally place out of the top ninety.

THE PLAYERS

Ann: Great

This player is one of the top players on the tour. She is single, easy-going, and very pleasant. In her early thirties, on the tour for 10 years, and fairly consistent, she earns on the average $150,000 a year, and wins one tournament a year. Consistently in the top 10 and the top 10 on the all-time money list. After two weak years, this year represented a major comeback year for her. She hit a solid hot streak towards the later part of the summer in the year she was interviewed. She finished among the top three in the annual rankings.

Beth: Up and Coming

She is a top player, finishing in the top fifteen in the annual rankings. She is relatively young—only in her fifth year on the tour—to be ranked so high. In her short career she has chalked up two tournament wins and four top-sixty finishes.

Cara: Up and Coming

This is a fifth-year pro in her late twenties. She is a fairly solid player, in no fear of losing her card and looking forward to doing very well. At the time of the interview, she was finishing in the top ten in tournaments and was ranked in the top twenty-five in the rankings. Later in the year, she came in second in a tournament. She ended the year ranked around 20th, making over $100,000. She is occasionally invited to the press room as she is frequently in contention and articulate.

Cathy: Up and Coming

This player is a young player doing extremely well, consistently placing in the top forty. She attributes her success to Mid-Western sensibilities which guide her life off the tour. Although, she can be very negative on the course if she is not playing well, she does seem to play better than some players with better-looking swings.

She was married to her caddy at the time of the interview. It was one of the many relationships that would not last on tour. Within a year of this interview, they were divorced. The year of the interview, she ranked close to 25th and earned $90,000.

Denise: Great

This player was possibly the most articulate player interviewed and proved to be an insightful informant. She has over ten years on the tour, and is very successful (consistently ranked in the top twenty-five). The last few years, however, have been somewhat of a struggle. She won a tournament toward the end of the year, confirming her assertion in the interview that she is on the way back. She finished in the top forty, making close to $90,000, after finishing out of the top one hundred the year before.

Doris: Up and Coming

This player sought me out and volunteered to be interviewed. She was a rookie at the time of the interview. One of a growing number of foreign-born players, but seasoned in the U.S. collegiate system, she finished around 40th, ahead of all the U.S.-born rookies.

She enjoyed a business-like sponsorship from an international automobile company. Part of her success she attributes to her guaranteed financial security.

Dorothy: Up and Coming

This player is in her fourth year on the tour. She is coming into her own as a player, gaining exemption after her third year and at the time of the interview was playing fairly well. She was ranked in the top fifty.

Her looks and actions resemble those of a young suburban housewife. Somewhat less tolerant of her fellow players and clearly dislikes the lifestyle of the tour. She is the earner of the smaller income in a two-income family, and says she will eventually leave the tour to raise a family.

Ethel: Great

A successful long-time player with almost fifteen years on the tour. She is winding down her career. Although she is still confident in her abilities, she is planning for life after the tour.

She is highly respected by peers and the press. She is a past officer in the LPGA organization. In her prime she did not win a lot of tournaments, but is a very good player, consistently finishing in the top forty in the annual rankings.

Fran: Steady

She has been on the tour for ten years and consistently finished in top 60 in the annual rankings. She has never won a tournament.

It took her four tries to get her card in qualifying school. Once getting on tour, however, she did quite well. She was rookie of the year followed by three more solid years. After the third year, she started having children and her rankings slipped.

Freeda: Steady

This player is a mother of one. She is a consistent player. Potentially a top-twenty player, she has never been one of the best. She ends the year between $45,000 and $65,000. She has been on tour seven years, struggled only during the year she gave birth to her child.

Gerri: Steady

This player is a veteran. She has one win, and has made a good living on the tour. Her play over the years has been erratic. In the interview she eludes to the fact personal issues interfere with her ability to play. She has finished as high as 20 on the annual money list. She was listed in the top 75 in career earnings at the time of the interview.

However, she struggled for four or five years after two good years. Last year she got it back together and was back in the top sixty, earning as much as had when she finished in the top twenty. She ended this year in the top sixty again.

She is around forty years of age and has been on tour for over ten years.

Gerta: Great

A forty-five-year-old golfer who began her career late, she is from a working-class background and is self-taught. Up until this point in her career she has consistently finished in the top sixty. She has won one major tournament and one minor. She is in the top 50 in career earnings and ended up 51st in the annual rankings this year.

Hattie: Steady

On tour since 1980, with an exempt status. She has been in the top sixty twice in her career and has won one tournament. Her exempt status was maintained by the win and the recent top-sixty finish. Otherwise, she has had only one other year in the top ninety. She is in an unusual position in that her status on tour is pretty secure but often finishes the year among the conditional players.

Helen: Up and coming

A rookie when she was interviewed, she was having a fairly successful first season. She was a highly regarded college player from an athletic family. A pleasant women who is sincerely excited about being on tour and playing well. Has not had to worry about making ends meet, which is unusual for a rookie without a sponsor. She also rarely worries about hiring a caddy, as friends and relatives always seem to be toting her bag.

Holly: Great

Holly is one of the most respected players on the tour. She is from a golfing family, and is a former official of the organization. She is polite, soft-spoken, and known throughout the golfing community for her teaching abilities. She is frequently requested to do teaching clinics and fellow players often ask her for help.

She is in her early forties, has won a tournament, and consistently finsihes in the top sixty. The year following the interview she took a semi-retired approach to tournament play.

Jane: Up and Coming

Fifth year on tour. Although she didn't make more than $10,000 in her first three years, in the fourth year she made over $25,000 and scored in the top ninety for the first time. The year of the interview she finished in the top ninety and made close to $35,000. In the years following the interview, Jane plays steady golf, consistently finishing in the top 90.

She is respected by peers, and is a player representative.

June: Up and Coming

This is a young player, in her fourth year. She is having some success. In her second and third year, she finished around 45th in the annual rankings. I interviewed in her fourth year when she was not playing as well. She is an emotional player, which is appealing to many fans, particularly when she is playing well. She is hard talking, openly defiant, and determined to win. Those in the know expect that she will be a top player, when she learns to manage her emotions.

Karen: Up and Coming

This interview took place in a campground. She travels and lives in a RV and a car with her partner/caddy.

She is enjoying some success after a long struggle on the mini tour. She is in her second year on the tour and finished in the top ninety ($35,000). Her first year was a financial disaster—she finished around 120.

Lynn: Steady

An average player who is struggling on the tour. She has been on tour for eight years. She started with three good years, finishing in the top ninety twice and once in the top sixty. Now she struggles to retain status. After three years as a conditional player she has regained her exempt status. This year she once again hovered around ninety on the annual earnings, but finished the season poorly and ended under the cut-off with just under $30,000 in prize money.

She retires after playing ten years.

Molly: Steady

She is a career player, fairly stable on the tour, but not a big winner on the tour over her twelve years. She has never won a tournament but has scored in the top ten in a couple of tournaments. Consistently between 60 and 100 in the year-end ranking on the tour, she has never broken into the top sixty. Lately she has been having trouble making the top ninety. She ended the year around 100.

Three years after this interview, Molly is still chipping and putting for a living.

Nat: Marginal

A sixth-year non-exempt player, she was ranked around 110 at the end of the season. This was her best year. She played in eighteen tournaments and made $15,000. She has lost money or broken even in each of her six years on tour, and did turn a profit for three years on the mini tour. During the year she was interviewed she seem torn between maintaining a relationship with her caddy and breaking even financially.

Nora: Marginal

She joined the tour just before Title IX and the collegiate golf boom increased the quality of the tour. Successfull early on, the tour seems to have passed her by. She struggles, in part, as a result of some personal troubles. She is a divorced, single mother, with minimal support from the father.

Although she finished ranked in the top twenty in the early eighties and won one tournament, she finished out of the top 90 for the next five years and lost her exempt status. She was struggling to get caught up again. The year of the interview she finishes ranked about 110, although she played some good golf at times.

Pam: Marginal

A rookie player, she is struggling this year just to make cuts. She lost her exemption at the end of the year, finishing around 120. She returned the following year and played better. Although she is not a big driver, she has an execptional approach shot, and thus has the potential to become a fixture on the tour.

Pauline: Marginal

One of the few younger players on the tour from a working-class background. She is in her late twenties and she is in her fourth year on tour. She is struggling to stay on the tour. She has been unable to establish a pattern after pregnancy interrupted her play.

So far she has finished 130 or above. The year she was interviewed she improved slightly, ending up around 120.

Roslynn: Steady

This player has been on the tour for about ten years. She has struggled most of the time. She is more than likely to be non-exempt, although early in her career she ranked between 60 and 90 three years in a row. This year she did not play particularly well on the LPGA circuit, but had a very good U.S. Open.

Sara: Marginal

She is a 24-year-old non-exempt rookie. She is another of the growing number of foreign-born, U.S. college-trained players on tour. She is fairly low in the pecking order and does not get in many tournaments. She ended up around 140 in annual earnings and played in about fifteen tournaments. She made less than $5,000. Fortunately, she had a sponsor. But later she was not able to find the backing to come out again.

Sue: Marginal

This interview was with a husband and wife team. They are a young team, in their second year. She does not hit it far, but hits it straight. She will never be great, but stands a chance at difficult courses. Her father is a pro.

She ended up around 140 the year she was interviewed. However, in the next season she began to make some money, finishing 110 and scoring very well at the U.S. Open.

Toni: Great

She joined the tour in the early 1960s and never earned more than $30,000 in one year. But she has won 11 tournaments during her career, the last one in the mid-1970s.

One of the first mothers on tour, she has two children. She has played a limited schedule since the children were born, and continues to play about fifteen tournaments a year. Due to her limited schedule, she has been in the top 90 only once in the last ten years. She finished around 150 the year we talked.

Tara: Great

She ended up 175 on the tour this year and is seriously considering leaving the tour. She has not been in the top ninety in the last five years and realizes she will lose her exempt status soon.

She has been on the tour since the early sixties and is one of the last of her peer group to be playing full time.

Tracy: Great

She is possibly the most respected elder player on the tour. Her best playing days are over, as she is in her late forties/early fifties. She is not a threat to win a tournament but has demonstrated a strong interest in improving the tour. She is an official in the LPGA organization.

Although she finished the year around 100 in annual earnings, her career earnings should keep her status exempt for a few more years.

Val: Marginal

A sixth-year player who is not able to make it on tour. She lost her card early on and has been playing non-exempt for some time. At the time of the interview, she was in the midst of rethinking golf as a career. The year the interview took place was her last year on the tour. She played only a couple of tournaments. She did not earn any money.

APPENDIX B

THE METHODS

In contrast to all the hardships I had heard about doing field research, my experience was both supportive and rewarding. Although I took off after the tour in my pickup truck, equipped with sleeping bag and pad and all the comforts of camping, studying the LPGA proved to be a boon to the quality of my life. I rarely slept in the truck as I generally had friends who took me in for the week. At the tournament site I enjoyed the luxury of a press pass.[1] With access to the press room I usually received three free meals a day, frequently prepared by the host country club's kitchen staff. The press pass, it turned out, was better than most academic grants a social scientist could hope to receive.

Data were fairly easy to acquire and record. At each site I was given a spot at one of the tables reserved for the press. Press tents or rooms came complete with electricity for my computer and phones. In addition, a media staff person was usually on hand to answer technical questions, and introduce me to "gatekeepers" at each tournament site. Most players, caddies, and other folks associated with the tour, were willing participants. No one seemed to mind my doing a study, and I did not feel particularly conspicuous.

The ease and the comfort of the setting was further complemented by the summer sun and lush bucolic settings. When I needed a break from research or transcription, the field site presented itself as free entertainment. I grew to enjoy the drama of a tournament, silently cheering for players who had given me good interviews.

METHODOLOGY

The primary methodological strategy of this study is qualitative sociological research. This type of research has been a major method of data collection for investigations of sport. For example, such sports as little league baseball (Fine, 1987), body building (Klein, 1986), minor league professional hockey (Gallmeier, 1987, 1988), and pool hustling (Polsky, 1969) have been studied by researchers employing qualitative methods. This study is a continuation of that tradition.

I have chosen qualitative methodology for a number of reasons. First, and possibly foremost, I have been trained as a qualitative researcher. As a graduate student in the Sociology Department at Brandeis University I was trained by some of the leading figures in ethnographic research and qualitative methods.[2] This strategy is the one with which I feel most qualified and comfortable. In turn, my expertise in this methodological strategy shapes the sort of study I have undertaken.

I would be skeptical of any exploratory research which attempts to capture the breadth and the complexity of the women's professional golf tour through quantifiable data. To paraphrase Robert Park, it is my belief that to understand a social world a sociologist must spend time in the field with the subjects they intend to study.[3] Particularly, when exploring aspects of society that fall outside the mainstream, a social scientist must stay very close to the selected area of study to limit researcher bias. The data collecting tools of qualitative research, participant observation, "hanging out," and open-ended interviews ensure this sort of proximity.

GROUNDED THEORY

Although I apply a subworld analysis to the LPGA, my intent is not to test theories or definitions of social world. My intention is to capture as completely as possible the everyday life of the tour. I employ a grounded-theory approach which has its roots in the Chicago School that was systematized by Glaser and Strauss (1967), and more recently advanced by Charmaz (1983). Quite simply, grounded theory is the process of generating and constructing theory directly from the data. Grounded theory arises out of the data and provides a way to analyze it. Grounded theory depends on gathering "rich" complex data which can yield explanatory frameworks. Although qualitative methods do not necessitate a grounded-theory approach, grounded theory suggests the employment of qualitative methods which are more apt to produce "rich" data than other methods.

Grounded theory stands in contrast to many conventional practices. For example, rather than identifying the desire to study a subculture first and then choosing women's golf to test the dominant theories and definitions, I chose the site first. Further, in conventional hypothesis testing, only the knowledge and use of one explanatory theory is necessary. The selected theory is usually tested against the findings gathered by the researcher.

In the grounded-theory approach, data collection, analysis, and theory building take place simultaneously. Throughout this process, numerous analytic strategies may present themselves. During data gathering a variety of concepts and theoretical positions can be explored as possible explanatory theories. The task of the researcher is to discover the best frameworks to communicate the reality of the social world under investigation. In this case, a subworld analysis was chosen well after the data had been collected. Prior to settling on subworld, I had toyed with[4] using Merton's notion of deviance (1968) Simmel's notion of the stranger (1950) and a variety of notions of subculture as explanatory tools. The subworld framework, however, is strongly suggested by the data. The very way the players refer to their place as "out here" suggests a separate and distinct sphere within the social world of golf.

CODING AND THEORY BUILDING

Because of the initial open-endedness of this method, one of the primary limitations of grounded theory and qualitative methods is the difficulty of getting a handle on the data. Qualitative researchers "code" data as a way managing it. Coding is the process of labeling, separating, compiling, and organizing the data (Charmaz, 1983). Codes are generally words or phrases which label chunks of data (text) and enable the research to manipulate the data. For this research project I followed the two-step coding style outlined by Charmaz (1983). This process was computer assisted.[5] Through coding, analytical strategies emerge.

The analytical framwork which develops is shaped by the knowledge and talent of the researcher as a social theorist. The broader the knowledge of the researcher, the more explanatory tools he or she has to choose from. One way to facilitate theory building is to surround oneself with "a team" of good thinkers. Throughout this project, I consulted numerous bright sociologists, whose input was invaluable.

THE SAMPLE

The data set consists of 55 interviews, a survey, and observations recorded between May 1988 and August 1989. A total of 60 people affiliated with the LPGA were interviewed. Interviews lasted between 40 minutes and two hours. Most of the interviews were conducted during a tournament week at the site of a tournament. One tournament director was interviewed at her office in the off season.

Professional women golfers make up the majority of the sample. Thirty-one different active players were interviewed. The data sample includes thirty-four interviews with active players. Three of these interviews were follow-up interviews conducted one year after the first interview. Two of the player interviews were ones in which the player and the caddy were interviewed as a team. In addition, two staff members and a caddy interviewed were former professional golfers. In total, thirty-four different active and former professional golfers were interviewed on tape.

In addition to the interviews where both player and caddy were present, eleven individual interviews were conducted specifically with caddies. Two of these caddies were interviewed twice, one year apart. One caddy was interviewed with his partner, who traveled with the tour, but had no formal association with the tour. Three of the caddies were also the life partners of players on tour.

The rest of the interviews include: a player's life partner; seven participants in pro-am tournaments; six individual interviews with LPGA paid staff and local volunteers or staff. In addition, numerous brief conversations were conducted with fans and pro-am participants which were recorded in field notes. One retired player was interviewed over the phone regarding the early history of the tour and that conversation was also recorded in field notes.

PROBLEMS AND SOLUTIONS

Each researcher brings into the setting certain limitations which need to be acknowledged. I was limited in two aspects. First, my sex prohibited me access to the locker room. While the locker room in golf is not as important as it is in team sports or individual sports in which participants begin and end competition together, it does serve as a private space for golfers and thus an excellent setting to collect data. In a setting in which the players "literally rub elbows" with the fans, the locker room serves as a safe haven for tour members. Frequently they will eat their meals and socialize in the locker room.

Second, I was given access to the LPGA tournaments through a press pass. This was both a blessing and a curse. The pass enabled me to enter the setting and facilitated contact with the players. It is rare that an independent sociologist gains access to a major professional sports world. However, the press pass, like a ticket, must be visible while on the course, particularly around the club house where security people are the most prevalent. This is also the area in which initial contact with players is most often made. The players first impression of me was inevitably as a member of the press. Players, I found, are generally "on guard" when dealing with the press and reluctant to reveal aspects of their "private" lives, preferring instead to talk in clichés typical of media-athlete interactions. These pat answers might make for easily consumable media bites and good quotes, which are the press' primary reason for conducting interviews, but they make poor sociology.

These limitations were overcome in a number of ways. Most notable was the fact that one of the players on the tour is a personal friend, Kim Shipman. This connection went a long way to gaining trust (Douglas, 1976) with other players. Players were generally approached to do an interview one week and interviewed the next. I often mentioned my friend Kim or another player I had interviewed when discussing the possibility of doing an interview. Most players would "check me out" by discussing my project with a mutual contact during the week. Only two of the thirty-three active players approached refused to participate in the study.

Invariably many interviews started out with a discussion of how I got to know Kim. We had met in college where I was also a national-caliber athlete, albeit in another sport. The fact that I had experiential knowledge of an elite sport added to my credibility and further distinguished me from the press.

I also found that if I spent time going out and watching the players I planned to interview, they were more open to me during the interview. This action, I suspect, also set me apart from most of the press, who hung around the clubhouse and press room and waited for players to finish their round.

Further, I spent considerable time explaining who I was and how I was conducting this study with each interview participant. Each interviewee signed a release form to indicate that they were willing participants and guaranteed their anonymity. These actions also helped to distinguish me from the press.

Another way I debunked the notion that I was a member of press was by asking questions which were far different from the standard press questions. I rarely asked questions about competition, club selection, and the like. My questions were primarily about tour life. Most players found the interviews to be a pleasant change from answering the same question over and over week after week. Usually players warmed up to the interview as we went along. Most found the process enjoyable.

When it came to collecting field notes unobtrusively and engaging in conversation with fans, however, the identity of press was very helpful. Unlike players, fans were very willing to talk to someone they perceived to be press. More often they approached me rather than other way around. When I introduced myself as a sociologist, fans were less willing to engage in conversation. As a sociologist I was someone with whom they were unfamiliar. They did not know how or were hesitant to interact with me. As long as fans related to me as a member of the press they were more willing to chat.[6]

VALIDITY

Issues of validity and reliability are always a concern for the social scientist. It may be a larger concern in qualitative research where the primary instrument for data analysis is the researcher. A frequently cited weakness of qualitative methods is that they lack "scientific" objectivity and the data is anecdotal. To ensure accuracy I systematically selected a variety of informants and observations. In the case of the players, for example, I interviewed players of diverse ages, rankings, and lifestyles.

The interviews, the primary data set for this study, were structured according to the concerns of the players. In some of my early interviews I simply explained what I was doing and asked what aspect of the tour the player would like to talk about. From the information of these early interviews I was able to design interview questions. As I learned more about the tour from the perspective of a player, I asked more specific questions within this context. By the end of the field research I had developed a fairly broad outline which helped me facilitate the interview. This method of developing questions reduces the personal biases a researcher brings to the field site and produces grounded questions.

To ensure accuracy, all interviews were recorded on tape and transcribed. Then each interview was systematically analyzed and coded. The coded interviews were entered into a computer. This allowed me to group the information according to content, enabling me to identify social patterns and themes the players share. The quotes used throughout this study are not merely anecdotal. They arise out of rigorous and disciplined data analysis, and I believe they are representative of the players' shared experiences.

To ensure validity, a combination of methods were employed in this study. While interview data are the primary source for this research, other methods were employed to corroborate this data. Mixing strategies of data gathering minimizes the chance of systematic bias (Douglas, 1976; Conrad, 1976). In addition to interview data, I also took extensive field notes. A good part of any day was spent mingling with fans, volunteers, and caddies, engaging in conversations, and observing the everyday life as it evolved. These conversations and observations were recorded as field notes, usually at the end of the day.

As further confirmation of the interview data I conducted a short written survey. This survey was designed as a check of the interview data and to gather some specific information about the background of the golfers. It was conducted during my last week out on tour. Of the 140 surveys distributed to the players, 58 were returned, a response rate of 41 percent.

Given the breadth and depth of the data and the rigor with which it was analyzed, I am confident of the validity of this research.

LIMITATIONS OF THIS STUDY

This research is limited in scope. I do not pretend to cover all aspects of the tour. In particular, this study is not a study of competitive golf. Although playing golf is the central concern of the players on the tour, it is not a primary concern of this study. Readers hoping to discover the players' grips, club selections, and player-caddy conversations will be sorely disappointed. The world inside the ropes was not accessible to me, nor would I have had the knowledge to differentiate between what was critical to performance and what was, say, a nervous habit.

Further, this study does not focus on what players do when they are away from the tour. This is a constraint of the setting—the tournament site. Players live in all areas of the country and the world. Exploring their lives off the tour was impractical and unfeasible. These two social realms; inside the ropes and off the road would need to be included in a complete study of professional golfers' lives.

This study, however, does focus on life on the tour and presents a sociological analysis of the social relations within the Ladies' Professional Golf Tour at tournament sites. In sum, this study is best seen as a preliminary ethnographic investigation into the subworld of professional women's golf.

APPENDIX C

Intergenerational Class and Occupational Mobility
of Professional Women Golfers' Families, 1989

Age	Public Course	Socio-Economic Assess-ment	Working Class	Middle Class	Upper Class	Change
19	N	M - M		PGF/M	F	+
21	N	M - U		M/F	PGF	+
23	Y	——		PGF	F	+
23	N	M - M		PGF/M	F	+
23	N	L - M	PGF	F		+
23	N	M - M	PGF	M/F		+
24	N	M - M		PGF/M/F		=
24	N	M - M			PGF/F	=
24	N	M - M			PGF/F	=
24	N	L - M	PGF		F	+
25	N	M - M		PGF	F	+
25	Y	M - M		PGF/F		=
26	N	M - M		MGF	F	+
26	N	M - M		PGF/F		=
26	N	LM - M		PGF/M	F	+
26	N	L - M	PGF	F		+
27	N	M - M			PGF/F	=
27	N	L - U	PGF		F	+
28	Y	L - M	F	PGM/M		+
28	N	M - M	PGF	F		+
28	N	M - M			PGF/F	=
28	N	M - UM		PGF	F	+
29	N	M - M	MGF	F		+

(continued on next page)

Age	Public Course	Socio-Economic Assessment	Working Class	Middle Class	Upper Class	Change
29	Y	M - M		PGF	F	+
29	N	M - M		PGF/F		=
29	N	L - M		PGF	F	+
29	N	L - M	PGF		F	+
29	N	L - M	PGF	F		+
29	Y	M - M		PGF/F		=
29	N	LM - M	PGF		F	+
30	Y	L - M	MGF	M		+
30	N	U - U			PGF/F	=
30	N	M - M		PGF/F		=
30	N	M - U			PGF/F	+
31	N	M - M			PGF/F	=
31	N	L - M	PGF	F		+
31	N	M - U	MGF		F	+
31	N	L - M	PGF		F	+
31	N	M - M		PGF/M	F	+
33	Y	L - M		PGF/M/F		+
34	N	L - M		PGF	F	+
36	Y	L - M	PGF	M/F		+
37	Y	L - L	MGF/F			=
38	N	M - M			PGF/F	=
38	N	M - U		PGF	F	+
39	Y	L - M	PGF	F		+
39	N	LM - M	PGF	F		+
39	N	M - M		PGF	F	+
40	N	L - M	PGF		F	+
48	Y	M - LM		PGF/F		-
49	N	M - M	PGF	F		+

Age = Age of player when surveyed
Public = Type of training facility as a youth
    N = private   Y = public
Socio-Economic Assessment = the player's assessment of class mobility from paternal grandparents to her family when she was a child*
Class = Assessment of parents' and paternal grandfather's occupations*

F = Player's father   M = Player's mother   PGF = Player's father's father
PGM = Player's father's mother   MGF = Player's mother's father

Change = Overall assessment of intergenerational mobility

*Note: Maternal grandfather was used when paternal grandfather was not applicable.

NOTES

INTRODUCTION

1. By subworld I mean a segment of a social world. David Unruh (1983) defines a social world as a large and highly permeable social organization made up of people sharing common interests. Golf is one social object around which a social world has developed. The LPGA is a world within that world.

2. The average earnings from winnings of players competing in seventeen or more tournaments in 1989 was over $64,000. The median income from winnings was just over $35,000. These figures are based on final rankings for the year 1989 compiled by the LPGA. Players' total gross earnings were actually more as a result of income brought in from endorsements, clinics, and private pro-ams. The average income of women in the United States between the ages of 24-35 who were employed full time and college graduates was $24,688 in 1989. (*Statistical Abstract of the United States, 1991*, table no. 740)

1. OUT HERE

1. Tara is a pseudonym for a player on tour interviewed for this study. All the players interviewed for this study did so under the assumption that their identity would not be revealed. In addition to the names, dates, places, and other data that might reveal a player's identity have been changed, but not to the point of misrepresenting the reality of the tour. For a complete list of players interviewed, see appendix A.

2. See Graffis, *The PGA: The Official History of the Professional Golfers' Association of America*, p. 29.

3. See Polsky, *Hustlers, Beats and Others*.

4. See Adelman, *A Sporting Time*.

5. Green, *Fit for America: Health, Fitness and Sport in American Society*, pp. 154-55

6. Green, *Fit for America*, pp. 151-52.

7. See Graffis, *The PGA*, pp. 40-42.

8. See Kimmel "Baseball and the Reconstitiution of American Masculinity" and Mary P. Ryan, *Womenhood in America*.

9. See Green, *Fit For America*; Barbara Ehrenreich and Deirdre English, *For Her Own Good*.

10. See Kimmel,"Baseball and the Reconstitiution of American Masculinity"; Adelman, *A Sporting Time*; Lorber, "Believing Is Seeing: Biology as Ideology."

11. See Chambliss, "The Mundanity of Excellence: An Ethnographic Report on Stratification and Olympic Swimmers."

12. In 1956, Beverly Hanson was ranked 10th on the tour with a per-round average of 76.4. In 1974 a per-round average of 76.4 garnered a top 40 ranking. A top 120 finish in the 1987 annual rankings (the minimum to retain membership on the tour) required a player to average 75 per round or better. In 1993, the per-round average of the 120th ranked player was 73.8. Granted, some of this improvement can be explained by improved quality in the courses played. However, most of it has to do with the improved play and depth of the tour.

2. OUTSIDERS INSIDE THE TOURNAMENT

1. Fred Corcoran, *Unplayable Lies*.

2. Graffis, *The PGA*, p. 91.

3. Graffis, *The PGA*.

4. Betty Hicks, "Next to Marriage We'll Take Golf," p. 94

5. See Corcoran, *Unplayable Lies*, p. 246

6. Early professionals made money via gambling and giving exhibitions. Professionals began to endorse manufacturers as early as 1901 with the introduction of the Vardon woods and irons manufactured by Spalding Sporting Goods. These products were named after a British champion, Harry Vardon. Shortly thereafter, US Rubber's golf ball division signed Walter Hagen to promote golf balls. Wilson and Spalding soon thereafter corraled professionals into "advisory boards" with free equipment, a small salary, and bonuses for victorious play, in exchange for public endorsements. See Graffis, *The PGA*, pp. 61-65.

7. The importance of the connection between manufacturers and sports is a crucial yet underexaminined aspect of the development of sport. See Stephen

Hardy, "'Adopted by all the Leading Clubs': Sporting Goods and the Shaping of Leisure, 1800-1900," in *For Fun and Profit*, ed. R. Butsch (Philadephia: Temple University Press, 1990), pp. 71-101. For golf-specific information, see Graffis, *The PGA*, chapter 4.

8. Corcoran, *Unplayable Lies*, chapter 5

9. Ibid., chapter 13 and Betty Hicks, Personal Correspondence, 1956, LPGA Archives.

10. Corcoran, *Unplayable Lies*, p. 60.

11 Graffis, *The PGA*, p. 233

12 Graffis, *The PGA*, pp. 126-27, gives Crosby primary credit for the creation of the modern tournament, and downplays Corcoran's contributions, most likely as a result of his friendship with Bob Harlow. Nonetheless, Graffis details the advantages of the celebrity pro-am tournament and locates it as the roots of the contemporary tournament.

13. Mills, *The Power Elite*, pp. 71-95.

14. Weber, *The Theory of Social and Economic Organizations*.

15. Mill, *The Power Eilte*, p. 74.

16. Corcoran, *Unplayable Lies*, chapter 13.

17. Graffis, *The PGA*, p. 355

18. For a detailed discussion of the difficulties women's sports faced, see Susan Cahn's *Coming on Strong: Gender and Sexuality in Twentith-Century Women's Sport*; see also, Lenskyj, *Out of Bounds: Women, Sport and Sexuality*.

3. RADICALS AMONG THE POWER ELITE

1. Much of the information for this section comes from letters found in the archives of the LPGA. The three most helpful letters for piecing together the early years of the tour are from Lois Hayhurst (1958), Fred Corcoran (1974), and Betty Hicks (1956), all written in response to requests from the LPGA for historical information. This record of the difficult transition from the WPGA to the LPGA stands in contrast to "official" LPGA literature.

2. Lois Hayhurst says as much in her 1958 letter, and Hicks indicates that PGA golf promoter Bob Harlow noted to a friend in 1940 that professional women's golf was possible following Berg's national amateur victory. See also Nancy Theberge's dissertation "An Occupational Analysis of Women's Professional Golf," pp. 33-38.

3. Hicks, Personal Correspondence to LPGA, 1956, LPGA Archives.

4. Ibid.

5. Ibid.; Graffis, *The PGA*, p. 241.

6. Hicks, Personal Correspondence to LPGA, 1956, LPGA Archives.

7. Ibid.

8. Hicks recalls that no one took minutes of meetings in those early years.

9. For a discussion of these practices, see Clack, *Ladies Professional Golf Association*; Graffis, *The PGA*, pp. 61-65.

10. It is not clear when this change took place, but Hicks names herself as the first president, and in 1950 *Sport Magazine*, November 1950 refers to Dettweiler as the former president of the WPGA.

11. Again the records are a bit fuzzy as to how many tournaments she won in a row. See Theberge, "An Occupational Analysis of Women's Professional Golf," p. 33, for a discussion.

12. Corcoran, *Unplayable Lies*, p. 178.

13. Betty Hicks, "The Ladies of the Fairway Circus," *Sport Magazine*, November 1950, pp. 44-45 and 91-92.

14. Corcoran, *Unplayable Lies*, chapter 13; Graffis, *The PGA*, pp. 207-8.

15. Corcoran, *Unplayable Lies*; Hicks, *Sport Magazine*, November 1950, pp. 44-45.

16. Hicks, Personal Correspondence to LPGA, 1956, LPGA Archives.

17. Corcoran, Personal Correpondence to the LPGA, 1974, LPGA Archives, and *Unplayable Lies*, chapter 13.

18. Corcoran, Personal Correspondence to the LPGA, 1974, LPGA Archives.

19. Hicks, *Sport Magazine*, November 1950, p. 91.

20. Ibid.

21. *Golf World*, 15 November 1950.

22. Corcoran, Personal Correspondence to the LPGA, 1974, LPGA Archives.

23. Corcoran, *Unplayable Lies*, p. 172

24. It appears that Hayhurst's 1958 account was used as the basis for the LPGA's public relations material throughout the sixties.

25. Personal communication with Berg, January 1989.

26. In the late 1800s a similar tension arose between the players and the owners/manufacturers in American baseball. Led by lawyer and fellow ballplayer John M. Ward, the players started their own league. Albert Spalding, owner and sporting goods manufacturer, ultimately crushed the player revolt. See David Q. Voigt, *American Baseball: From Gentleman's Sport to the Commissioner System*, for details.

27. See Gregory Stone's classic article "American Sports: Play and Display."

28 See Ryan, *Womanhood in America.*

29. After a 1953 operation, Didrikson returned to the tour. She won the 1954 USGA-sponsored U.S. Open and continued to play a leadership role in the LPGA over the next two years. She died in 1956.

30. Betty Hicks, "Next to Marraige We'll Take Golf," p. 92.

31. I found the memo in the LPGA Archives. Unfortunately, the by-laws were no longer attached.

32. LPGA 1989 Media Guide.

33. Wright played in only eleven tournaments in 1965. Through the last half of the sixtiess she played an abbreviated schedule, and only sporadically after 1969.

34. Clack, *Ladies Professional Golf Association.*

35. Ibid.

36. The statistics for Baugh, Stephenson, and Lopez were compiled by the author from LPGA media guides.

37. Clack, *Ladies Professional Golf Association.*

38. This information is based primarily on interview data, particularly interviews with Ethel, who was a player representative in the early eighties.

39. The leadership of the LPGA are part of what G. Willaim Domhoff calls a "network of interlocking directorates," a group of powerful and wealthy individuals with overlapping duties and social lives. See Domhoff, *The Powers That Be.*

4. GETTING IN AND STAYING OUT

1. A small but significant number of LPGA professionals are the offspring of teaching professionals.

2. Similar mentoring relationships in the developmental stage of athletes have been found in other sports. These coaches are not necessarily the most

knowledgeable technicians, but caring parental figures who share their love of the game with young athletes. Carlson and Engstrom in their study of high-ranking Swedish male junior tennis players found that those who developed into touring professionals developed their basic skills under the guidance of a nurturing mentor. Access to court time was liberal and casual. Parental pressure was minimal, and the athletes generally chose the sport themselves. The elite Swedish tennis players experience mirrors that of the LPGA professionals. See Carlson and Engstrom, "The Swedish Tennis Wonder of the 80s: An Analysis of the Players' Background and Development."

3. In the years prior to 1970, to join the LPGA, a woman simply declared herself a professional and paid the entry fee and played in tournaments. If she played reasonably well, placing in the top two-thirds of the field, she became a member of the LPGA.

4. The number fluctuates on account of players tying for the final opening at qualifying school.

5. Exempt players are less likely to skip a major tournament and very few spots are available for conditional players in these tournaments.

6. It also increases the likelihood that the outcome of the tournament will not be known until the last players have finished. This heightens the drama and keeps spectators interested as long as possible.

7. This experience is not unique to golf. For athletes competing on the elite level, sport is experienced as a rather everyday and mundane activity. See Chambliss, "The Mundanity of Excellence."

8. Of the players surveyed claiming pro-ams as their primary means of income, all earned less than $10,000 from competition golf and all were age 30 or over and averaged nine years on the tour.

9. The majority of LPGA players don't play their best golf until they are 28 or older.

10. 88% of the sample (n=50) claimed endorsements accounted for 20% or less of their annual income. 19 = 0%, 24 = 20% or less, 6 = 20% to 50%, 1 = 50% or more. These findings do not vary significantly from those of Theberge, "The System of Rewards in Women's Professional Golf," p. 30.

11. In her 1975 research, Theberge discovered a similar emphasis on non-monetary rewards. See Theberge, "The System of Rewards in Women's Professional Golf."

5. DOING GENDER AND THE PROWESS ETHIC

1. For further discussion on this point, see Fields, "Slavery, Race and Ideology in the United States of America."

2. There are a number of studies which illustrate the connections between masculinity and sport, including Goffman, *The Presentation of Self in Everyday Life*; Veblen, *The Theory of the Leisure Class*; Lenskyj, *Out of Bounds*; Messner, *Power at Play*; Adelman, *A Sporting Time*; and *Men, Sport and the Gender Order*, a fine collection of essays edited by Messner and Sabo.

3. The beginning of the industrial period is usually cited as around 1750 in England, and the beginning of modern sport is usually considered to be around 1850. The ideological battles to which I am referring seem to have been most heated during the last three decades of the 1800s in the United States. See Adelman, *A Sporting Time* for a more complete discussion of modernity, sport, and the development of masculine ideology.

4. See Fields, "Slavery, Race and Ideology in the United States of America."

5. See Lorber, "Believing Is Seeing: Biology as Ideology."

6. Ibid.

7. See Michel Foucault, *The History of Sexuality*.

8. See Carol Smith-Rosenberg, *Disorderly Conduct*; Adelman, *A Sporting Time*; and Kimmel, "Baseball and the Reconstitution of American Masculinty, 1880-1920."

9. See Lenskyj, *Out of Bounds*; Carol Smith-Rosenberg and Charles Rosenberg, "The Female Animal: Medical and Biological Views of Women and the Role in Nineteenth-century America."

10. See Mrozek, "The Amazon and the American 'Lady': Sexual Fears of Women as Athletes"; Susan Kahn, *Coming on Strong*.

11. See West and Zimmerman, "Doing Gender," pp. 125-27.

12. Ibid., p. 136

13. For seminal discussions of the social construction of gender, see Goffman, "The Arrangement between the Sexes" and *The Presentation of Self in Everyday Life*; Lorber, "Believing Is Seeing: Biology as Ideology"; Connell, *Gender and Power*; West and Zimmerman, "Doing Gender."

14. This finding confirms the findings of Theberge "An Occupational Analysis of Women's Professional Golf." This ability of women athletes to manage a feminine identity seems to cut across all sports; see Sabo, "Psychological Impacts of Athletic Participation on American Women: Facts and Fables," and Duff and Hong, "Self-Images and Women Body-Builders."

15. Connell, *Gender and Power*.

16. These comments from the players confirm Thorne's (*Gender Play*)

speculation that integrated play in childhood will have lasting and signficant impact on children's "sense of the possible."

17. Lorber, in her study of women physicans, notes a similar double bind. See Judith Lorber, *Women Physicians*, p. 41; West and Zimmerman, "Doing Gender."

18. Brownmiller, *Femininity*.

19. Sexy is a social construct that expresses heterosexuality and femininity.

20. Eitzen and Zinn, "The De-Athleticization of Women: The Naming and Gender-Marking of Collegiate Sport Teams."

21. For further discussion of women athletes and display of heterosexual femininity, see Duncan, "Sports Photographs and Sexual Difference: Images of Women and Men in the 1984 and 1988 Olympic Games."

22. See Brownmiller, *Femininity*, pp. 219-31.

23. See Corcoran, *Unplayable Lies*, chapter 13 for a more detailed discussion of the event.

24. MacKinnon, *Feminism Unmodified*, p. 50 actually dissolves the distinction between sexuality and gender.

25. West and Zimmerman "Doing Gender," p. 145.

26. "Tomboy" is so pervasive that it normalizes athletic activity for girls, yet continues to carry a stigma with it. As such it constitutes a type of positive deviance discussed in Matza, *Delinquency and Drift*. Recent studies of children indicate that the label "tomboy" is losing favor and may indicate that athletic prowess for girls is less deviant. See Thorne, *Gender Play*, p. 115.

27. West and Zimmerman, "Doing Gender."

28. See Kidd, "The Men's Cultural Centre: Sports and the Dynamic of Women's Oppression/Men's Repression."

29. Bryson, "Sport and the Maintenance of Masculine Hegemony."

30. Ibid.

31. Chambliss has argued that talent fails as an explanation for athletic success, on conceptual grounds. To use talent as a means of explaining performance is to resort to a tautology. The action of performing is reified, and we call it talent. Further, it mystifies excellence, subsuming a complex set of discrete actions behind a single undifferentiated concept. As compelling as Chambliss' arguments are, the players understand themselves as having talent. See Chambliss "The Mundanity of Excellence."

32. What is particularly interesting about such statements is that the judgment involved is the assesment of talent. In "The Mundanity of Excellence," Chambliss notes that athletes are rarely recognized as having talent until they have achieved some success. Therefore, the player with a flash of success is more likely to have her character questioned than a player who struggles, but works hard, to keep her card.

33. Prerequisites for membership into the Hall of Fame are that a player must have been a member in good standing for ten consecutive years and have won at least 30 official events, including two different major championships, or have won 35 official events with one major title, or have won 40 official events.

34. See Messner, *Power at Play*, for a complete discussion of the dilemmas retired male athletes face.

6. THE PROWESS ETHIC AND THE PARENT CULTURE

1. The socio-occupational scale used is from Bourdieu, *Distinctions*, pp. 526-45. See appendix for details.

2. Paternal grandfathers were used except when none were listed, in these cases the maternal grandfather was used as an index of class mobility.

3. Bourdieu, *Distinctions*.

4. Details can be found in Karen, "Achievement and Ascription in Admission to an Elite College: A Political-Organization Analysis." Sport as middle-class culture is not new. It has a long history. In his historical exploration of sports in New York City, Adelman (*A Sporting Time*) notes that it was not the upper-class social clubs, which are often given credit, that acted as the primary catalysts for the development of baseball, but clubs made up of the upwardly mobile middle-class men.

5. See Aldrich, *Old Money: The Mythology of America's Upper Class.*

6. Sportsmanship does seem to differ from prowess in that sportsmanship is used to delineate and enforce class distinctions and prowess is used for the individual to stand out on her own with less emphasis on class or social group.

7. Aldrich, *Old Money*, p. 100.

8. Bourdieu, *Distinctions*, p. 388.

9. Sennet and Cobb, *The Hidden Injuries of Class.*

10. Aldrich, *Old Money*.

11. Weber, *The Protestant Ethic and the Spirit of Capitalism.*

7. THE IMAGE MAKERS

1. See Fine, *With the Boys*; West and Zimmerman, "Doing Gender"; Byson, "Sport and the Maintenance of Masculine Hegemony."

2. See West and Zimmerman, "Doing Gender," p. 146.

3. See Bryson, "Sport and the Maintenance of Masculine Hegemony"; Duncan and Messner, "Gender Stereotyping in Televised Sports"; Duncan and Hasbrook, "Denial of Power in Televised Sports"; Duncan, "Sports Photographs and Sexual Difference: Images of Women and Men in the 1984 and 1988 Olympic Games."

4. See Coakley, *Sport in Society: Issues and Controversies*, pp. 330-56.

5. Nelson, *Are We Winning Yet*, pp. 148-49.

6. Similar observations are made by Nelson, *Are We Winning Yet*, pp. 132-54.

7. There are several male sexual fantasies common in popular culture from which the tour can draw: groups of women without male control (women in prison, all-female high schools, and convents), women traveling alone (the female hitchhiker, the young widow), and highly successful women whose career ambitions represents a misdirected or repressed desire for a man.

8. Lack of player attendance at such events may be changing. New rules require that players attend a certain number of social events each year.

8. INTERPERSONAL RELATIONS ON THE TOUR

1. Even if other players are around, it is likely that they will not be able to celebrate fully or share in the victor's happiness as it represents their loss.

2. For a detailed discussion of emotion management and emotional labor, see Hochschild, *The Managed Heart*.

3. The seventies can be viewed as a period of transformation. The Blalock affair in the early seventies marked the beginning of the transformation, which culminated with the emergence of Nancy Lopez as a public figure around 1980. As discussed in chapter 3, Jane Blalock, a rising star of the tour, was caught cheating and was barred from the game by her peers. The punitive measure imposed by the LPGA members against Blalock, loss of status by separating her from her craft, hints at how player saw themselves and their work. This type of punishment, loss of status, is most often associated with "generative work" (see Margolis, "Considering Women's Experience"), such as motherhood or medicine. Professional golf requires a certain professional ethic, which the players felt Blalock failed to uphold.

Blalock sued the LPGA and won. In contrast to the players, the court viewed golf as a product to be sold and consumed, professional golf an occupation, and the golfer an independent business person. While the court did not exonerate Blalock of cheating, the court ruled in favor of Blalock, arguing that she could not be denied access to making a living by her competitors.

4. I have in mind here Durkheim's notion of excessive individualsim, found in *Suicide*.

5. For a discussion of transcendence of self through achievement, see Sennett and Cobb, *Hidden Injuries of Class*.

6. Theberge discusses this uncertainty of LPGA tour life in her dissertation "An Occupational Analysis of Women's Professional Golf."

7. Durkheim, *Suicide*; Giddens, *The Consequences of Modernity*, p. 121.

8. Durkheim, *Suicide*, p. 210.

9. Giddens, *The Consequences of Modernity*, p. 120.

10. Ibid., p. 119.

11. As Theberge ("An Occupational Analysis of Women's Professional Golf") notes, player demands on caddies vary. Some players would prefer not to have caddies at all, or view the caddies' primary function to carry the bag. Others rely heavily on the caddies' technical advice. I found most players' expectation of their caddy falls somewhere in between these two extremes.

12. There are a few but significant number of caddies who are also family members, or current lovers. This transforms the player/caddy relationship from paid labor to unpaid, fixing the establishment of trust within the norms and mores of family.

13. See, for example, "Gender Differences in Friendship Formation" in Rubin, *Just Friends*, and the discussion of emotion work, in Hochschild, *The Managed Heart*, pp. 162-70.

14. Rubin, *Just Friends*.

15. M. Greenspan, "The Fear of Being Alone: Female Psychology and Women's Work"; Rubin, *Just Friends*, pp. 63-65.

16. Kanter, *Men and Women of the Corporation*, pp. 101-3.

17. Fienstein, *Hard Courts*.

18. Rubin, *Just Friends*, p. 81.

19. J. Lever, "Sex Differences in the Games Children Play," *Social Problems* 23 (1976): 478-87; Gilligan, *In a Different Voice*. See also Thorne's discussion of the management of meaning of competition when girls play in *Gender Play*, pp. 105-6.

20. Rubin, *Just Friends*, pp. 85-86.

21. Hochschild, *The Managed Heart*, pp. 167-69.

22. Ibid.

23. See bell hooks, *Feminist Theory: From the Margin to the Center*, pp. 85-93.

24. I am obviously not the first to make this point. For a discussion of professional women, see also Gordon, *Prisoners of Men's Dreams*, and see the conclusion of Lorber, *Women Physicians*. See also Margolis, "Considering Women's Experience" and her discussion of women in service positions.

9. FANS, STATUS, AND THE GIFT OF GOLF

1. Mauss, *The Gift*, p. 45.

2. Margolis, "Considering Women's Experience."

3. Hyde, *The Gift: Imagination and the Erotic Life of Property*. See also A. Klein's discussion of the feudal economy of bodybuilding in *Little Big Men*.

4. Ibid., p. xii.

5. For further discussion of generative power, see Margolis, "Considering Women's Experience," pp. 404-6.

6. Hyde, *The Gift: Imagination and the Erotic Life of Property*, pp. 57-73.

7. Caplow, "Rule Enforcement without Visible Means: Christmas Gift Giving in Middletown," p. 1307.

8. Ibid., pp. 1320-22.

9. Margolis, "Considering Women's Experience," p. 395.

10. Blalock, as was discussed earlier, appealed the ruling in terms of the punishment which impacted her ablity to compete in the market. For comparison of justice within the exchange market and status orders, see Jacobs, *Systems of Survival* (1992), or D. Margolis, "Considering Women's Experience."

11. Mauss, *The Gift*, pp. 1-18.

12. Mills, *Power Elite*, pp. 71-93.

13. Ibid., pp. 71-72.

14. Ibid., p. 72.

15. Margolis, "Considering Women's Experience," p. 405.

16. Hochshild, *The Managed Heart*, pp. 162-84.

17. Margolis, "Considering Women's Experience," pp. 398-99, and Hochshild, *The Managed Heart*, pp. 162-81.

10. THE CORPORATE IMAGE

1. Clack, *Ladies Professional Golf Association*.

2. Diaz, "Find the Golf Here?," p. 60.

3. Memorandum dated July 1985, LPGA Archives.

4. Standards adopted by the Better Business Bureau's Philanthropic Advisory Service suggests "that fundraising costs should not exceed 35 percent of related contributions. Total fundraising and administrative cost should not exceed 50 percent of total income." Moore and Williams, "Setting Standards for Non-Profits."

5. Hodgkinson and Weitzman, *Giving and Volunteering*, p. 36.

6. I am grateful to Susan Ostrander for this observation.

7. Duncan and Messner, "Gender Stereotyping in Televised Sports"; Duncan and Hasbrook, "Denial of Power in Televised Sports"; Duncan, "Sports Photographs and Sexual Difference: Images of Women and Men in the 1984 and 1988 Olympic Games."

8. For example, see Goldstein, "Babes in Tourland," and Pastena, "Pros in Paradise."

9. Goffman, *Stigma: Notes on the Management of Spoiled Identity*.

10. For a critical discussion of the interconnections between sport and the political industrial elite, see Sage, *Power and Ideology in American Sport*.

11. PROWESS AND TRANSFORMATION

1. See Morgan, "'Radical' Social Theory of Sport: A Critique and a Conceptual Emendation."

2. See Bloch, "Everyday Life, Sensuality and Body Culture"; Heikkala, "Discipline and Excel: Techniques of the Self and the Body and the Logic of Competing."

3. James, *Beyond a Boundary*. James is political theorist and essayist and, in his youth, was an accomplished cricket player. He writes: "My Puritan soul

burnt with indignation at injustice in the sphere of sport. Cricket had plunged me into politics long before I was aware of it. When I did turn to politics I did not have too much to learn" (p. 71).

4. For a general discussion of culture/meaning radiating inward onto a subgroup as well as outward, see Willis, *Common Culture*. For sport-specific discussion, see Bloch "Everyday Life, Sensuality and Body Culture"; Blinde, Taub, and Han, "Sport Participation and Women's Personal Empowerment: Experience of the College Athlete"; and for a broad theoretical discussion which incorporates the body, see Theberge, "Sport and Women's Empowerment," and MacKinnon, *Feminism Unmodified*.

5. Polsky, *Hustlers, Beats and Others*.

6. Willis, *Profane Culture*.

7. Ibid.

8. Thorne, *Gender Play*, pp. 129-31.

9. Ibid., p. 133.

10. Duncan, "Sport Photographs and Sexual Difference"; Duncan and Hasbrook, "Denial of Power in Televised Women's Sports."

12. FEMINISM AND THE TOUR

1. See O'Donnell, "Look Who's No Longer Missing the Links," p. 68.

2. For a discussion of the legal tactics employed by recreational golfers, see Kehoe, "Getting Equal."

3. For a general discussion of ideology, see Fields, "Slavery, Race and Ideology." For a discussion of gender, ideology, and sport, see Messner, "Sports and Male Domination."

4. See Lenskyj, *Out of Bounds*.

5. The later work of Foucault is dedicated to exploring how the body and the regulation of it became central in modern society. See, in particular, *The History of Sexuality*, vol. 1.

6. See Margolis, "Considering Women's Experience."

7. For discussions of the justification of the dominance via biological or racial explanation as a product of the modern era, see Smith-Rosenberg, *Disorderly Conduct*; Lorber, "Believing Is Seeing: Biology as Ideology"; and Fields, "Slavery, Race and Ideology."

8. See, for example, the discussion in Fields, "Slavery, Race and Ideology."

9. For a discussion of the social meaning of sport and the impact of women's increasing participation on men and male identity, see Kidd, "Men's Cultural Centre: Sports and the Dynamic of Women's Oppression/Men's Repression."

10. Messner, "Sports and Male Dominations: The Female Athlete as Contested Ideological Terrain."

11. James, *Beyond a Boundary*; Klein, *Sugarball*; Lever, *Soccer Madness*; Foley, "The Great American Football Ritual: Reproducing Race, Class and Gender Inequality"; Messner, "Sports and Male Domination: The Female Athlete as Contested Ideological Terrain"; Lenskyj, "Female Sexuality and Women's Sport."

12. Lenskyj, *Out of Bounds*.

13. Duncan, "Sports Photographs and Sexual Difference."

14. See, for example, Messner, *Power at Play*; Duncan and Hasbrook, "Denial of Power in Televised Women's Sports"; Bryson, "Sport and the Maintenance of Masculine Hegemony"; Eitzen and Zinn, "The De-Athleticization of Women: The Naming and Gender Marking of Collegiate Sport Teams."

15. Friedan, *The Feminine Mystique*.

16. MacKinnon, *Feminism Unmodified*.

17. See, Bennett et al., "Changing the Rules of the Game: Reflections Toward a Feminist Analysis of Sport."

18. Blinde, Taub, and Han, "Sport as a Site for Women's Group and Societal Empowerment: Perspectives from the College Athlete"; Cahn, *Coming on Strong*, discusses the lack of connection between women athletes and feminist leadership in sport (pp. 259-61).

19. Willis, "Women in Sport in Ideology."

13. CLASS, RACE, AND THE INCREASING EXCLUSIVITY OF THE TOUR

1. See, for example, Page, "The World of Sport and Its Study."

2. Gerson, *Hard Choices*, pp. 9-22.

3. Parents' occupations in this group included, laborer, mason, and logger, occupations not typically associated with the golfing set.

4. The break at five years is not arbitrary. Total training time prior to entering the tour is about eight years, four in college, and four prior to college. Those players who have been on the tour for five years or less took up the game of golf in the late seventies and eighties and were influenced by the collegiate sporting boom, Title IX, Nancy Lopez, and standardization of professional women's golf.

5. National Golf Foundation, *1988 Golf Participation in the United States.*

6. Sweda, "Foreign Powers."

7. Ashe, *Hard Road to Glory.*

8. Petersen, *Only the Ball Was White.*

9. Staple, "Where are the Black Fans?"

14. GENDER EQUALITY AND THE LPGA

1. See, for example, Lorber, *Women Physicians.*

2. See Connell's discussion of "Liberated Zones" in *Gender and Power.*

3. See Lorber, *Women Physicians.* The concern here seemed to be about how to climb the career ladder within an old boy network. In William's 1989 study of male nurses and women in the military, gender-identity maintenance seemed a primary concern. In both cases, the researcher's attention is drawn to how the gender order is reproduced on the job.

4. See Walby, "Theorising Patriarchy" for a discussion of the various structures which make up patriarchy and the need for multiple and persistent challenges to the gender order.

5. For a general discussion of the adaptation to the latest wave of feminism, see Faludi, *Blacklash.* For a discussion of the adoption to the increase in women athletes, see Bryson, "Sport and the Maintenance of Masculine Hegemony."

6. Acker, "Heirarchies, Jobs, Bodies: A Theory of Gendered Organizations."

7. Gerson, *Hard Choices* and Gordon, *Prisoners of Men's Dreams.*

8. See Adleman, *A Sporting Time.*

9. Lober, *Women Physicians*; Lorber, "Dismantling Noah's Ark."

10. Morgan, "'Radical' Social Theory of Sport: A Critique and a Conceptual Emendation."

11. Chambliss, "The Mundanity of Excellence," argues that excellence has much less to do with talent than the habitual practice of small skills and activities. Framed in this manner, with less emphasis on talent or biology, athletic excellence would seem to be even more subversive.

12. Ibid.

13. Ibid.

14. Messner, *Power at Play*, p. 169.

15. Lenskyj, *Out of Bounds* and Cahn, *Coming on Strong*.

APPENDIX B: THE METHODS

1. The LPGA granted my formal request for a press pass. After a couple of tournaments I became something of a regular fixture on the tour and entry to a press room did not go through formal channels. I would just show up at the tournament and the LPGA media staff would confirm my identity and purpose to local volunteers. I would be handed a press pass.

2. The methods course taught by Shulamit Reinharz was influential in this regard. Reinharz' book *On Becoming a Social Scientist* (1979) frames the Brandeis philosophy (if there is such a thing) data collection and theory building. This approach was nurtured by lively discussion with fellow graduate students, in particular, Joan Alway and Jim Ptacek.

3. The actual phase is "Get your hands dirty with real research."

4. In Charmaz' terms, "wrote memo's."

5. I used FYI 3000 Plus software from FYI Inc.

6. The fans have an impression that the press has influence over the sport. Fans often expressed how they would change things about the tour.

BIBLIOGRAPHY

Acker, Joan. 1991. "Hierarchies, Jobs, Bodies: A Theory of Gendered Organizations." In J. Lorber and S. A. Farrell (eds.), *The Social Construction of Gender.*

Adelman, Melvin L. 1986. *A Sporting Time.* Urbana: University of Illinois Press.

Aldrich, Nelson W. Jr. 1989. *Old Money: The Mythology of America's Upper Class.* New York: Vintage Books.

Ashe, Arthur. 1988. *A Hard Road to Glory: A History of the African-American Athlete.* Westport, CN: Greenwood Press.

Bennett, Roberta S., Whitaker, K. Gail, Woolley Smith, Nina Jo, and Sablove, Anne. 1987. "Changing the Rules of the Game: Reflections Toward a Feminist Analysis of Sport." *Women's Studies International Forum,* 10(4):369-79.

Blinde, Elaine M. and Taub, Diane. 1993. "Sport Participation and Women's Personal Empowerment: Expereinces of the College Athlete." *Journal of Sport and Social Issues* 17(1).

Blinde, Elaine M., Taub, Diane and Han, Lingling. 1994. "Sport as a Site for Women's Group and Societal Empowerment: Perspectives from the College Athlete." *Sociology of Sport Journal* 11(1):51-59.

Bloch, Charlotte. 1987. "Everyday Life, Sensuality and Body Culture." *Women's Studies International Forum,* 10(4):433-42.

Bourdieu, Pierre. 1984. *Distinction: A Social Critique of the Judgement of Taste.* Cambridge, MA: Harvard University Press.

———. 1988. "Program for a Sociology of Sport." *Sociology of Sport Journal* 5(2):153-61.

Brownmiller, Susan. 1984. *Femininity.* New York: Fawcett Columbine.

Bryson, Lois. 1987. "Sport and the Maintenance of Masculine Hegemony." *Women's Studies International Forum* 10(4):349-60.

Cahn, Susan. 1994. *Coming on Strong: Gender and Sexuality in Twentieth-Century Women's Sport*. New York: Free Press.

Caplow, Theodore. 1984. "Rule Enforcement without Visible Means: Christmas Gift Giving in Middletown." *Amercian Journal of Sociology* 89(6):1306-23.

Carlson, Rolf and Engstrom, Lars-Magnus. 1986. "The Swedish Tennis Wonder of the 80s: An Analysis of the Players Background and Development." Paper presented at the Multi-Disciplinary Conference for Sport Sciences, Lillehammer, Norway.

Chambliss, Dan. 1989. "The Mundanity of Excellence." *Sociological Theory* 7(1):70-86.

Charmaz, Kathy. 1983. "The Grounded Theory Method: An Explication and Interpretation." In R. M. Emerson (ed.), Contemporary Field Research. Boston: Little Brown.

Clack, Jeff. 1978. *Ladies Professional Golf Association*. Boston: Intercollegiate Case Clearing House.

Coakley, Jay J. 1994. *Sport in Society*. St. Louis: Times Mirror/Mosby.

Cohen, A. K. 1955. *Delinquent Boys*. Glencoe, IL: Free Press.

Collins, Patricia Hill. 1990. *Black Feminist Thought: Knowledge, Consciousness and the Politics of Empowerment*. Boston: Unwin Hyman.

Connell, R. W. 1987. *Gendered Power*. Stanford, CA: Stanford University Press.

Conrad, Peter. 1976. *Identifying Hyperactive Children*. Lexington, MA: Lexington Books.

Corcoran, Fred J. 1974. Personal Correspondence to Mr E. M. Erickson. LPGA Archives.

Cowen, Henry P. 1954. Personal Corresponcence to Louise Suggs and Beverly Hanson. LPGA Archives.

Domhoff, G. William. 1979. *The Powers That Be*. New York: Vintage Press.

Donnelly, Peter. 1985. "Sport Subcultures." Exercise and Sport Science Reviews 13:539-78.

Douglas, Jack D. 1976. *Investigative Social Research*. Beverly Hills: Sage Publications.

Duff, Robert W. and Hong, Lawrence K. 1984. "Self Images and Women Body Builders." *Sociology of Sport Journal* 1(4):374-80.

Duncan, Margaret Carlisle. 1990. "Sport Photographs and Sexual Difference: Images of Women and Men in the 1984 and 1988 Olympic Games." *Sociology of Sport Journal* 7:22-43.

Duncan, Margaret Carlisle and Brummett, Barry. 1989. "Types and Sources of Pleasure in Televised Sports." *Sociology of Sport Journal* 6:195-211.

Duncan, Margaret Carlisle and Cynthia A. Hasbrook. 1988. "Denial of Power in Televised Women's Sport." *Sociology of Sport Journal* 5:1-21.

Duncan, Margaret Carlisle and Messner, Micheal. 1990. "Gender Stereotyping in Televised Sports." Los Angeles: The Amateur Athletic Association of Los Angeles.

Durkheim, Emile. 1968. *Suicide.* New York: The Free Press.

Ehrenrich, Barbara and English, Deirdre. 1979. *For Her Own Good.* Garden City, NY: Anchor Press.

Eitzen, Stanley D. and Zinn, Maxine Baca. 1989. "The De-Athleticization of Women: The Naming and Gender of Collegiate Sport Teams." *Sociology of Sport Journal* 6(4):362-70.

Faludi, Susan. 1991. *Backlash: The Undeclared War against American Women.* New York: Crown.

Feinstein, John. 1992. *Hard Courts.* New York: Villard.

Fields, Barbara. 1990. "Slavery, Race and Ideology in the United States of America." *New Left Review* 181:95-118.

Fine, Gary Alan. 1979. "Small Groups and Culture Creation: The Idioculture of Little League Baseball Teams." *American Sociological Review* 44:733-44.

———. 1987. *With the Boys: Little League Baseball and Preadolescent Culture.* Chicago: University of Chicago Press.

Fine, Gary Alan and Klienman, Sherryl. 1979. "Rethinking Subculture: An Interactionsit Analysis." *American Journal of Sociology* 85:1-19.

Foucault, Michel. 1980. *The History of Sexuality: An Introduction.* New York: Vintage Press.

Fox, Kathryn Joan. 1987. "Real Punks and Pretenders: The Social Organization of a Counterculture." *Journal of Contemporary Ethnography* 16:344-70.

Freidan, Betty. 1963. *The Feminine Mystique.* New York: Dell Publishing.

Gallmeier, Charles P. 1987. "Putting on the Game Face: The Staging of Emotions in Professional Hockey." *Sociology of Sport Journal* 4(4):347-61.

———. 1988. "Methodological Issues in Qualitative Sport Research: Participant Observation among Hockey Players." *Sociological Spectrum* 8:213-35.

Gerson, Kathleen. 1985. *Hard Choices.* Berkeley: University of California Press.

Giddens, Anthony. 1990. *The Consequences of Modernity*. Stanford: Stanford University Press.

Gilligan, Carol. 1982. *In a Different Voice*. Cambridge, MA: Harvard University Press.

Glaser, Barney G. and Strauss, Anselm. 1967. *The Discovery of Grounded Theory*. New York: Aldine.

Graffis, Herb. 1975. *The PGA: The Official History of the Professional Golfers' Association of America*. New York: Crowell.

Green, Harvey. 1986. *Fit for America: Health, Fitness, Sport and American Society*. New York: Pantheon.

Greenspan, Miriam. 1984. "The Fear of Being Alone: Female Psychology and Women's Work." *Socialist Reveiw* 14(1):93-112.

Goffman, Erving. 1959. *The Presentation of Self in Everyday Life*. Garden City, NY: Doubleday Anchor.

———. 1977. "The Arrangement between the Sexes." *Theory and Society* 4:301-31.

———. 1963. *Stigma: Notes on the Management of Spoiled Identity*. New York: Simon & Schuster.

Goldstein, John. 1988. "Babes in Tourland." *Fairway*, pp. 8-13.

Gordon, Suzanne. 1991. *Prisoners of Men's Dreams: Striking out for a New Feminine Future*. Boston: Little, Brown.

Heikkala, Juha. 1993. "Discipline and Excel: Techniques of the Self and the Body and the Logic of Competing." *Sociology of Sport Journal* 10(4).

Hayhurst, Lois. 1958. "History of the LPGA." Personal correspondence, LPGA Archives.

Hicks, Betty. 1950. "The Ladies of the Fairway Circus." *Sport Magazine*, November 1950, pp. 44-45 and 91-92.

———. 1954. "Next to Marriage We'll Take Golf." *Saturday Evening Post*, February 1954, pp. 36-37 and 92-95.

———. 1956. Personal correspondence, LPGA Archives.

Hoberman, John M. 1984. *Sport and Political Ideology*. Austin: University of Texas Press.

Hobsbawm, Eric. 1984. "Mass-Producing Traditions." In E. Hobsbawm and T. Ranger (eds.), *The Invention of Tradition*. Cambridge: Cambridge University Press.

Hochschild, Arlie Russell. 1973. *The Unexpected Community: Portrait of an Old Age Community.* Berkeley: University of California Press.

———. 1983. *The Managed Heart: Commercialization of Human Feeling.* Berkeley: University of California Press.

Hodgkinson, Virgina and Weitzman, Murray. 1992. *Giving and Volunteering 1992.* Washington, DC: Independent Sector.

Hooks, Bell. 1984. *Feminist Theory: From the Margin to the Center.* Boston: South End Press.

Hyde, Lewis. 1983. *The Gift: Imagination and the Erotic Life of Property.* New York: Random House.

Jacobs, Jane. 1992. *Two Systems of Survival: A Dialogue on the Moral Foundations of Commerce and Politics.* New York: Random House.

James, C. L. R. 1983. *Beyond a Boundary.* New York: Pantheon.

Kanter, Rosabeth Moss. 1977. *Men and Women of the Corporation.* New York: Basic Books.

Karen, David. 1991. "'Achievement' and 'Ascription' in Admission to an Elite College: A Political-Organizational Analysis." *Sociological Forum* 6(2):349-80.

Kehoe, George. 1993. "Getting Equal." *Golf for Women* 6(1):22-26.

Kidd, Bruce. 1987. "Sports and Masculinity." In M. Kaufman (ed.), *Beyond Patriarchy.* Oxford: Oxford University Press.

Klein, Alan M. 1986. "Pumping Irony: Crisis and Contradiction in Bodybuilding." *Sociology of Sport Journal* 3(2):112-33.

———. 1991. *Sugarball.* New Haven: Yale University Press.

———. 1993. *Little Big Men.* Albany: State University of New York Press.

Laqueur, Thomas. 1987. "Orgasm, Generation and the Politics of Reproductive Biology." In C. Gallagher and T. Laqueur (eds.), *The Making the Modern Body.* Berkeley: University of California Press.

Lenskyj, Helen. 1986. *Out of Bounds: Women, Sport and Sexuality.* Toronto: The Women's Press.

Lever, Janet. 1976. "Sex Differences in the Games Children Play." *Social Problems* 23:478-87.

———. 1983. *Soccer Madness.* Chicago: University of Chicago Press.

Levine, Peter. 1985. *A. G. Spalding and the Rise of Baseball.* Oxford: Oxford University Press.

Lorber, Judith. 1984. *Women Physicians*. New York: Travistack.

―――. 1991. "Dismantling Noah's Ark." In J. Lorber and S. A. Farrell (eds.), *The Social Construction of Gender*. Newbury Park: Sage.

―――. 1993. "Believing Is Seeing: Biology as Ideology." *Gender and Society* 7:568-81.

MacKinnon, Catherine A. 1987. *Feminism Unmodified: Discourses of Life and Law*. Cambridge, MA: Harvard University Press.

Margolis, Diane Rothbard. 1989. "Considering Women's Experience: A Reformulation of Power Theory." *Theory and Society* 18:387-416.

Massengale, John. 1974. "Coaching as an Occupational Subculture." *Phi Delta Kappen* 56(2):140-42.

Matza, David. 1990. *Delinquency and Drift*. New Brunswick: Transaction Publishers.

Mauss, Marcel. 1990. *The Gift: Forms and Reason for Exchange in Archaic Societies*. New York: W. W. Norton.

Merton, Robert K. 1968. *Social Theory and Social Structure*. New York: The Free Press.

Messner, Micheal A. 1988. "Sports and Male Domination: The Female Athlete as Contested Ideological Terrain." *Sociology of Sport* Journal 5(3):197-211.

―――. 1992. *Power at Play*. Boston: Beacon Press.

Miller, Jean Baker. 1976. *Toward a New Psychology of Women*. Boston: Beacon Press.

Mills, C. Wright. 1956. *The Power Elite*. Oxford: Oxford University Press.

―――. 1959. *The Sociological Imagination*. Oxford: Oxford University Press

Morgan William J. 1985. "'Radical' Social Theory of Sport: A Critique and a Conceptual Emendation." *Sociology of Sport Journal* 2(1):56-71.

Moore, Jennifer and Williams, Grant. 1991. "Setting Standards for Non-Profits." *The Chronicle of Philanthropy*, 9 April 1991.

Mrozek, Donald J. 1987. "The Amazon and the American 'Lady': Sexual Fears of Women as Athletes." In J.A. Mangan and R.J. Park (eds.), *From Fair Sex to Feminism*. London: Cass.

National Golf Foundation. 1988. *Golf Participation in the United States*.

Nelson, Burton Mariah. 1991. *Are We Winning Yet?* New York: Random House.

Novak, Michael. 1976. *The Joy of Sports*. New York: Basic Books.

O'Donnell. 1993. "Look Who's No Longer Missing the Links." *Newsweek*, 14 March, p. 68.

Page, Charles. 1973. "The World of Sport and its Study." In J. Talamini and C. Page (eds.), *Sport and Society.* Boston: Little, Brown.

Pastena, Vincent J. 1989. "Pros in Paradise." *Fairway*, pp. 18-25.

Pearson, Kent. 1979. *Surfing Subcultures of Australia and New Zealand.* Queensland: University of Queensland Press.

Petersen, Robert. 1970. *Only the Ball Was White: A History of Legendary Black Players and All-Black Professional Teams.* Oxford: Oxford University Press.

Polsky, Ned. 1969. *Hustlers, Beats and Others.* New York: Doubleday Anchor Books.

Reinharz, Shulamit. 1979. *On Becoming a Social Scientist.* San Francisco: Jossey-Bass.

————. 1992. *Feminist Methods in Social Research.* New York: Oxford University Press

Rosecrance, John. 1985. "The Invisible Horseman: The Social World of the Backstretch." *Qualitative Sociology* 8(3):248-65.

Rubin, Lillian B. 1985. *Just Friends.* New York: Harper & Row.

Ryan, Mary P. 1979. *Womanhood in America.* New York: New Viewpoints.

Sabo, Don. 1993. "Psychological Impacts of Athletic Participation on American Women: Facts and Fables." In D. S. Eitzen (ed.), *Sport in Contemporary Society.* New York: St. Martins.

Sage, George. 1990. *Power and Ideology in American Sport.* Champaign: Human Kinetics Books.

Scott, Marvin. 1968. *The Racing Game.* Chicago: Aldine.

Sennett, Richard and Cobb, Jonathan. 1973. *The Hidden Injuries of Class.* New York: Vintage.

Simmel, Georg. 1950. *The Sociology of Georg Simmel.* New York: Free Press.

Staple, Brent. 1987. "Where Are the Black Fans?" *New York Times Magazine*, 17 May.

Stone, Gregory P. 1955. "American Sports: Play and Display." *Chicago Review* 9:83-100.

Sweda, George. 1989. "Foreign Powers." *Fairway*, pp. 27-35.

Taylor, Ian. 1987. "Putting the Boot into a Working-Class Sport: British Soccer." *Sociology of Sport Journal* 4(2):171-91.

Telander, Rick. 1984. "The Written Word: Player-Press Relationships in American Sports." *Sociology of Sport Journal* 1(1):3-14.

Theberge, Nancy. 1977. "An Occupational Analysis of Women's Professional Golf." Ph.D. dissertation, University of Massachusetts, Amherst.

———. 1980. "The System of Rewards in Women's Professional Golf." *International Review of Sport Sociology* 15(2):387-93.

———. 1987. "Sport and Women's Empowerment." *Women's Studies International Forum* 10(4):387-93.

Unruh, David. 1983. *Invisible Lives: Social Worlds of the Aged.* Beverly Hills: Sage.

Veblen, Thorstein. 1953. *The Theory of the Leisure Class.* New York: Mentor Book.

Voigt, David Q. 1966. *American Baseball: From Gentleman's Sport to the Commissioner System.* Norman: University of Oklahoma Press.

Walby, Sylvia. 1989. "Theorising Patriarchy." *Sociology* 23(2):213-34.

Weber, Max. 1958. *The Protestant Ethic and the Spirit of Capitalism.* New York: Scribner.

———. 1964. *The Theory of Social and Economic Organizations.* New York: Free Press.

West, Candace and Zimmerman, Don. 1987. "Doing Gender." *Gender and Society* 1(2):125-51.

Williams, Christine. 1989. *Gender Differences at Work.* Berkeley, CA: University of California Press.

Willis, Paul. 1978. *Profane Culture.* London: RKP.

———. 1982. "Women in Sport in Ideology." In J. Hardgraves (ed.), *Sport, Culture and Ideology.* London: RKP.

———. 1990. *Common Culture.* Boulder: Westview Press.

Yinger, Milton. 1960. "Contraculture and Subculture." *American Sociological Review* 25(5):625-35.

Young, Kevin. 1988. "Performance, Control and Public Image of Behavior in a Deviant Subculture: The Case of Rugby." *Deviant Behavior* 9:275-93.

Young, Kevin and Gallup, Beth. 1989. "On Boardheads: Windsurfing, Bourdieu and Cultural Capital." Paper presented at the Joint Conference of the North American Society for the Sociology of Sport and Philosophic Society for the Study of Sport, Washington DC, 8-12 November.

INDEX

273